The Forgotten Tragedy

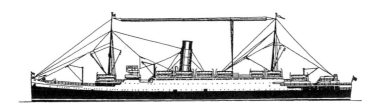

1. Commander Harry Grattidge

THE FORGOTTEN TRAGEDY

THE STORY OF THE SINKING
OF
HMT *LANCASTRIA*

BRIAN JAMES CRABB

SHAUN TYAS

DONINGTON

2 0 0 2

Typeset and designed
using the discs of the author
by the publisher

SHAUN TYAS
(an imprint of 'Paul Watkins')
1 High Street
Donington
Lincolnshire
PE11 4TA

ISBN
1 900289 50 4

Dedicated to my daughters Anna and Helen,
and all those who lost their lives on or after 17 June 1940
as a result of the sinking of HMT *Lancastria*, the greatest
maritime disaster in Britain's history.

By the same author:
Passage to Destiny; The sinking of the
SS *Khedive Ismail* in the sea war against Japan
(Paul Watkins, 1997)
In Harm's Way; The story of HMS *Kenya*,
a Second World War Cruiser
(Paul Watkins, 1998)

Printed and bound by Woolnoughs of Irthlingborough

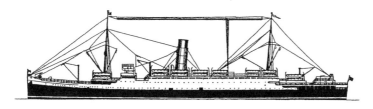

CONTENTS

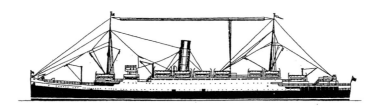

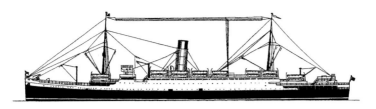

ACKNOWLEDGEMENTS

My own interest in this tragic story originates from my publisher, Shaun Tyas, who published a book about the loss of the *Laconia* in 1994. Three years later he published my own book, the story of the sinking of the *Khedive Ismail.* Between them the loss of these two ships represented the second- and third-worst British Merchant Navy disasters in the Second World War. In later discussions he revealed interest in publishing a book about Britain's *worst* maritime disaster, the sinking of His Majesty's Troopship *Lancastria.* Thanks are long overdue to him for his friendship, professional advice, expert layout and flawless editing.

Initially I contacted Harry Pettit, a survivor of the tragedy and a former member of an inactive group who called themselves 'Lancastria Survivors'. Due to illness Harry forwarded a letter I had written him in December 1998, to Robert Miller, who is the Honorary Secretary of 'The HMT *Lancastria* Association'. Robert corresponded and, after a discussion with other members of the Association, it was decided to accept my proposition and assist me in any way they could.

Therefore, I would first like to thank Robert Miller for his genuine enthusiasm and help. If the sources at the back of this book look impressive, it is partly due to him; he kindly supplied some of the material held at the Public Record Office, Kew, saving me hours of research and hundreds of miles travelling along the monotonous M4 motorway with its notorious traffic jams near Richmond. Brian Reynolds (President of 'The HMT *Lancastria* Association') has also been extremely helpful with last-minute details, which has helped me to solve many details necessary to link the finer points of this amazing story. Pierre L. Guillou, who was a pilot in the Loire estuary for many years, has also been extremely helpful with my questions concerning the wreck of the *Lancastria.* Eric Smith, who was a leading seaman in the Royal Navy, has collated ship's casualty rolls for both the Royal and Merchant Navies in both World Wars. Therefore I am extremely grateful to him for supplying his list of known personnel lost in the *Lancastria* (Robert Miller checked Eric's list and kindly supplied several hundred more; mainly Royal Air Force personnel). Because I decided to provide as much information as possible about each (known or supposed) person lost in the *Lancastria*, it has been necessary to check every name for myself, sifting through the relevant registers published by the Commonwealth War Graves Commission. This painstaking task revealed many more names to the large list. Having no easy way of discovering the names of the civilians lost, connected with Avions Fairey, who were based in Belgium in 1940 and escaped through France to gain passage in the *Lancastria*, I must thank survivor Roger Legroux, who lost his father in the tragedy. He returned to Belgium, with his mother and sister, who also survived the disaster, after the war and kindly supplied them. In France, in June 2001, I was fortunate to meet Jim Wood, a gardener employed by the Commonwealth War Graves Commission. He has been extremely helpful supplying information about personnel buried at Pornic War Cemetery. Pat Boardman has also been very helpful discovering some unknown facts concerning one survivor, who died nearly seven years after the incident and is listed by the CWGC as a casualty. Richard Cornish has also been a great help supplying details of awards given to people involved in the rescue of survivors. Bill Chatterton Dixon kindly checked my list of Honours and Awards with *Seedie's Roll of Naval Honours and Awards 1939–59*, published by Ripley Registers, and added a few omissions.

Concerning the German records of the attack, I would like to express my gratitude to Karl Bühler, a member of the KG 30 Association, Herr Roeske of the Bundesarchiv at Berlin, Frau Jansen of the Bundesarchiv-Militärarchiv at Freiburg and Herr Euteneuer of the magazine *Luftwaffenring* at Bonn. The German Air Ministry was wrecked by Allied bombing in 1943, destroying a great many records of the Luftwaffe's activities in the early part of the 1939–45 conflict, but German records of anti-shipping activities off the French coast do exist for this period, some in the National US Archives in Maryland, but they are too vague to be of specific assistance for the attack on the *Lancastria*. In the survivors' narratives and reports there are many contradictions, especially concerning the identity of the German aircraft that bombed the ship. It is known that aircraft of II./KG 30 were attacking ships in the Loire estuary at the time of the sinking of the *Lancastria*, and that all three *Gruppen* belonging to KG 30 exclusively flew Junkers Ju 88s, but identification of the initial group of attacking aircraft, which also belonged to KG 30, has proved impossible to discover. However, they were definitely from either I. or III. *Gruppe*.

ACKNOWLEDGEMENTS

Some photographs have been generously supplied without the levying of copyright fees, namely from Cunard Line, Cunard White Star Ltd., the National Archives of Canada (Ottawa), Mr T. T. Aspinall (Librarian at the Museum of London), Michael Cassar (Malta), Jim Crissup, MN and many members of 'The HMT *Lancastria* Association'. Dick White also spent time locating one of the postcards depicted in this book. I would like to thank author Neil McCart for helping me locate the source of an interesting photograph of the *Lancastria* under tow in the Thames. Thanks are also due to Philip Colebourne for allowing me to use a copy of his late father's (Norman Colebourne) last painting; a scene of Liverpool dock, featuring the *Lancastria*.

The problem of translating texts from foreign languages was dealt with by Gillian Hull (Spanish and French), Jacqueline Duggan (French), John Duggan (French), Gigi Lebert (French), Martine and Donovan Hawley (French), Sarah Stevens (German), and Ute Bommersbach (German). To all eight I am truly grateful.

Ted Hooton, an author and expert on the history of the Luftwaffe, has been extremely helpful with his advise and guidance, as well as reading my draft account of the aerial attack and the early history of KG 30; he made constructive comments and added extra information and material. Harry Hutson, an author and specialist on Grimsby trawlers, kindly provided me with relevant information about the anti-submarine trawler *Cambridgeshire*. Author and personal friend David Miller has also been instrumental in pointing me in the right direction for reliable information on many specific questions. Bill Knight, MN, author, good friend, annual dining companion and ex-merchant mariner with Port Line Ltd. (a subsidiary of Cunard), has helped me with certain technical details, including the glossary. Robert Blackwell, MN, a marine artist and long established friend has also helped with technical information. I would also like to thank author Ian Johnston for lending me some interesting photographs of the *Tyrrhenia/Lancastria*, which he discovered while researching and writing his book about the history of William Beardmore & Co. Ltd., entitled *Beardmore Built*. Although I am a reasonably experienced marine engineer, specific technical aspects described in this book could not have been dealt with without the help of Captain Nicholas Trott, MN; Chief Engineer Paul Siddons, MN; Chief Engineer Ken Pointon, MN; Engineer Paul Arnold, MN; Nigel Foster, MN; Gilbert Wan, MN; Engineer John Fey, MN; Major Clive Owen; Bill Boardman, RN; Terry Wan; Paul Grainger; Simon Purvis and Michael Steer.

For help with background information and reading I am truly grateful to Lieutenant Commander Geoffrey Mason, RN, Lol Petch, RN, Steve Watts and Patrick Pearson, Communications Manager of Fairey Group plc.

In other areas of research I would like to thank George Gardner, Archive Technician at the Archives and Business Records Centre, University of Glasgow, David Powell, Katie Hooper and Nicola Ashbridge, Library Assistants at the University of Liverpool, Mrs Eileen Edwards, Assistant Curator of Merseyside Maritime Archives, Miss F. A. Penfold, Miss Lynn Farrell, Mrs B. Wilson and Mrs Maureen Annetts, all of the Enquiries Section at the Commonwealth War Graves Commission, Maidenhead, Mr William Spencer, Librarian and Researcher at the Public Record Office, Kew, Iain Goode and Anthony Bowry, both Deputy Departmental Record Officers at the Ministry of Defence, and the librarians (of whom there are many) at the Imperial War Museum Archives Department and the Guildhall, Bridgwater, Bristol and Portishead libraries (Portishead librarians have been exemplary in locating 'out of print' copies of published material for perusal and inclusion).

This amazing and tragic story could not have been given proper justice without the stories of the survivors of the disaster. Many are recorded in John L. West's earlier book *The Loss of Lancastria* and many more in an unpublished collection called 'The HMT *Lancastria* Narratives', put together by members of 'The HMT *Lancastria* Association'. During the 60th Pilgrimage I was privileged to join and interview a large number of survivors, all of whom are included in the list below. These contributors' names are without rank or service details, as these details are recorded elsewhere in the book. They are listed as they appear in the story († denotes that the survivor has now died): H. Strudwick†, Sidney H. Dunmall, Leslie Bailey, G. Skelton†, Charles 'Fred' Coe, Tom Hutchison, John Lees West†, C. W. 'Oscar' Cornish, J. H. Drummond, E. M. C. Shipp, MBE, Clement Stott, F. E. Griggs, A. Picken†, G. Youngs, Frank Brogden†, Michael Sheehan, Michael 'Jesse' Fenton, Edgar Blant, George Crew, J. Mansfield, William Rose, Percy Brown, Tom W. Payne, Jacqueline Tanner (*née* Tillyer), William McGinty, J. Broadbent, William Slater, N. Fuller, OBE†, M. B. Andexser, R. Hayes, P. K. Barker†, C. Brooke†, Norman de Coudray Tronson†, Fernande Tips, Harry Pack, E. J. Mansfield, C. Green, Norman Driver, P. H. Fairfax, J. L. Langley, Stanley Flowers, Neal Howard, Gaston Noblanc, Morris Lashbrook, Dennis Maloney, Joe Sweeney, G. Miller† and S. Clarke, MBE. I would

ACKNOWLEDGEMENTS

also like to thank Angela Johnson, who kindly lent me a letter written by her father, Major J. A. McAllister, RE, thanking and commending Captain Brown, master of the *Baharistan*.

The additional help of The HMT *Lancastria* Association's committee members: Mrs Raye Dancocks (Chairman) and Colin Clarke (Honorary Treasurer) is also appreciated.

The commanding officer of the French minehunter FS *Verseau*, Lieutenant Commander Guillaume de Roquefeuil, and his second-in-command, Lieutenant Bertrand de Lorgeril, also deserve a special mention for the interesting information revealed about the wreck of the *Lancastria*.

Nigel Dyer, who has always shown interest in the different stages of the research process, also deserves a mention for lending a sympathetic ear. I would also like to thank my good friend Richard Skuse, who has given tremendous support and encouragement throughout my writing career. Christine Mahany deserves my thanks for spotting some remaining errors in the publisher's penultimate text. Helen Crabb, my youngest daughter, also deserves a mention for her help typing a document which appears near the end of this book. Finally, I would like to thank my wife Angela for all her encouragement and help since I started researching and writing in 1992, without which none of this would have been possible.

Brian Crabb
December 2001

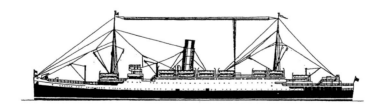

1(b). Anchor Line's new 'T' class liner, the *Tuscania*, built in 1922 by Fairfield's, Glasgow.

1 (c). The new Cunard liner, *Ascania*, one of the six 'A' class ships built to replace Cunard's heavy losses in World War I. All were similar in design to the *Lancastria*; illustrated in a Cunard postcard, showing her leaving Liverpool.

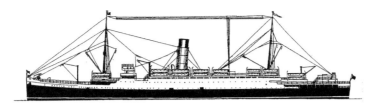

INTRODUCTION

The story you are about to read reveals the truth about the worst disaster in Britain's maritime history, though the exact figure of how many lives were lost on that fateful day will never be known. Anchored in Charpentier Roads at the mouth of the River Loire, near the French port of Saint-Nazaire, the troopship *Lancastria* was awaiting the embarkation of troops in other ships, and the departure of a naval escort which was to escort them back to England. The Cunard White Star liner was carrying approximately six thousand people: British troops, RAF personnel, British and Belgian civilians and the ship's crew. Some 2,000 people are known to have been lost on Monday afternoon, 17 June 1940, when the *Lancastria* was bombed by German Ju 88 bombers, rolled over onto her port side and sank in just twenty minutes. There was two brief mentions of the disaster in the confidential copies of *Lloyd's List and Shipping Gazette* for 22 and 24 June. The first entry stated: '*Lancastria* – London, June 21 – Steamer *Lancastria* has been bombed by aircraft and was reported to be sinking'. The second entry reported: '*Lancastria* – London, June 22 – Steamer *Lancastria* has sunk'.

Such was the size of the disaster that Winston Churchill immediately issued a D notice, suspending publication of any news about the event. In a later account, published in his book *The Second World War*, Volume III, he wrote:

> At Brest·and the western ports the evacuations were numerous. The German air attack on the transports was heavy. One frightful incident occurred on the 17 June at Saint-Nazaire. The 20,000-ton liner *Lancastria*, with five thousand men on board, was bombed just as she was about to leave. Upwards of three thousand men perished. The rest were rescued under continued air attack by the devotion of the small craft. When this news came to me in the quiet Cabinet Room during the afternoon I forbade its publication, saying: "The newspapers have got quite enough disaster for today at least." I had intended to release the news a few days later, but events crowded upon us so black and so quickly that I forgot to lift the ban, and it was some time before the knowledge of this horror became public.

The convenient postponement, which lasted five and half weeks, was brought to the British peoples' attention in a late edition of *The Times* newspaper on Thursday 25 July 1940, and in more detail the following day. The story was not disclosed by Winston Churchill, however, but by the *New York Sun*, which published the story on 24 July. *The Times* used a normal sized column to publicise the disaster, heading it:

TROOPSHIP LOST

—

BOMBED IN B.E.F. EVACUATION

—

HEAVY CASUALTIES

The report went on to say:

> ...As reported in our later editions yesterday, the loss of the Cunard White Star liner *Lancastria* off the French port of Saint-Nazaire, as she was evacuating members of the B.E.F. on the day the Pétain Government capitulated, has now been revealed from an American source.
>
> Nobody knows exactly how many were on board, but the number was probably about 5,000, of whom about 2,500 were saved.
>
> Most of the casualties were British soldiers, but there were also on board about 600 RAF officers and men and a few British civilians who had held official positions in France. Nearly all of them had come from Nantes, which had been used as an assembling ground for British troops of all units. Saint-Nazaire was one of the last ports available for the evacuation of British troops, and many thousands embarked there.
>
> A number of air raids had already been carried out on Saint-Nazaire, but the damage done had been slight and the casualties surprisingly few. The embarkation had just been completed when the shipping was attacked by a strong formation of Junkers 87 dive-bombers [*sic*]. Three bombs hit the *Lancastria*.
>
> RAFTS MACHINE-GUNNED
>
> The liner heeled over almost immediately and sank within about half hour. Many men who had survived the explosion were machine-gunned as they tried to make for the shore in small boats and in rafts. The Junkers also dived to within a short distance of the sea to fire on helpless survivors struggling in the water. Many soldiers and airmen were killed, and many others were drowned before help could reach them.
>
> Fortunately, the anti-aircraft fire had driven off most of the Junkers, and the arrival of the RAF Hurricanes sent others scurrying. One German machine was shot down into the sea by a Hurricane, and at least one more was badly damaged.

Out of the large number of ships evacuating troops from Saint-Nazaire the *Lancastria* was the only one that was lost, in spite of almost constant raids. Among those lost were a number of RAF officers and men who had arrived at the port that day from Blois, on the River Loire, which had been used by units of the Advanced Air Striking Force. One was a squadron leader padre, who had refused to embark in an earlier ship because he did not want to leave behind a crate full of bibles. Others were Army officers and men who had been in camp outside Nantes. The casualties also included men from the Royal Corps of Signals and other regiments who had been assisting the AASF in ground work.

On the same day, the *Daily Mirror* gave a more dramatic headline, stating actual numbers:

2,823 LOST IN BOMBED LINER

...Of the 5,300 people on board the Cunard White Star liner *Lancastria* (16,243 tons), when she was bombed and sunk at Saint-Nazaire, 2,823 people are missing.

This was revealed last night when the story of her loss was told in full for the first time.

Lancastria had just completed embarking personnel when enemy aircraft attacked her.

For half an hour the raiders' attempts to score direct hits failed. Then she was struck by a salvo of bombs.

Immediately she took a heavy list which severely hampered the launching of the ship's lifeboats...

Quite how these numbers were calculated is not known. (For other newspaper reports see Appendix 11).

In the official record of debates in the British Parliament, named Hansard after its first printer, the following questions were asked of Right Honourable Sir Alfred Duff Cooper, the Minister of Information, on 31 July 1940:

Mr. Granville asked: "Why it was that the news of the bombing and sinking of the *Lancastria*, and the story of the heroism of the British troops on board, was not published in this country until after it had appeared in the American Press?" The question was immediately followed by Lieutenant Colonel Sir Assheton Pownall, who asked: "What were the reasons which caused him to withhold for five weeks the news as to the sinking of the *Lancastria*?" The line of questioning did not stop there. Mr. Shinwell asked: "... whether he can explain why a request by the *Journal of Commerce*, submitted on 24 June, to publish a paragraph on the sinking of the steamship *Lancastria* was refused; why, though the Minister promised to make a report on 2 July, no report appeared until 24 July, when the

American Press disclosed the facts; and is he aware that the attitude of the Ministry has caused bewilderment in Liverpool and in shipping circles, where facts were known three days after the event?"

Cooper's reply stated: "The reasons for holding the news of the bombing and sinking of the steamship *Lancastria* were the following: This ship was engaged on a military operation, and it was evident from the German wireless announcement that the enemy were totally unaware of the identity of the ship which had been sunk. Further, it is contrary to the general policy of His Majesty's Government to announce the loss of individual merchant ships. The number and total tonnage of merchant ships lost is given in a weekly statement. The tonnage of the steamship *Lancastria* was included in the statement issued on 2 July. This policy is well known, and I cannot, therefore, understand why on this occasion bewilderment should have been caused in Liverpool and shipping circles."

Further questioning did ensue, which merely elicited further confirmation of Cooper's first answer. The last question concerned the relatives of those lost on board the *Lancastria*, who were reported, by Cunard representative Mr. Logan, not to have been notified of their loss; he was assured, by Mr. Cooper, that the need to confirm the correct identity of those lost was the only reason for the delay.

Very little further news of the ship was reported in the British press for the rest of the War.

This book uncovers the early history of the ship, in addition to recording the truth concerning *Lancastria*'s tragic destruction.

Captain Rudolph Sharp, a Cunard man of great experience, was master of the *Lancastria* at the time of her loss, but he was amongst the rescued and subsequently became master of the 19,695-ton troopship *Laconia*, the loss of which became Britain's second worst Merchant Navy disaster, when she was torpedoed and sunk in the South Atlantic by *U-156* on 12 September 1942, with the loss of 1,614 lives. In the second tragedy he chose to go down with his ship. The third worst British Merchant Navy disaster in the 1939–45 conflict was the loss of the troopship *Khedive Ismail* when she was sunk in the Indian Ocean on 12 February 1944, torpedoed by the Japanese submarine *I-27*; 1,219 men, 77 women and one baby boy died as a result of the sinking.

The loss of these ships and many of their passengers and crew are significant events, not just for their grim statistics and the human tragedy therein, but also because of their military significance. They deserved to be remembered more than they have been, and the loss of *Lancastria* most of all.

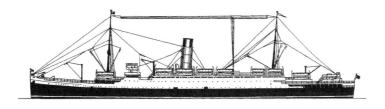

I

THE EARLY HISTORY OF SS *TYRRHENIA/LANCASTRIA*

During November/December 1911 the Cunard Steam Ship Company acquired the share capital of Anchor Line, gaining overall control of that company. Four years later Anchor Line took over the passenger ships of Donaldson Line, adding them to the number of ships already under Cunard administration. During the First World War Cunard's ships were requisitioned for government service as troopships and armed cruisers. As a result, the shipping group sustained an abnormal number of losses during the four-year conflict, including most of their modern ships. Cunard alone lost twenty-two ships, half of which were ocean-going liners. So, at the end of hostilities a huge Government-subsidised building programme was set in motion, all of which was administered from Cunard's new headquarters at Liverpool Pier Head, the building of which was completed in 1917. In addition, the German liner *Imperator* was handed over to Cunard as part-reparation for war losses; she was renamed *Berengaria.*

Six large liners were assigned to Anchor Line, incorporating three C class ships for the New York run (the *Cameronia, California* and *Caledonia*) and three T class for the Mediterranean–New York service (the *Tyrrhenia, Tuscania* and *Transylvania*). For the Cunard company itself, and excluding the austere *Albania* (a hybrid of pre-war A class design, though smaller, without any upper accommodation and therefore only capable of carrying 500 cabin-class passengers. She looked like and was, in many respects, a cargo ship), there were to be eleven new ships; five in the 20,000-ton 'Scythia' class (*Scythia, Samaria, Laconia, Franconia* and *Carinthia*) for the alternating destinations of New York and Boston, and six 16,000-ton 'A' class (*Andania, Antonia, Ausonia, Aurania, Alaunia* and *Ascania*) for the Canadian service. Shortly after the *Tyrrhenia*'s keel was laid, however, ownership was changed to Cunard itself.

2. Lady Invernairn poses for the official photographer on 18 May 1920, pretending to push the launching button. The launch was delayed, however, because of very high winds. No doubt to save face, she merely named the ship. Lord Invernairn is looking up at the *Tyrrhenia*'s towering bow while the Marquis of Graham, with the bowler hat and brolly, stands to her left.

The SS *Tyrrhenia* was built by William Beardmore & Company Limited, Dalmuir, Glasgow and was initially ordered by Anchor Line as a sister ship to the *Cameronia*, which was built at the same shipyard. Her keel was laid on 2 June 1919, nearly three months after that of the *Cameronia*. In 1916, when Anchor Line first approached the shipyard, concerning the building of *Cameronia* and *Tyrrhenia*, the original specifications had required the installation of Ljungström turbo-electric machinery. However, both liners were completed with the tried-and-tested geared turbine technology.

The *Tyrrhenia* was to have been launched by Lady Invernairn, in the company of her husband Lord Invernairn (Sir William Beardmore) and the Marquis of Graham (Joseph Beardmore) on 18 May 1920. All three attended the ceremony, but the actual launch was cancelled because of the gale force winds. Instead, Lady Invernairn performed a naming ceremony.

The *Tyrrhenia* was eventually launched by Colonel J. Smith-Park, who was acting on behalf of the chairman's wife, on 31 May becoming the

6

3. The *Tyrrhenia, Cameronia* and *Conto Rosso* in the fitting out berth on 7 April 1921, during the delay caused by the joiners' strike which lasted nearly nine months

first Cunard ship with a cruiser stern, a design mode that had evolved after World War I, when access to the model experiment tank, at the National Physical Laboratory, became available to cargo vessel builders. The tests proved conclusive and the importance of streamlining hull shapes was soon recognised, resulting in better aft end design and cruiser sterns. She was then towed to the fitting-out berth alongside her sister ship *Cameronia* and the cruiser HMS *Raleigh.* Her contractual price, including extras, was £1,359,907. She cost Beardmore's £1,220,908 to build, grossing the company a handsome £138,999 profit.

All three 'T' class liners had names beginning with this letter and were intended to be used for the same route, but *Tyrrhenia* proved to be an unpopular name and she was eventually renamed *Lancastria* in 1924. As for the other two members of the class, the *Transylvania*, which unusually had *three* funnels, was requisitioned as an Armed Merchant Cruiser in August 1939. However, on 10 August 1940 she was torpedoed by *U-56* and taken in tow, but foundered off Malin Head, in position 55° 50′N 08° 03′W. Over 300 people were rescued and 48 people lost their lives. The *Tuscania* was sold to the General Steam Navigation Co. of Greece in 1939 and renamed *Nea Hellas*; she survived the War.

4. The *Tyrrhenia* in No. 3 graving dock at Govan in 1922. She is undergoing a hull inspection before receiving a fresh coat of anti-fouling paint prior to delivery. A Glasgow tramcar, which is travelling along Govan Road, illustrates the enormity of the new liner.

For the next two years the *Tyrrhenia* was fitted out, transforming shipyard job No. 557 into an ocean-going liner. Paint alone increased her weight by some sixty tons. In the early 1920s, however, the shipbuilding industry was hit by a series of prolonged strikes when the employers decided to remove special wartime and post-war bonuses in an attempt to reduce rising costs. Four thousand joiners went on strike on 1 December 1920, delaying the completion of all vessels under construction, including the *Tyrrhenia*. The 'expired' bonuses had been some twelve shillings extra salary per week, a substantial supplement to the average weekly shipyard wage of £4. The joiners eventually resumed work on 26 August 1921, but the employers had won the day. Half the bonuses were removed with immediate effect, while the remainder was removed in two equal amounts in October and December the same year.

The *Tyrrhenia*'s sea trials were conducted on the River Clyde with Captain F. G. Brown at the helm and, on 12 June 1922, she was handed over to her new owners, beginning her maiden voyage from Glasgow to Montreal (via Quebec) the next day. Her official number in the Lloyd's Register of Shipping was 145943 and her call sign KMGS.

The *Tyrrhenia*'s gross weight was 16,243 tons and she was registered as 552.8 feet long (170 metres), 70.4 feet wide (21.6 metres), with a moulded depth of 38.8 feet (nearly 12 metres); her actual overall length was recorded by Lloyd's as 579 feet (178 metres). On a draught of 29 feet her displacement came out at around 23,500 tons, while her dead-weight capacity was 11,200 tons.

She was fitted for oil fuel (even though her original plans did show provision for coal storage) and propelled by two sets of HP/IP/LP Brown-Curtis steam turbines driven through double reduction gearboxes to two screwed shafts, developing a total of 12,500 shaft horse power. In each set a HP (high pressure) and IP (intermediate pressure) turbine, in tandem, drove one pinion while the LP (low pressure) turbine drove the other. Astern turbines were incorporated in the IP and LP casings. She had three single-ended and three double-ended boilers mounted in one boiler room, with a total of 36 corrugated furnaces, all of which could be easily converted to burn coal. Both types of boiler were 17½ feet in diameter with the single-ended 11½ feet and the double-ended 22½ feet long, developing super-heated steam at 220 pounds per square inch with superheaters and forced draft. The total heating surface was 29,163 square feet.

With the HP turbine rotating at 3,000 r.p.m. and the LP at 1,700 r.p.m., she could readily achieve 16½ knots with a shaft speed of 80 r.p.m., 17 knots being her maximum speed. Her fuel capacity was 1,380 tons, which was carried in bunker, settling and double bottom tanks.

She was designed to carry 265 first-class, 370 second-class and 1,150 third-class passengers with a crew of 320; a total complement of 2,105 people, but this specification was slightly different from the original plans, which show room for 250 first-class, 339 second-class, 1,258 third-class and 379 crew. The plans redrawn by the author for this book show the final specifications. According to early crew lists at the Public Record Office, however, she carried 375 crew. The first-class cabins were mainly situated midships on B deck (the upper deck) with a few more forward of the main companionway, on the starboard side of C deck. Second-class passengers were accommodated aft of the first-class accommodation on the same deck levels. The third-class accommodation (mostly used for emigrants) was on D and E decks. The first- and second-class dining saloons (which could seat 220 and 300 passengers respectively) and lounges were on A deck and, like the accommodation, was of the highest Cunard standard.

Cargo was carried in seven holds and 'tween decks; four for'd and three aft. There were eleven main watertight bulkheads and four mechanically operated watertight doors, which could be closed from B deck (see drawing of side elevation of ship). The quadrant-type steering gear, winches and windlass were all electrically powered.

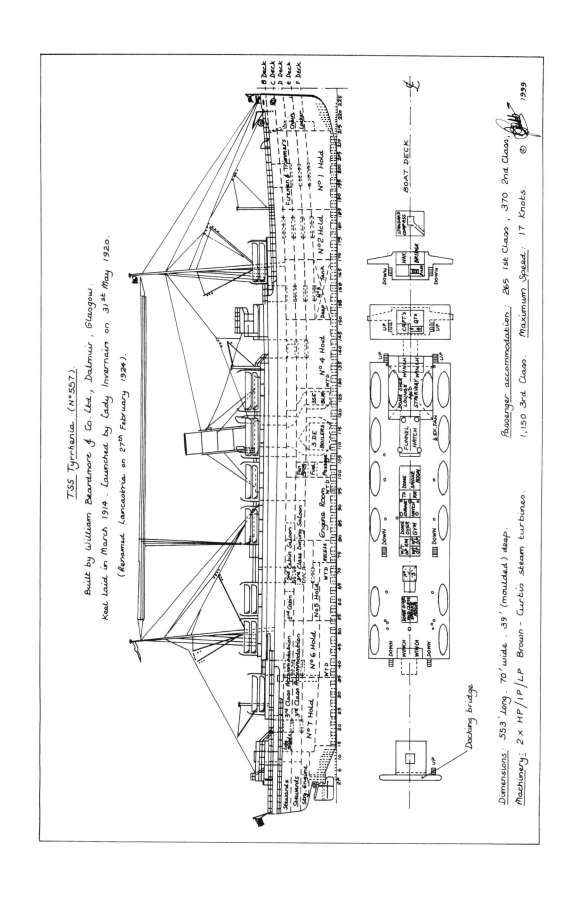

TSS Tyrrhenia (Nº557).

Built by William Beardmore & Co. Ltd., Dalmuir, Glasgow.

Keel laid in March 1914. Launched by Lady Invernairn on 31st May 1920.

(Renamed Lancastria on 27th February 1924).

BOAT DECK

Docking bridge

Dimensions: 553' long. 70' wide. 39' (moulded) deep.

Machinery: 2 × HP/IP/LP Brown-Curtis steam turbines.

Passenger accommodation: 265 1st Class, 370 2nd Class, 1,150 3rd Class. *Maximum Speed:* 17 Knots.

© 1999

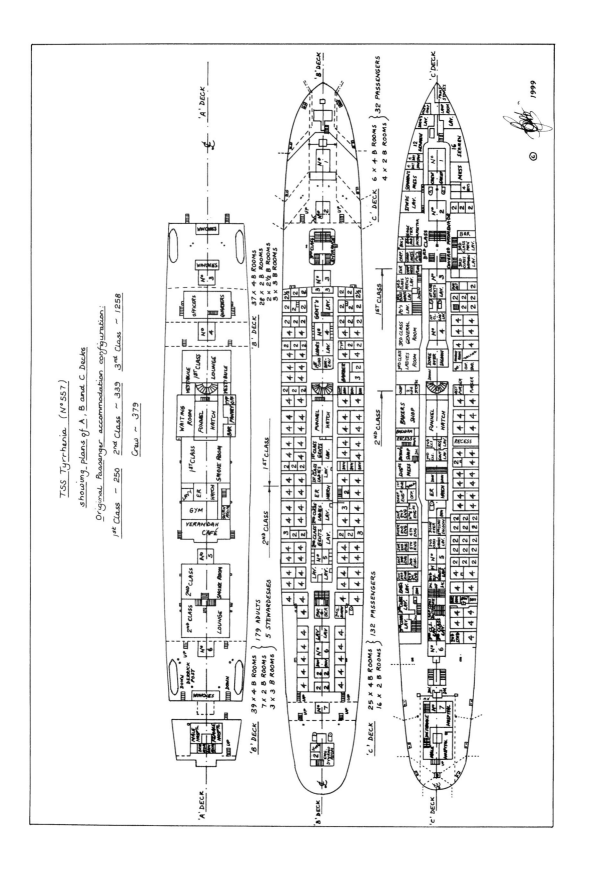

TSS Tyrrhenia (No 557)

showing plans of A, B and C Decks

Original Passenger accommodation configuration:

1st Class ~ 250   2nd Class ~ 339   3rd Class ~ 1258

Crew ~ 379

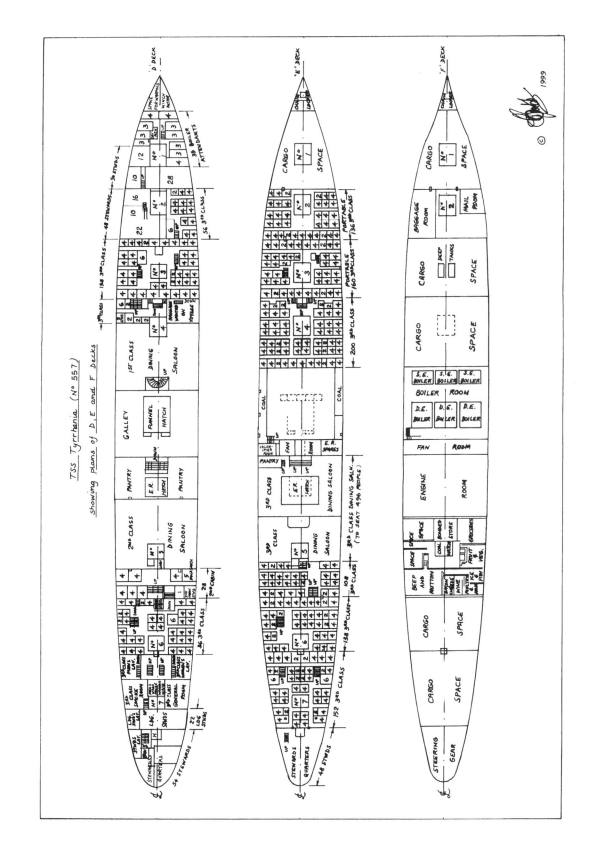

TSS Tyrrhenia (N° 557)

showing plans of D, E and F Decks

1999

She had three full length steel decks (C, D and E), C being a shelter deck – in other words, the eleven main bulkheads did not continue to this deck but stopped at D deck. Nos 1, 2 and 3 holds had an orlop deck (F deck). Access for loading cargo into the holds was through individual hatchways down vertical trunkways which, after loading, would be sealed off with watertight covers at the lower 'tween (or orlop deck) and the uppermost deck. The space in the trunkway between the two hatch covers was sometimes used to carry extra cargo.

8. *Tyrrhenia*'s sister ship *Cameronia*, in Liverpool, boasting her Admiralty cowled funnel, the distinctive feature which distinguishes her from her sister.

Viewed from the for'd port or starboard quarter the *Tyrrhenia* was a beautifully proportioned ship, a classic of 1920s design. Although she was a sister ship to Anchor Line's *Cameronia*, in profile, there was one easy way of distinguishing each ship. The *Cameronia* boasted an Admiralty cowled top to her funnel. The *Tuscania*, although similar in shape to both the *Cameronia* and the *Tyrrhenia*, was also easily distinguishable because it had an extra 'midships deck.

The *Tyrrhenia* continued on the transatlantic passage with the new and 'odd' *Albania* and the Donaldson Line ships *Cassandra* and *Saturnia*. Throughout 1922 these four ships made regular journeys to Boston, New York, Halifax and Montreal. On 13 November 1922 the *Tyrrhenia* was

13

taken over by Captain W. H. Hossack and in early December the liner sailed from New York on a cruise to the Mediterranean, calling at Gibraltar, Naples and Genoa as well as other ports. On 27 December she arrived back at Liverpool for a three-week overhaul before sailing to New York on 20 January 1923.

The *Andania* was the first of the new A class ships to join the run, followed by the arrival of the rest of the class from 1922 to 1925, when the *Tyrrhenia* was switched to the Hamburg–Southampton–New York run, which she began on 21 February.

On 16 July 1923 one of the *Tyrrhenia's* IP turbines developed a mechanical problem. The turbine casing was lifted at Hamburg to discover that nine blades had sheared off from the forward IP turbine, near the last diaphragm; three more blades were fractured at the root. Temporary repairs consisted of cutting out the damaged row of blades and disconnecting the IP turbine. Permanent repairs were effected at Plymouth and completed on 27 September.

During the winter months of 1923–4 her passenger accommodation was modified to 580 cabin- and 1,000 third-class. This costly alteration was in response to the new US immigration quota system, which rendered her large emigrant accommodation redundant. Two swimming pools were also constructed port and starboard, towards the rear of the promenade deck, creating an area known as the sun deck. The conversion made her more suitable for cruising, a role she performed regularly until the outbreak of war.

On 27 February 1924 the *Tyrrhenia* was renamed *Lancastria*, testing the credulity of an age old superstition. As early as the fourteenth century it had become traditional to bless a ship at the launch, placing her under the divine protection of a god or saint. Although the change of name was welcomed by some, because of the old name's complexity, the act of changing a ship's name, in the eyes of many, courted disaster. It was not without reason; many ships with changed names, before and after the sinking of the *Lancastria*, have suffered a similar fate. One name that did disappear after the name change, however, was the *Tyrrhenia's* nickname, 'Soup Tureen'; a typically British adaptation of a word that is difficult to pronounce.

The *Lancastria* began her 'maiden' voyage on the New York service, sailing from Liverpool on 22 March 1924, when her call sign was changed to GJCB. In the beginning of June 1926 she joined the *Carmania*, *Caronia* and *Tuscania* to maintain a weekly service from London to New York, via Le Havre and Southampton. Nearing the end of her first voyage the *Lancastria* suffered another engine defect, when one of her LP turbines stripped on 16 June, as she neared New York (via Boston). Again the damaged turbine was uncoupled and she completed the voyage at reduced speed. Permanent repairs were carried out at the end of the return passage, when she arrived in the Royal Victoria Dock, London.

9. One of Cunard Line's early postcards depicting the *Lancastria* with an 'exaggerated' funnel. Virtually all of the early Cunard postcards attempted to make the ships look even bigger than they really were.

On 17 January 1927 the *Lancastria* docked at Southampton, having sailed from London. While manoeuvring to her designated berth she sustained damage to her davits, boat rails and plates when she collided with another Cunard steamer, the 52,226-ton *Berengaria*, in Ocean Dock. Cruising from Helsingfors (now known as Helsinki) the *Lancastria* snagged a buoy around one of her propellers on 9 July, while proceeding through the Kiel Canal. She then touched the bank at Kaiser Wilhelm Canal, 41 miles from the Brunsbuttelkoog entrance. She was refloated with tug boat assistance. A diver's inspection confirmed no apparent damage and, after obtaining a 'Certificate of Seaworthiness', she proceeded to London.

The earliest Lloyd's Voyage Record Card details, for any merchant ship, begin on 1 October 1927 (these 'yearly', A5-size, cards record brief

10. An impressive view of the *Lancastria* at top speed in choppy weather off Liverpool.

R.M.S. BERENGARIA.

11. Stern view of the *Berengaria*; she was involved in a collision with the *Lancastria* in Ocean Dock, Southampton.

12. *Lancastria* in the Thames, under tow by two 'Sun' tugs en route to King George V dock, in the mid-1920s.

details of a ship's arrivals [in black] and sailings/speakings [in red]. A 'speaking' is made when a ship's position is reported to Lloyd's by another vessel, a coast guard station or by radio. The maritime origin of the word is derived from the days of sailing vessels which, on chance encounters, would signal their name and position to each other for subsequent transmission when each vessel reached port. The Voyage Record Card also reveals a coded reference to every entry in Lloyds's List, concerning casualties, collisions, mechanical problems, etc., so by means of the microfilm and ships' card index, a complete voyage record of all ocean-going vessels can be obtained. All are held at the Guildhall Library, Aldermanbury, London). *Lancastria's* first card records her at sea (a speaking), off Cornwall, on passage from New York. After calling in to Plymouth on 2 October, she proceeded to London. During the early hours of 4 October Captain R. G. Malin was left with no other alternative but to drop anchor off Chapman Light at Gravesend, due to dense fog. At 02.27 the *Lancastria*, while swinging on her anchor, fouled the steamship *River Fisher*, damaging one of her starboard portholes and denting a hull plate. In the darkness and obscurity it was first thought that the *River Fisher's* cable was fouled around the *Lancastria's* starboard propeller. However, daylight confirmed that she was clear and the liner proceeded up the Thames later that morning.

13 (right). Embarkation notice showing the *Lancastria*'s scheduled departure from Southampton to Halifax and New York on Saturday 1 December 1928. The four-funneled illustration is that of either the *Mauretania* or *Aquitania*.

14 (opposite). The last painting by Norman Colebourne, showing a typical view of Princes landing stage at Liverpool in the 1930s. The North Wales steamer *St Tudno* is shown astern of the *Lancastria*. The Seacombe-bound Wallasey ferry *Francis Storey* is depicted right.

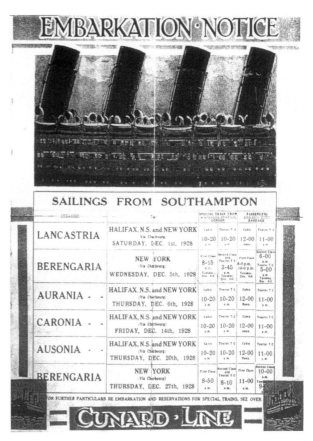

EMBARKATION·NOTICE

SAILINGS FROM SOUTHAMPTON

STEAMER	To	SPECIAL TRAIN FROM LONDON		PASSENGERS BAGGAGE	
		Cabin	Tourist T.C	Cabin	Tourist T.C
LANCASTRIA	HALIFAX, N.S. and NEW YORK Via Cherbourg SATURDAY, DEC. 1st, 1928	10-20 a.m.	10-20 a.m.	12-00 noon	11-00 a.m.
BERENGARIA	NEW YORK Via Cherbourg WEDNESDAY, DEC. 5th, 1928	First Class 8-15 a.m.	Second Class and Tourist T.C 3-45 p.m. Tuesday, Dec. 4th	First Class 6-0 p.m. 10-0 p.m. Tuesday, Dec. 4th	Second Class 6-00 p.m. Tourist T.C 5-00 p.m. Tuesday, Dec. 4th
AURANIA - -	HALIFAX, N.S. and NEW YORK Via Cherbourg THURSDAY, DEC. 6th, 1928	Cabin 10-20 a.m.	Tourist T.C 10-20 a.m.	Cabin 12-00 Noon	Tourist T.C 11-00 a.m.
CARONIA - -	HALIFAX, N.S. and NEW YORK Via Cherbourg FRIDAY, DEC. 14th, 1928	Cabin 10-20 a.m.	Tourist T.C 10-20 a.m.	Cabin 12-00 noon.	Tourist T.C 11-00 a.m.
AUSONIA - -	HALIFAX, N.S. and NEW YORK Via Cherbourg THURSDAY, DEC. 20th, 1928	Cabin 10-20 a.m.	Tourist T.C 10-20 a.m.	Cabin 12-00 Noon.	Tourist T.C 11-00 a.m.
BERENGARIA	NEW YORK Via Cherbourg THURSDAY, DEC. 27th, 1928	First Class 8-50 a.m.	Second Class and Tourist T.C 8-10 a.m.	First Class 11-00 a.m.	Second Class 10-00 a.m. Tourist T.C 9-00

FOR FURTHER PARTICULARS RE EMBARKATION AND RESERVATIONS FOR SPECIAL TRAINS, SEE OVER.

CUNARD·LINE

For the remaining months of 1927 the *Lancastria* carried out three more voyages to New York. For the first three months of 1928 she sailed on two Mediterranean cruises and in April she cruised to the Canary Islands and Madeira before reverting back to the New York run. In July, she combined a Mediterranean cruise with a voyage to the Norwegian fjords. From August 1928 until the end of June 1929 she plied between the British Isles and New York. Her voyage schedule followed a similar pattern in the forthcoming years (with the omission of Spanish ports during the country's Civil War of 1936–9).

The *Lancastria* left Southampton on 6 December 1929, arriving at Cherbourg the same day. Bound for New York, via Halifax, she ran into a storm and was struck by lightning on 8 December. Electricians and engineers repaired defects to her wireless transmitter and other electrical equipment. She sheltered in Cork's port of Queenstown (now known as Cobh), taking on more passengers before continuing her passage to North America. On 9 June 1930, while en route from New York to Helsinki, the *Lancastria* struck a 'dolphin' (a wooden pile/piles used for mooring) in the Kiel Canal. The ship was undamaged (exactly two years

18

to the day, again in the Kiel Canal, the *Lancastria* grounded with no apparent damage).

After the Wall Street Crash on 24 October 1929, which threw first the USA and then the world economy into recession, trade on the scheduled service routes gradually diminished, forcing Cunard to switch many of its ships to long periods of cruising during the bleak years of the early 1930s. During the latter part of August 1931, the *Lancastria* set off from New York to complete a mini-cruise to the Caribbean, stopping at Puerto Rico, Caracas, Curaçao and Colon, before returning to New York.

Rudolph Sharp, RNR, had joined the ship as First Officer (Mate) on 16 June 1930 and in October 1932 was already on his fifth voyage with her (see Appendix 4 for his career details) when, during a stormy night on 10 October, the *Lancastria* received a distress signal from the 4,889-ton steamship *Scheldestadt*. Her plotted position placed her 50 miles away, in the Bay of Biscay; her engine room was flooded. She had belonged to the Zeevartmaats company of Scheldestroom and had recently been purchased for breaking by an Italian company. Three other vessels were standing by, as a hurricane-force gale whipped up huge seas. A volunteer

19

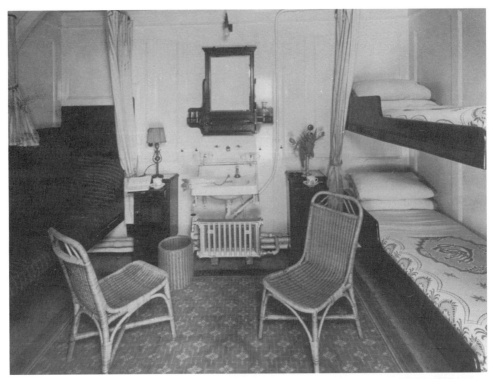

15 (above). Interior view of one of *Lancastria*'s tourist state rooms in March 1932.

16–18 (right and opposite). Views showing the grandeur of *Lancastria*'s dining saloons, also dated March 1932. A bomb would plunge through this deck on 17 June 1940.

21 (above). Smoking room in March 1932.

19 (opposite, top). *Lancastria*'s verandah café.

20 (opposite, below). Writing room in March 1932.

crew from the *Lancastria*, under the command of deck officer A. J. Denby, were the first to take the initiative and succeeded in launching No. 9 lifeboat. After a hard pull they managed to close the *Scheldestadt* and rescue the Italian captain, 20 crew and a Belgian wireless operator at 11.30. Although all the crew were rescued, the adverse weather conditions had dictated the decision to abandon the lifeboat; but not before the officer of the watch had reported its last known position. The *Lancastria* then proceeded to Lisbon where it landed the *Scheldestadt*'s crew. On 15 October, arriving at Casablanca, the master of the Danish steamer *Bodil* reported the sighting of *Lancastria*'s lifeboat adrift in the Bay of Biscay.

On 24 December 1932 the *Lancastria* was entrusted with a special cargo: gold bullion worth £1,500,000, which was safely discharged at New York on 3 January 1933.

During 1933, after negotiations which began in October 1932, the Cunard Steam Ship Company conditionally merged with the White Star Line as part of a deal initiated by the Government to reduce competition

22. *Lancastria* under way in the River Mersey.

in what was currently a loss-making industry. Even the construction of the *Queen Mary*, the keel of which had been laid at John Brown's shipyard on the Clyde during December 1930, had been halted for the duration of the economic difficulties. Mr Neville Chamberlain, who was Chancellor of the Exchequer at the time, made it known that he was keen to promote a strong British shipping company for the Atlantic trade. Therefore, as part of a low-interest loan, the Government advanced £3 million to complete the new liner, £1½ million as working capital and £5 million for the building of a second giant vessel (subsequently named *Queen Elizabeth*). By February 1934 a formal agreement had been reached and the two companies amal- gamated, forming the new Cunard White Star Limited three months later. As a result, the junior partner, White Star Line brought eight new ships into Cunard's fleet, although one of these, the old *Adriatic* (II), was sold in November the same year.

The *Lancastria* began another voyage to New York on 22 April and, as she steamed out into the estuary of the River Mersey into the Crosby Channel the ship touched the bottom. However, the damage was considered inconsequential and she proceeded into the North Atlantic without further incident. On 8 August 1933, under the command of Captain G. R. Dolphin, the *Lancastria* lost an anchor and about 100 fathoms of cable while leaving Santander bound for Corunna. Both the anchor and cable were recovered later, after the ship had left harbour.

23–4. Two tourist postcards of the *Lancastria*. The above painting by Kenneth Shoesmith is rare, but the card below is not uncommon.

Cunard White Star.

Engine trouble delayed the *Lancastria*'s arrival at Liverpool by twenty-four hours when returning from a cruise in the Mediterranean on 5 September. On 25 March 1934 the *Lancastria* lost her port anchor and cable while entering the Mersey Channel, after calling into Dublin and completing another Mediterranean cruise.

25 (above). Another tourist postcard, this time a photograph showing *Lancastria* just after dropping off the pilot and proceeding towards the open sea.

26 (right and opposite). Cover and opening pages of the third-class passenger list booklet issued to Margerie Duxbury at the beginning of a voyage in the *Lancastria* from New York on 18 October 1935.

List of Passengers

●

CUNARD WHITE STAR

On 21 July the *Lancastria* sailed to Bergen, arriving three days later at the start of a Scandinavian cruise to Norway and Denmark. At 00.30 on 25 July, while en route to Loen in Nordfjord, the liner ran into dense fog and was forced to stop. From the bridge the Norwegian pilot could just make out the Tussen Lighthouse, at the east end of the island of Smaleo. Unaware of her peril, the *Lancastria* was slowly drifting, stern first, to the set of the current, and at 01.12 she struck an uncharted rock, the noise echoing through the ship's hull and causing unseen damage. The voyage was not aborted, however, for she called in to Mandal, Oslo and

WELCOME—

We want you to know that every officer and member of the crew is interested in your welfare and will spare no effort to see that you enjoy the utmost comfort and happiness during your voyage.

We sincerely hope that your crossing will be so pleasant that we will again have the pleasure of arranging your passage.

CUNARD WHITE STAR LIMITED

A Record of My Trip

on the

CUNARD WHITE STAR LINER

LANCASTRIA

Sailing from New York

October 18, 1935

And a List of

Fellow Passengers

S. S. LANCASTRIA

———

OFFICERS

CAPTAIN:
E. EDKIN, O.B.E., R.D., A.D.C., R.N.R.

CHIEF ENGINEER:
J. DUNBAR

CHIEF OFFICER:
E. M. FALL, D.S.C., R.D., R.N.R.

SURGEON:
R. W. G. STEWART

PURSER:
G. N. BAILDON, R.D., R.N.R.

ASSISTANT PURSER:
J. P. COULTON, R.N.R.

CHIEF STEWARD:
T. BRENNAN

CHIEF THIRD STEWARD:
T. CRAIG

S. S. LANCASTRIA

From New York, October 18, 1935

THIRD PASSENGER LIST

*Aalto, Mr. Towo
*Allen, Mr. Percy
Anderson, Miss Esther
*Ashton family
Austin, Mr. John
Austin, Mrs.

Bowman, Mr. J.
Brady, Mrs. Mary
Brady, Miss Elizabeth
Brady, Mr. Frederick
Brown, Mr. William
Brown, Mrs.
Brown, Master Henry
Brown, Master Dennis
Burke, Mr. James
Burke, Mrs.

Carroll, Mr. William
Clarke, Mr. H. L.
Clarke, Mrs.
Clarke, Miss Mollie
Conaboy, Miss Margaret
Connell, Mrs. Mary
Connell, Miss Mary
*Conroy, Mr. Michael J.
*Cook, Mr. Peter

*Embarking at Boston

Copenhagen before returning to Liverpool on 3 August. There she was dry docked at Cammel Laird's shipyard and taken out of service until 8 September; no less than twenty-eight bottom plates had been damaged during the luckless collision. The *Laurentic* took over the duties of her scheduled service.

On 1 May 1936 the *Lancastria* sailed from Liverpool to begin another Mediterranean cruise. After calling into Gibraltar she arrived at Valletta on 7 May. On board were 611 survivors of the First World War, who were greeted and shown around the local sights of the island by members of the Malta Branch of the Salonica Reunion Association. However, this was not the main purpose of their visit. The *Lancastria* was scheduled to visit the Turkish port of Gelibolu, in the Dardanelles, near the battlefields of Gallipoli. The pilgrimage, led by British Field Marshall Sir William Birdwood (1865–1951, who was the first commander of the Australian and New Zealand Army Corps [ANZAC]), Admiral of the Fleet Sir Roger J. B. Keyes, RN (1872–1945, Chief of Staff to the commander of the Gallipoli campaign) and Captain Edward Unwin, VC, RN (1864–1951, who commanded the collier *River Clyde* at the V Beach landing) laid wreaths at the battleground on 12 May. Two days later the ship arrived at Salonica (now known as Thessaloniki), mainland Greece, where a similar ceremony took place at Colonial Hill.

27. *Lancastria* laid up alongside another liner in Liverpool Dock, near the Bootle Cold Storage building. The date is unknown.

28–9. Bow and stern views showing the *Lancastria* high and dry after the tide had receded off Egremont Pier, Cheshire. She had ran aground during the early hours of 20 October 1936 in a gale-force wind, when returning from a Mediterranean cruise.

30. A superb view of the *Lancastria* in Cunard's colours. She was a
classic ship of 1920s design.

On 19 October, after returning from a 16-day Mediterranean
cruise, she was held up for seventeen hours in Liverpool Bay, due to a
hurricane force gale which gusted up to 80 mph. Shortly after 04.00 the
next morning, while following the *Scythia* (sister ship of the ill-fated
Laconia) up the Mersey, a gust of wind caught her and she gently
grounded off Egremont Pier in Cheshire. As the tide receded she was left,
embarrassingly, high and dry until the next tide. She was refloated at
11.30 the same day and pulled the final half mile to the landing stage by
tugs. A precautionary inspection in the Huskisson Dock, even though she
had been lying on a flat sandy bottom, revealed no damage. After an
overhaul she sailed for Boston and New York on 21 November. Shortly
after this incident her hull was painted white, the new livery used by
Cunard White Star Line for most of their cruise ships. The *Lancastria* was
openly described as 'beautiful' by anyone who revered ships.

Another mishap befell the *Lancastria* when she sailed from the
Tunisian port of Bizerta on 25 September 1937. Bound for Catania, Sicily,
she was clear of the main wharf when she drifted in a fresh breeze and
struck the head of a small stone pier three times along her port side. The
pilot reported that the shocks were hardly felt on the bridge and that he
did not think that the ship had sustained much damage. However, big
stone blocks of the pier were moved or split. The liner proceeded to her
next port of call without delay.

31. Cunard advertisement depicting the *Lancastria*. It was possibly this poster that some of the survivors reported seeing when they landed back in England in June 1940.

32. Port side view of the *Lancastria* at anchor and bunkering through the 'gunport' doors. She is dressed overall for the Coronation Fleet Review in May 1937.

From the beginning of June until the end of July 1938 the *Lancastria* sailed on three cruises to Scandinavia before completing four cruises to the Mediterranean and the Atlantic Isles. At that time, prices for a 13-day Mediterranean cruise started at 13 guineas (£13.65p), while a 22-day cruise, taking in Gibraltar, Tangier, Lisbon and the Atlantic Isles, started at 23 guineas (£24.15p). These prices included all 'standard' shore excursions and were specifically marketed to appeal to workers fortunate enough to be still employed during the recession, offering holidays of a lifetime at bargain prices. From 1 October to the beginning of February 1939 the *Lancastria* underwent a refit at Liverpool.

On 3 March she sailed from Liverpool bound for Queenstown, Boston and New York, arriving there on 15 March. Three days later she was chartered by Furness Withy & Co., and began a series of four-day and five-day cruises to Bermuda, which continued until the end of April, when the cruises were extended to six days and her destination changed to the Bahamas. After the outbreak of war against Germany, on 3 September 1939, the *Lancastria*, under the command of Captain E. M. Fall, completed her last cruise from Nassau on 8 September and berthed in New York, where she remained for two weeks. During this time she was painted grey and her portholes were blacked out. She sailed from New York on 22 September bound for Halifax, where she loaded cargo. She sailed, unescorted, on 25 September, arriving at Royal Victoria Dock, in London, during the afternoon of 5 October. Here she was requisitioned by the Ministry of War Transport for use as a troopship, converted and armed with a number of defensive guns. Her war work now began.

A month later she sailed to New York, a trip she repeated before returning to Liverpool on 12 January 1940. In the same month she went into dry dock. She sailed from Liverpool on 26 January, arriving at Halifax on 3 February and New York three days later. These voyages had two uses; on the westbound passage she carried mainly Canadian civilians who wanted to return home, eastbound she carried cargo and war materials, including cased aircraft which she carried as deck cargo.

The *Lancastria* arrived at Liverpool from New York on 24 February. On 5 March Captain Rudolph Sharp took over command of the *Lancastria* from Captain H. R. Oulsnam for the first time; the ship sailed for America on 9 March. During this last voyage to the 'Big Apple' the *Lancastria* sustained slight weather damage on 21 March as she neared New York; seven seamen were injured. She sailed down the River Hudson, passing the Statue of Liberty for the last time, on 28 March, arriving at Liverpool on 6 April and sailing to Glasgow ten days later.

33. *Lancastria* photographed on her last trip to New York in March
1940, three months before she was sunk. She is now a troopship.
Note her grey hull, blacked-out port holes and 4-inch low-angle gun.

Germany invaded Denmark and Norway on 9 April 1940
(Operation Weserübung) prompting Britain into discussions with the
Government of Iceland. The talks resulted in an agreement which
allowed them to form naval bases at strategic fjords around the island.

On 1 May FP 3, a Narvik-bound troop convoy carrying expedi-
tionary forces to Norway, including the French Foreign Legion Demi-
Brigade (Colonel Magrin-Verneret) and the Polish Brigade (General
Bohusz) sailed from the Clyde in the transports *Colombie, Mexique,
Chenonceaux, Algérie, Monarch of Bermuda* and *Empress of Australia*; they were
accompanied as far as Scapa Flow by *Reina del Pacifico, Lancastria, Duchess
of Atholl, Batory* and *Sobieski*. The naval escort comprised the destroyers
Atherstone and *Warwick*, the French destroyers *Epervier* and *Foudroyant* and
the minesweeping sloops *Jason* and *Gleaner*, which joined from Ardrossan.
While the five troopships anchored in Scapa, during the afternoon of 2
May, plans to use these ships for more landings north of Narvik were
cancelled. Convoy FP 3 arrived safely at Harstad and Tromsø on 5 May
while the supply convoy FS 3, with the cargo ships *Albert le Borgne, Enseigne
Maurice Préchac, Saint Clair* and *Vulcain*, arrived the following day.

33

The manning and defence arrangements of selected Icelandic bases began on 10 May and was code-named 'Alabaster'. On 14 May convoy 'Alabaster' sailed from Glasgow at 15.00 bound for Reykjavík. It consisted of two troopships, the *Franconia* (Commodore Vice Admiral M. Lennon Goldsmith, DSO, RN) and the *Lancastria*; naval escort was provided by the destroyers *Foxhound* and *Havant* (ex-*Javary*). Both troopships were full of all manner of stores. The *Franconia* was carrying 1,860 officers and troops, 22 nurses, Captain M. Macdonald (the newly promoted Naval Officer in Command of Reykjavík) and his seven staff. The *Lancastria* was carrying 1,846 officers and troops. The speed of the convoy was 16 knots and zig-zagging was carried out throughout the voyage. The route taken was outside the Hebrides, as directed by the Admiralty at Greenock.

At 01.00 on 17 May the convoy was closed and challenged by the armed merchant cruiser HMS *Salopian* (ex-*Shropshire*). The convoy arrived safely at Hvalfjord at noon the same day. The embarkation of troops and stores was completed on 21 May while the *Foxhound* and *Havant* refuelled from the *Franconia*. Meanwhile the *Franconia* embarked 35 marines and one officer, and the *Lancastria* 548 marines, including officers, five British consular staff and four prisoners. The auxiliary netlayer *Guardian*, which had been damaged when she hit an uncharted rock while laying net defences at the entrance to Hvalfjord, joined the convoy for passage to Belfast for repairs. The convoy sailed at 21.00 on 21 May with progress reduced to 11¾ knots due to the *Guardian*'s damage. Responding to the orders of the Commander-in-Chief, Home Fleet, the *Guardian* parted company at 00.30 on 25 May, off the Mull of Kintyre. The convoy arrived safely at Greenock at 07.00 the same day, despite Lord Haw Haw's earlier propagandist claim that both troopships had been sunk.

Days later the *Lancastria* was allocated to the Norwegian campaign to assist in the evacuation of troops from Harstad, about 30 miles south-west of Narvik. She formed part of Group 1, which sailed unescorted from Greenock on 28 May and included the troopships *Monarch of Bermuda*, *Franconia* and *Georgic*. The *Batory* and *Sobieski*, which also formed part of Group 1, sailed unescorted from Greenock the following day. Group 2, comprised of five more troopships, three Irish Channel packet-boats and an armed boarding vessel (see Appendix 6), which were to be sent in later. They were met by the cruiser *Coventry* (Rear Admiral Vivian) about 180 miles from the Norwegian coast. At the two separate rendezvous areas each group was given instructions. Group 1 was the first to be sent in, anchoring in various inlets and small subsidiary fjords in Andfjord. The troops were embarked from destroyers, which themselves had been loaded from smaller craft.

34. An interesting picture showing the *Lancastria* about to leave Glasgow as part of convoy 'Alabaster' on 14 May 1940, while a Scottish band plays them off. Her decks are crammed with troops, a scenario that would be repeated almost three-fold in June the same year.

Although daylight persisted around the clock, the embarkation was carried out, mostly, during 'night-time' hours, due to restrictive sorties by the Luftwaffe. Aerial protection was provided by RAF fighters from Bardufoss, Fleet Air Arm Skuas from the aircraft carrier *Ark Royal* and surviving Gloster Gladiators of 263 Squadron from HMS *Glorious*. The six troopships of Group 1 embarked 14,700 troops during three consecutive 'nights', which was completed on 4 June.

Group 1 reassembled at the distant rendezvous area the following day; from where they set course for home waters, escorted by the cadet training ship *Vindictive* (ex-cruiser *Cavendish*). It was not without incident; the convoy was attacked by German high-level bombers, resulting in the *Lancastria* (which was carrying around 2,600 troops – a figure she would more than double at Saint-Nazaire two weeks later) being near-missed by two bombs – no damage was done.

Lord Cork, who was the Naval Commander and overall commander of the operation, due to the absence of an appointed Supreme Commander, had originally intended to hold Group 1 at the rendezvous area until Group 2 had completed embarkation. The joint convoy could then have been afforded the added protection of two cruisers and five destroyers. However, the Admiralty were anxious for Group 1's return because of pressing demands elsewhere. Group 1 arrived safely at Scapa Flow on 8 June. The *Lancastria* then returned to the Clyde on 10 June (the day Italy entered the War) before sailing to Liverpool, where she arrived three days later in readiness for much needed repairs. However, this was not to be, for she was required for another important operation. The ensuing voyage would prove to be her last.

Group 2 left Harstad on 7 June, with a further 9,800 troops, arriving safely at Scapa Flow three days later, but their return home was nearly intercepted by a German squadron, under the command of Fleet Commander Admiral Marschall, code-named *Juno*. It consisted of the battleships *Gneisenau* (Captain Netzbandt) and *Scharnhorst* (Captain Hoffman), the heavy cruiser *Admiral Hipper* (Captain Heye) and the destroyers *Erich Steinbrinck*, *Hans Lody*, *Hermann Schoemann* and *Karl Galster*, which was intended to intercept the British transports west of Harstad. On their way, however, they came across another group of ships, sinking the troopship *Orama* (19,840 tons), which was carrying German prisoners of war, the tanker *Oilpioneer* (5,666 tons) and the trawler *Juniper* (505 tons), all on 8 June. Perhaps surprisingly, the immunity of the hospital ship *Atlantis*, which was with the *Orama* when she was sunk, was respected.

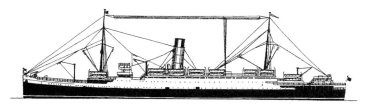

II

OPERATION AERIAL

The miraculous rescue of 338,226 men from the beaches of Dunkirk and De Panne, which began on 27 May 1940, had taken nine days. It was far and above the Allies' estimated number of 25,000 men in two days. Had Hitler decided to push the British Expeditionary Forces into the sea the War may well have taken a very different course. However, this particular operation, codenamed 'Dynamo', was by no means the end of evacuations from western Europe.

With most of the main British Expeditionary Forces safely evacuated, and the surrender of all French forces north of the River Somme, the Germans were free to push south and attack the next line of defence the French had taken up. The line broadly followed the courses of the rivers Somme and Aisne and terminated at the end of the Maginot Line forts in the east. On 5 June Germany began its new offensive, an operation code-named 'Rot' (Red) using greater numbers of men than the French had at their disposal, and broke through the line in a number of places. The French defence soon crumbled.

As Field Marshal Paul von Kleist's two Panzer groups rumbled south, penetrating the French countryside, the large ports of Cherbourg, Brest and Saint-Nazaire were threatened. In overall control of 120 divisions, Field Marshal Fedor von Boch's Army Group B reached the Seine, south of Paris, on 9 June. Meanwhile, Field Marshal Karl Rudolf Gerd von Rundstedt, who commanded Army Group A, was delayed by French resistance and counter-attacked until 12 June, when the Germans broke through at Chalons, assisted by one of Kleist's Panzer groups. The French forces were compelled to enact a headlong retreat all along their line, leaving Paris and much of the Loire abandoned by the following day. Paris fell on 14 June and the Germans broke through at Saarbrücken the same day, and Colmar the day after.

As the German forces pushed southward into France, Britain's navy and air force retained control of the English Channel and the approaches to the British Isles. Control of the Channel had to be maintained in order to enable the rescue of large numbers of British and Allied troops retreating before the German advance.

Meanwhile, Paul Reynaud, France's President, recalled Marshal Henri Philippe Omer Pétain, who was the French Ambassador in Spain, to act as Vice-President. In early June Pétain had been in favour of surrender, strongly rejecting Reynaud's proposal of unifying French forces with Britain's, which he also felt was doomed to defeat. Consequently, Reynaud resigned on 16 June and was replaced by Pétain, who offered the Germans an armistice the following day, and this came into effect on 22 June, leaving Germany in control of the country from Belgium to the Spanish border. A proviso that the French Fleet was to be assembled in specified ports, ready for demobilisation and disarmament, by either the Germans or the Italians, was also agreed.

Originally the British War Cabinet had intended to return the British Expeditionary Force to France, as soon as it was reorganised and re-equipped. Indeed, two divisions still remained in France. Being south of the River Somme when the Germans broke through the defensive line at Abbeville, the 1 Armoured and the 51 (Highland) divisions had become detached from the rest of the British forces under Lord Gort. Approximately 150,000 men were employed at bases or on the Lines of Communication. Most, in the course of recent events, were surplus to requirement, and plans were set in motion to evacuate these men first, along with residual stores and equipment.

'Operation Cycle' involved the evacuation of men from ports along the north-west coast of France, including Le Havre. Demolition parties had been sent over from Britain towards the end of May, while the Luftwaffe began bombing the town and port of Le Havre in the early part of June. Dieppe was almost completely blocked by two ships that were deliberately sunk in the approach channel on 10 June. A third ship struck a mine just outside the harbour, preventing the blockade of the inner entrance to the port. On the same day fog hindered Admiral James' last ditch attempt to rescue the detached 51 Highland Division and French forces. They had become separated from the main French armies when the Germans split the Allied forces by capturing Rouen and the lower Seine. Meanwhile, near the tall cliffed beaches of St Valéry-en-Caux, at Veules, south of Dieppe, only 2,137 British and 1,184 French soldiers were taken off, leaving some 6,000 men of the 51 Highland Regiment, including Divisional Headquarters, to surrender the following day.

On 7 June German aircraft did a great deal of damage to the port and city of Le Havre, leaving the Admiralty with little option but to order

Commander-in-Chief, Portsmouth, Admiral Sir William James, to send seven British and two Canadian destroyers, and a number of smaller warships to rendezvous off the French coast in the early hours of 10 June. Large numbers of schuyts and small craft were also sent across the English Channel. Under heavy bombardment the evacuation proceeded, albeit with initial delays. On 11 June the personnel vessel *Bruges* was sunk by enemy aircraft. Learning from this, and other aerial attacks, Britain sent over strong patrols of home-based fighters, tipping the scales of air dominance in the opposite direction and keeping the enemy bombers, in and around Le Havre, at bay. The operation enabled 11,059 British troops to be successfully embarked from Le Havre between 10 and 13 June, although nearly 9,000 of these men were shipped to Cherbourg. The destroyers *Ambuscade, Boadicea* and *Bulldog* were damaged during the operation.

'Operation Aerial' was the British codename for the evacuation of the remainder of the British Expeditionary Forces from the ports of north-western France, which began on 15 June. The plan utilised the ports of Cherbourg, Saint-Malo, Brest, Saint-Nazaire and La Pallice. Following so soon after the harrowing nine-day evacuation of Dunkirk, it placed a heavy strain on the overtaxed forces of the southern naval commands. As a result flotilla vessels, required to escort troopships, were simply not available. Germany, at this point in time, had insufficient naval surface strength to combat Britain's superior forces, however.

The larger ships of the Operation were provided by the Home Fleet based at Scapa Flow, while smaller ships came from the southern ports of England. Air cover was provided by the RAF from home-based squadrons. The naval operation, which provided ships from the Merchant and Royal Navies for the evacuation from the ports of Cherbourg and Saint-Malo, was directed by Admiral James from Portsmouth, while the other three ports was controlled from Plymouth, by Admiral Dunbar-Nasmith, Commander-in-Chief, Western Approaches.

Admiral James had originally considered a convoy plan, but with insufficient escort ships he was compelled to organise a continuous flow of troopships, motor-transport and store-ships from Southampton to his allotted French ports. The designated shipping routes were patrolled by the few available warships, while coasters sailed from Poole and schuyts from Weymouth. Between 15 and 17 June most of the 52 Division had been taken off at Cherbourg. On 18 June men from various formations, known as the 'Norman Force', arrived at the port and were embarked in similar fashion. Meanwhile, as two destroyers provided cover for the withdrawal of the rearguard, fuel reserves at Caen and Cherbourg were destroyed. By late afternoon, most of the remaining men had embarked in the last troopship. This part of 'Aerial' had brought 30,630 men home, including the 9,000 men previously taken to Cherbourg from Le Havre. It had been successfully carried out without loss; no doubt assisted by the tireless work of the RAF, which had managed to keep the enemy's strengthening air power suppressed.

Meanwhile, on 16 June, the embarkation of the 1 Canadian Division had proceeded at Saint-Malo. No fewer than 21,474 men had been evacuated by the evening of the next day. As demolitions continued, a final search was made for stragglers, while the enemy closed in on Saint-Malo. As Admiral James concluded his part in the evacuation, Admiral Dunbar-Nasmith began an even larger evacuation programme from ports in the Bay of Biscay. On 16 June naval officers arrived at Brest and Saint-Nazaire to organise and accelerate embarkation procedures. The Admiralty took a special interest in Brest, where the newly constructed battleship *Richelieu* lay alongside nearing completion. Some personnel ships were already at Brest, while Dunbar-Nasmith despatched the large liners *Arandora Star*, *Otranto* and *Strathaird*. Smaller craft had been assembled in west country ports, but this time they were not needed.

Embarkation proceeded rapidly and, acting on orders from London, the evacuation at Brest was completed on time during the evening of 17 June. No fewer than 28,145 British Army and RAF personnel were evacuated; another 4,439 Allied soldiers were rescued, bringing the total rescued from Brest to 32,584. Although, in terms of men, the evacuation was a complete success, had British intelligence been more reliable, the operation could have continued for at least another twenty-four hours, allowing many more vehicles, equipment and stores to have been shipped back to Britain in motor-transport and storeships. Ships that had room for more men were redirected to Saint-Nazaire, while others, that were full, returned to home ports.

The Luftwaffe's only activity over Brest was the occasional sortie to lay mines, which only caused some delays which were summarily dealt with by minesweeping trawlers sent over specifically for that purpose. Without the luxury of escorting flotilla vessels, all the troopships from Brest were routed home independently. Meanwhile, on 18 June, the French, assisted by a British party, began demolitions in and around the port. Shortly after, at around 16.00, most of the French fleet sailed south to Casablanca and Dakar; only a few came to British ports to continue the fight. By 19 June the large naval base was clear of shipping and the demolition party was withdrawn in the destroyer *Broke*.

Further south, and concurrent with the evacuation from Brest, the port of Saint-Nazaire presented a very different problem. Strong tides and navigational hazards in the River Loire slowed the operation considerably. A second new French battleship, the *Jean Bart*, lay alongside Saint-Nazaire's dockyard, an unthinkable asset to the enemy should it fall into their hands. Knowing that between 40,000 and 60,000 British and Allied troops were retreating towards Nantes, some fifty miles up the River Loire from Saint-Nazaire, it was imperative to begin the evacuation as soon as possible. Meanwhile, on 15 June, Admiral Dunbar-Nasmith ordered the troopship *Lancastria* and a number of other troopships and cargo ships to sail to Saint-Nazaire.

On the morning of 16 June, the evacuation began with three destroyers ferrying troops to two British liners, *Georgic* and *Duchess of York*, and two Polish liners, *Batory* and *Sobieski*, which were anchored and waiting in Quiberon Bay, some twenty miles north-west of the Loire estuary. Although anti-submarine defences at Quiberon Bay were virtually non-existent, the area provided good anchorage for large ships. HMS *Havelock*, under the command of Captain E. B. K. Stevens, who was the leader of the 9th Destroyer Flotilla, was ably assisted by the destroyers *Wolverine* and *Beagle*. Almost unavoidably, a large number of valuable ships were accumulated in and around Quiberon Bay; ships that were susceptible to both air and submarine attack (although the latter never materialised, despite Admiral Raeder's orders, which placed seven U-boats along the supposed troopship routes). Regardless of German aircraft mining the channel, embarkation began on the afternoon of 16 June, allowing some 13,000 base troops, along with stores, equipment and transport, to be loaded into the four liners and appropriate cargo ships. Once loaded, the *Duchess of York*, *Georgic* and the two Polish liners sailed for home waters.

It was on the same day that the Luftwaffe attacked shipping in Quiberon Bay. Fortunately, they only managed to damage the liner *Franconia*. Throughout the night ships were loaded with stores while Admiral Dunbar-Nasmith diverted ships from Brest and sent more from England. The naval force was strengthened by the addition of the two destroyers *Highlander* and *Vanoc*, which joined Captain Stevens' flotilla.

As dawn broke on 17 June it revealed much activity, as small French and British ships, along with Captain Stevens' flotilla vessels, ferried troops out to two big ships anchored in Charpentier Roads. More ships were arriving as the RAF patrolled above. Throughout the morning the evacuation proceeded smoothly and efficiently, raising Allied hopes of achieving yet another successful operation. It was to prove a forlorn hope.

On board the liner *Lancastria* were over 5,000 personnel, including troops, RAF personnel and civilians awaiting passage home. The troopship *Oronsay* was anchored about 4 cables (about half a mile) from the *Lancastria*. She was the first ship to be attacked by the Luftwaffe, being bombed and hit on the bridge at 13.48, a forewarning of what was to come. At 15.35 the Luftwaffe launched a heavy air attack and struck the *Lancastria*. She briefly caught fire, rolled over and sank within twenty minutes, with heavy loss of life.

The two operations (Cycle and Aerial) had succeeded in rescuing nearly 200,000 British and Allied troops, civilians and a considerable amount of military equipment and transport. This number included 57,235 troops (54,471 British and 2,764 Allied) who were brought home from Saint-Nazaire and Nantes.

The new and unfinished French battleship *Richelieu* sailed for Dakar on 18 June. Meanwhile, Vice Admiral T. J. Hallett arrived north of Saint-Nazaire in the destroyer *Vanquisher*, at noon on the 18 June and waited in Quiberon Bay. He had been given Admiralty instructions to ensure that the *Richelieu*'s sister ship, the *Jean Bart*, either sailed or was destroyed by the next day. The French dockyard staff worked with great urgency to get the battleship undocked and seaworthy early on 19 June, the same day that the Germans entered Nantes. If they failed, it was their intention to destroy the great ship themselves. Meanwhile Hallett sent tugs to assist with the undocking procedures. The *Jean Bart*, which was in a similar unfinished state as the *Richelieu*, eventually rendezvoused with the *Vanquisher* and three French destroyers, but not before she had been near-missed by six bombs. The French Admiral of the Ouest command, flew his flag in the destroyer *Hardi*. Vice Admiral Hallett stayed in company until the French squadron turned south, for Casablanca. On the same day the *Mécanicien Principal Carvin*, which was carrying equipment for the *Jean Bart*, including a 380-mm gun, arrived at Saint-Nazaire. She was bombed and sunk two days later in the Gironde.

However, it must be noted that not all the French naval ships sailed south, for some captains opted to sail to Britain to continue the war on the Allied side. The old battleships *Paris* and *Courbet*, the large destroyers *Léopard* and *Le Triomphant* and the smaller *Mistral* and *Ouragan*, seven submarines, including the large *Surcouf*, six torpedo boats and several minesweepers arrived at British ports from 19 June.

The *Richelieu* was damaged by the British Navy on 8 July 1940, due to the defection of the French Navy. After the North African landings in November 1942 (Operation Torch) she joined the Allies and was refitted in America, becoming part of the Home Fleet at Scapa Flow towards the end of 1943. Meanwhile, the battleship *Jean Bart* sailed from Dakar during the African landings and was put out of action by the American battleship *Massachusetts*. Once France had surrendered, any ship of the French navy which had not sailed to Britain was considered an enemy vessel. France had fallen and a considerable number of Allied personnel had been rescued and brought home, but while the surviving British vessels of Operation Aerial were triumphantly sailing into home waters and a peace of sorts was descending over the French coast, the *Lancastria* and many of its passengers and crew were lying at the bottom of the Loire estuary.

34 (b). Rare aerial photograph of the *Lancastria*, in peacetime but not unlike the view which must have been seen by the pilot of the first Ju 88 to attack the ship on 17 June 1940.

III

THE EARLY HISTORY OF KG 30

Kampfgeschwader 30 or KG 30, known as the *Adler Geschwader* or Eagle Wing, was formed and expanded with the expressed purpose of attacking enemy shipping. As it will be seen, the Junkers Ju 88 (which was the only aircraft used by KG 30) played the major role in the sinking of HMT *Lancastria*.

The Luftwaffe's earlier plans, to build a number of heavy four-engined bombers, were dashed on the morning of 3 June 1936, when Generalleutnant Walther Wever, Chief of the General Air Staff, was killed in an air crash. He had been at the controls of a Heinkel He 70, with his flight engineer, but his aircraft crashed shortly after take off from Dresden airport, killing all on board. As Wever was the main advocate of a long-range strategic bombing arm, the idea died with him. His successors opposed his ideas, favouring instead the concept of dive-bombers and twin-engined medium-range bombers. The *Schnellbomber*, or high-speed bomber, which was already being developed at the Junkers works in Dessau, was considered adequate.

Initially the Ju 88 was designed as a high-speed, long-range bomber with a range of 1,080 nautical miles (2,000 kilometres) and capable of carrying a bomb load of one metric tonne (1,000 kgs or 2,200 lbs). The first prototype Ju 88 V1, which was powered by two 1,000-hp Daimler Benz DB 600Aa engines, made its maiden flight on 21 December 1936. However, it was lost during high-speed trials a few weeks later. Four more prototypes followed and these were closely watched by the then Generalfeldmarschall Hermann Göring. Towards the end of the summer of 1938 Göring revisited the Dessau works to witness further trials. He was so impressed by the new aircraft that he wrote to Junkers' managing director, Dr Heinrich Koppenberg, giving him permission to begin series production. The letter, dated 3 September 1938 (a year before Britain declared war against Germany), ended with the sentence 'And now build me a mighty bomber fleet of Ju 88s in the shortest time possible.'

In March 1939 the fifth prototype demonstrated the Ju 88's true potential. Powered by two 1,200-hp Junkers Jumo 211 engines, it established a new world air speed record for its class, completing a 1,000-km (621-mile) closed circuit flight between Dessau and Germany's highest Alpine peak (Zugspitze) at an average speed of 517 kmh (321 mph). In loose comparison, its design was similar to Britain's De Havilland Mosquito, although not in materials (for the Mosquito was largely made of wood). The Ju 88 was the brainchild of Diplom Ingenieur (Qualified or Certified Engineer) Ernst Zindel.

Generalleutnant Ernst Udet, who became responsible for aircraft development, insisted that all bombers were to have dive-bombing capability. However, Udet's requirement was not as simple to introduce as it sounded; the increased stresses experienced in a dive necessitated radical design modifications, including the strengthening of the airframe and the addition of dive brakes. Naturally this increased the weight of the aircraft, reducing the top speed by 40 mph (65 kmh); further government requirements saw the addition of defensive armament, making it essential to double the crew. These changes, coupled with the fact that the prototypes that Göring had initially seen were far from ready for mass production, all served to delay hopes of early delivery. In fact, instead of the anticipated 'mighty bomber fleet of Ju 88s', Germany began the Second World War with only twelve of the new aircraft ready for use, although even these were not operational.

Early in 1939 a development unit (*Erprobungkommando* 88) was created to inaugurate the Ju 88 into service, as well as developing and perfecting suitable bombing techniques. In September 1939 this became *Stab* (Staff) 1. and 2. *Staffel* of KG 25. On 7 September the short-lived KG 25 disappeared from Luftwaffe records when these two *Staffeln*, soon to be joined by a third, were redesignated I. *Gruppe*/KG 30; II. *Gruppe*/KG 30 was formed on 17 November 1939 and III. *Gruppe*/KG 30 on 1 January 1940, partly from *Lehrgruppe* 88, a demonstration unit which replaced *Erprobungsgruppe* 88. KG 30, with all three *Gruppen*, now consisted of between 90 and 120 aircraft.

Werner Baumbach, who was recognised as one of the Luftwaffe's leading bomber pilots in the 1939–45 conflict, stated the following in his book *Broken Swastika*: 'During the Second World War only three types of bombers, the He 111, the Do 217 and the Ju 88, in addition to the Ju 87 dive-bomber, were employed by us on a large scale ... The only twin-engined bomber with which successful dive-bombing could be effected was the Ju 88.' The Ju 88 was favoured as an alternative to the Ju 87 (Stuka) and adapted to attack shipping because it had a much longer range and could carry twice the bomb load (the Ju 88 aircraft which attacked *Lancastria* flew from Belgium, far too great a distance for the Ju 87 to achieve; the Ju 87 was a short-range dive bomber). A ship, at the best of times, is a very difficult target to hit, especially if the vessel is under way.

35. View inside the cockpit of a Ju 88 showing the observer pointing to the map while the pilot checks his position.

On 10 May 1940 the *Stab* (Headquarters) I., II. and III. *Gruppen* of KG 30 (Oberstleutnant Loebel) was assigned to *Luftflotte* 2's *Fliegerkorps* IV, under General der Flieger Alfred Keller, who had been one of the leading German bomber commanders in the First World War. The complete force of KG 30 took part in the invasion of Denmark and Norway in April 1940. In May and June no less than eight *Gruppen* of Ju 88 bombers were available for the assault on the Low Countries and France (KG 30, KG 51, and sections of KG 4 and LG 1). However, the Ju 88 was not used operationally to any great extent up to this point in the war, because they were simply in the minority and most were in Norway. Nevertheless, some units did have them for use in France by May 1940. Initially, most of the Ju 88s used in the Western Campaign, named *Fall Gelb* (Operation Yellow), were in Holland. The real acid test for the Ju 88s came in the Battle of Britain, as it did with other German bombers, when it was discovered that the defensive armament and protection was inadequate, necessitating further delays in development.

The first operational sortie by I./KG 30, which had just been transferred northwards from Jever (near Wilhelmshaven) to Westerland, on the island of Sylt, was a raid on British warships of the Home Fleet on 26 September 1939, north of the Great Fisher Bank in the North Sea. During the attack hits were mistakenly reported on the aircraft carrier *Ark Royal*. The target, which also included the battleships *Rodney* and *Nelson*, the battlecruisers *Hood* and *Renown*, the cruisers *Edinburgh*, *Newcastle* and *Norfolk* and destroyers of the 4th and 8th Flotillas, was initially reported by a Dornier Do 18 flying boat, belonging to II./*Küst fliegergruppe* 106 (2 Squadron, 106 Coastal Aviation Group) *Geschwader* of *Flieger* Division 10, Naval Group West, which was based at the East Frisian island of Nordeney. Nearby was the 2nd Cruiser Squadron, which comprised *Aurora*, *Glasgow*, *Sheffield* and *Southampton* and six destroyers of the 7th Flotilla. These had been sent out to recover the submarine *Spearfish*, which had been badly damaged in the North Sea.

By 11.00, barely a quarter of an hour after the sighting, alarms were ringing at the bomber base at Westerland, but the small force sent to attack such a large number of British ships was insufficient to say the least; only nine Heinkel He 111s of I./KG 26 and four Ju 88s of I./KG 30 were sent. The pilot of one of KG 30's aircraft, Gefreiter (Aircraftman First Class) Carl Francke, near-missed the *Ark Royal* with his second attempt while Oberleutnant Storp's aircraft, of the same *Geschwader*, hit the *Hood* with one bomb, but which failed to explode. Here is Francke's description of his attack on the *Ark Royal*:

> I initiated the second attack from 2700 metres (8856 feet). This time when I emerged from the clouds I was almost bang on target. A slight adjustment was all that was needed. The fire from the ship's flak made it stand out like some giant, illuminated advertising hoarding. But nothing hit us.
>
> At the correct altitude I pressed the bomb release button. The first bomb exploded in the water some 20 metres (65 feet) from the target, but the second hit the carrier on the starboard side.
>
> Unfortunately, at the moment of impact, I was fully occupied recovering from the dive, but the crew reported seeing black smoke and signs of fire.
>
> Aircraft of the reconnaissance squadron kept a close watch on the carrier. Although it remained with the fleet, it was listing badly and apparently unable to hold a steady course.
>
> The next day, when the fleet was sighted again, the two battlecruisers were on their own and there was no sign of the aircraft carrier. It had disappeared.

In actual fact the *Ark Royal* had not been sunk. The captain of the carrier had timed his manoeuvre to perfection, turning his ship away from the path of the falling 500-kg bomb. The bomb had narrowly missed by less than five metres (15 feet) throwing a huge column of white water over the for'd end of the flightdeck. The *Ark Royal* shuddered and was lifted upwards. Initially she took a list to starboard before coming slowly back on an even keel. Vice Admiral L. V. Wells, who was flying his flag in the *Ark Royal* at the time, dismissed the attack as 'no more than the breaking of a little crockery and splashing us with some water.'

Although Francke's subsequent radio report was guardedly optimistic, it stated:

> Dive-attack with two SC 500 bombs on aircraft carrier; first a near miss by ship's side, second a possible hit on bows. Effect not observed.

The German Propaganda Ministry immediately seized upon the story, claiming:

> German Luftwaffe sinks Britain's latest aircraft carrier! And with a single bomb!

36. HMS *Ark Royal*, seen here going astern. She was reported by the German Propaganda Ministry as being bombed and sunk by Gefreiter Carl Francke – a claim that was to cause him great embarrassment.

Even Göring was convinced by the claim, adding his seal of approval by promoting Francke to the rank of Leutnant and awarding him the Iron Cross, grades I. and II. The next time Göring met Francke was at the Luftwaffe test centre at Rechlin. Göring, who had since discovered the truth about the *Ark Royal* incident, is reported to have dolefully said: "You still owe me an aircraft carrier!" At around the same time aircraft of I./KG 26 had attacked the 2nd Cruiser Squadron without result.

Francke, an unwilling hero, had become a household name overnight, but as it became common knowledge that the *Ark Royal* was still afloat and had escaped damage his reputation deteriorated; meanwhile he continued test flying at Rechlin. At one point he even contemplated suicide, no doubt influenced by derisive remarks by fellow officers who despised the fact that he had been promoted and decorated for something he had not done. After volunteering for another operational posting, he was killed on the Eastern Front.

On 9 October 1939, another sortie on the cruisers *Edinburgh, Glasgow* and *Southampton*, the battlecruiser squadron, consisting of *Hood* and *Repulse*, the cruisers *Aurora* and *Sheffield* and four destroyers (known as the Humber Force) and the Home Fleet, with the battleships *Nelson* and *Rodney*, the carrier *Furious*, the cruiser *Newcastle* and eight destroyers, was initially brought about by the cunning use of a German naval task force. Using the battlecruiser *Gneisenau*, the cruiser *Köln* and nine destroyers, the Germans lured the Royal Navy into the North Sea. An aerial attack was contrived by Generalleutnant Geisler's staff using no fewer than 21 Ju 88s of I./KG 30, and 127 He 111s, mostly of KG 26 and reinforced by aircraft of II./LG 1. Once again the Germans failed to achieve any success, despite reports by some of I./KG 30's pilots, who claimed ten hits on British cruisers. The truth was that no British ship had been hit.

The *Gruppenkommandeur* of I./KG 30, Hauptmann Helmut Pohle, was furious at the failure and, when he was personally asked to explain the reasons, by telephone to Generalfeldmarschall Göring, he replied bitterly: "We were just sent to an area where there was no enemy!" The following morning Göring headed a big conference at the Reich Air Ministry in Berlin, demanding improvements to the Luftwaffe's recent failures on naval targets. The meeting was attended by Oberst Hans Jeschonnek, who had succeeded Stumpff as Chief of Air Staff in 1939; Generaloberst Erhard Milch, Secretary of State for Air; Oberstleutnant Josef Schmid, Chief of Air Intelligence; Generalleutnant Ernst Udet, Director of General Equipment of the Luftwaffe; Generalmajor Joachim Coeler, Chief of the Fleet Air Arm; Pohle and many others. Göring made it plain that he wanted the battlecruisers *Hood, Renown* and *Repulse* eradicated from the scene, in addition to the aircraft carriers, so that the *Scharnhorst* and the *Gneisenau* could dominate the North Sea.

On 15 October 1939, German aerial reconnaissance had reported the sighting of a British battlecruiser, presumed to be the *Hood*, off the east coast of Scotland. This was confirmed during the early hours of the next morning, when the battlecruiser was sighted entering the Firth of Forth. That same morning Jeschonnek contacted Pohle in Westerland, warning him that the Führer had insisted that if the battlecruiser was already in dock no attack was to be made. Apparently, Hitler did not want to be the first to draw civilian blood, a trait that the British were also keen to follow at this stage of the war. (Hitler, at this point in time, still hoped that the conflict with Britain could be appeased).

At 11.00 fifteen Ju 88s, belonging to I./KG 30, took off from Westerland, reaching the outer estuary of the Firth of Forth an hour-and-a-quarter later and from where Pohle led his bombers inland. The Luftwaffe's headquarters had mistakenly informed him that no Spitfires were stationed in Scotland. Unfortunately, for Pohle, this piece of intelligence was very inaccurate: 602 and 603 Squadrons, flying Spitfires, had been based at Turnhouse, near Edinburgh, by British Fighter Command some weeks earlier. To make matters worse, that very morning, 607 Squadron, flying Hurricanes, had landed at Drem, on the Firth's south bank. A local radar station was conveniently positioned to report any unscheduled aircraft movements, a luxury which normally provided British fighter pilots with plenty of time to get airborne, intercept and attack enemy aircraft out to sea. By mischance the radar station had suffered a power failure as the enemy approached; therefore no alarm was sounded until the drone of the Ju 88s was heard 12,000 feet above their bases. Valuable time had been lost, allowing the enemy aircraft the freedom of selecting targets without aerial resistance.

Pohle's pilots gained a clear view of Edinburgh, becoming the first German bomber unit to fly over the United Kingdom since the outbreak of war. They could also see the great bridge separating the inner and outer Firth of Forth, and beyond that, on the north bank, the docks at Rosyth naval base. Almost at once Pohle sighted the battlecruiser he had come to sink. Unfortunately, Hitler's explicit orders now robbed him of his prize, for the *Hood* was already in dry dock. Pohle decided not to waste a good opportunity, however, and put his machine into a dive, targeting the *Southampton*. The 9,100-ton cruiser immediately responded to the attack, opening fire with all her anti-aircraft guns. Pohle's aircraft was rocked by the explosions as he dived at eighty degrees, accelerating to nearly 400 miles per hour. Then disaster struck: first a short, sharp bang, then a cracking tearing sound, followed by an icy blast of air as the canopy roof blew off. Pohle had experienced this before, at Rechlin during flight tests. This aircraft certainly needed further development.

37. Reconnaissance picture taken of the attack on the cruisers *Southampton* and *Edinburgh* on 16 October 1939. The Firth of Forth railway bridge and Inch Garvie Island are on the left, while the accuracy of the bombing is very evident.

Determined to gain some sort of success he continued his dive, with the *Southampton* plumb in his sights. At 3,000 feet he released his 500-kg bomb, striking the modern cruiser amidships in the starboard superstructure, penetrating three decks obliquely before it emerged out the side of the ship and sank an Admiralty launch without exploding. Rather ironically, the Ju 88 had made its first kill, although hardly the size that Göring had expected. The bomber's crew had no time to study the effect of the attack. As Pohle pulled out of the dive his radio-operator screamed out "three Spitfires are attacking!" Pohle later reported:

> It was too late to take avoiding action. Our port engine was hit at once and started smoking. I turned seawards, hoping to reach the German fishing cutter *Hörnum*, which the Navy had proposed to station at a given point off the Scottish coast during our attack.

The Spitfires renewed their attack against Pohle's smoking Ju 88, but it was a one-sided battle. The only rear-aiming gun was a single MG 15 machine-gun but, against the superior gun power of the Spitfire, the Ju 88 was virtually defenceless. Both the rear gunner and the radio operator were hit as machine-gun bullets slammed into the fuselage. Passing Port Seton, in East Lothian, Pohle brought his aircraft down so low that he was almost skimming the surface of the sea. It made no difference. The Spitfires continued their attack, this time badly wounding the observer and damaging the starboard engine. Pohle went on to describe what happened:

> We were finished. I spied a trawler steaming north, and thought perhaps I could still reach it. After that I lost consciousness.

The trawler Pohle had spotted was British and his damaged aircraft crashed into the sea not far from it. Within minutes one of the fishing boat's dinghies came alongside the waterlogged and crumpled fuselage. Pohle was the only member of the crew still alive, and he was rescued. Five days later, while recovering in Port Edwards Hospital on the Firth of Forth's north bank, Pohle regained consciousness. He was lucky to be alive. During the same attack by I./KG 30 one other Ju 88 was lost. The cruisers *Southampton* and *Edinburgh,* and the destroyer *Mohawk* suffered slight damage. It was during an attack on the latter that Leutnant Horst von Riesen was to have an experience similar to Pohle's:

> During the dive a heavy flak shell must have exploded quite close to our machine. A loud bang momentarily drowned the sound of our engines, and then a strong wind howled through the cockpit. The right engine cowling had been blown off and the cabin canopy buckled inwards.

After pressing home his attack on the destroyer, von Riesen had also sought the safety of open sea with Spitfires in hot pursuit. He managed to limp back to Westerland on one engine.

On the following day, 17 October, under the command of their new *Gruppenkommandeur*, Hauptmann Fritz Dönch, four Ju 88s of I./KG 30 flew further north. This time their target was Scapa Flow. However, like Prien (who had managed to manoeuvre *U-47* into Scapa Flow barely 72 hours earlier and sink the *Royal Oak*) Dönch discovered that the anchorage was near empty. He therefore concentrated his attack on the Home Fleet's old base ship, the former battleship, *Iron Duke* (Admiral Jellicoe's flagship at the Battle of Jutland). The deluge of near-misses left the veteran battleship's captain no other alternative but to beach her. One of Dönch's aircraft was shot down by anti-aircraft fire, exploding on Hoy and becoming the first Luftwaffe aircraft to crash on British soil during the Second World War.

As a consequence of these two embarrassing attacks, the Admiralty temporarily withdrew the Home Fleet to the safer haven of Scottish ports along the west coast; while the waters between Kirkwall and Burwick were permanently barricaded with enormous concrete blocks. Aerial and sea defences were greatly improved, while two squadrons of modern fighters were based within easy reach of the naval base, in the north of Scotland. When the work was completed the Home Fleet returned to Scapa Flow. However, these defensive improvements did not deter the Luftwaffe's efforts, at least for the moment. Meanwhile Europe began to suffer a particularly hard winter, by far the severest for many years.

I./KG 30 carried out the occasional sortie without success. On 13 November the *Gruppe* entered the history books by becoming the first enemy aircraft to drop bombs on British soil (the previous attacks had either hit ships or landed in the sea). Their targets were military installations on the Shetland Islands, including an RAF flying-boat base at Sullom Voe. All four bombs dropped harmlessly into an open field, however. Typical of British humour, though, someone placed a dead rabbit (which had actually been purchased from a local butcher), in one of the bomb craters. The national press were quick to exploit the opportunity, using a photograph of the unfortunate 'bunny' for propaganda purposes.

On 22 December two Ju 88s of I./KG 30 flew over the Firth of Forth on a reconnaissance mission. They were chased away by Spitfires of 602 Squadron. However, one of the German aircraft crashed while returning to base. On New Year's Day 1940 six aircraft of I./KG 30 were flown over the Orkney and Shetland areas. One failed to return. On 3 February aircraft of I./KG 30 achieved their first confirmed success, when they sank the 875-ton minesweeping sloop HMS *Sphinx* off Moray Firth; another Ju 88 was lost. Six days later I./KG 30 achieved further success when they sank two small naval trawlers, the 550-ton *Fort Royal* and the 290-ton *Robert Bowen*, off Aberdeen, but again at the cost of one aircraft.

On 16 March, 18 Ju 88s of I./KG 30 attacked units of the British Home Fleet in Scapa Flow, while 16 He 111s of KG 26 concentrated their efforts on anti-aircraft positions and the airfields at Stromness, Barthhouse and Kirkwall. Despite lavish claims of hitting three battleships and one cruiser, only the last was correct. They had inflicted minor underwater damage to the 8-inch cruiser *Norfolk*, killing six of her crew. The *Iron Duke* was also slightly damaged from a trio of near misses. One civilian was also killed during the raid. I./KG 30 lost one of its aircraft, when it lost its bearings during the return flight and crash-landed on an island near Denmark, where the survivors were temporarily interned.

In late March II./KG 30 began operations in the North Sea led by *Gruppenkommandeur* Hauptmann Claus Hinkelbain. In less than a week he had lost three of his *Staffelkapitäns*. On 29 March Oberleutnant Rudolf Quadt was shot down by anti-aircraft fire while attacking a small coastal convoy off Northumberland. Oberleutnant Hauptmann Fritz Koch followed, four days later, when he crashed in bad weather in Germany, after returning from an evening attack on Scapa Flow. The following day, 3 April, Oberleutnant Karl Overweg was shot down by a Sunderland flying-boat, which was protecting a convoy to Bergen.

On 9 April, the day that Germany invaded Denmark and Norway, the Luftwaffe received a reconnaissance report that a large section of the British Home Fleet was near Bergen in Norway, under Commander-in-Chief, Admiral Sir Charles M. Forbes. Early that same morning Forbes had been joined by Admiral Layton (18th Cruiser Squadron) with two cruisers, and seven cruisers and thirteen destroyers under the command of Admiral Cunningham (1st Cruiser Squadron), Admiral Edward-Collins (2nd Cruiser Squadron) and the French Rear Admiral Derrien (with his own squadron of French ships). At 06.20 Admiral Forbes requested intelligence reports, regarding the enemy's strength at Bergen, which he intended to attack. At 11.30 Forbes detached Admiral Layton, with the cruisers *Glasgow, Manchester, Sheffield* and *Southampton* and the Tribal class destroyers *Afridi, Gurkha, Mashona, Matabele, Mohawk, Sikh* and *Somali*, to attack Bergen. At this point in time the Home Fleet was some eighty miles south-west of Bergen and heavy seas were hampering their progress. Early in the afternoon the RAF reported that two German cruisers of the Köln class were in harbour. Shortly after, the Admiralty cancelled the attack believing, incorrectly, that the Norwegian shore defences were in German hands and that Forbes' combined force was insufficient in both numbers and size.

Meanwhile, the weather had cleared and German reconnaissance aircraft had resumed shadowing duties. The first enemy attack, consisting of 47 Ju 88s of all three *Gruppen*'s of KG 30 and 41 He 111s of KG 26, concentrated on Layton's splinter group. The *Gurkha* was sunk and the cruisers *Galatea* and *Southampton* were damaged by near misses. The main body of the fleet was also attacked and the *Rodney* was hit by a bomb which failed to penetrate her six-inch armoured deck. The *Devonshire, Glasgow* and *Sheffield* were slightly damaged by near misses. Four Ju 88s were shot down, including Oberleutnant Hauptmann Siegfried Mahrenholtz who was the *Gruppenkommadeur* of III./KG 30.

The following evening nineteen Ju 88s of I. and II./KG 30 set course for Scapa Flow. This time their objective was the Royal Navy's fuel depots. Attacking at dusk, two more aircraft fell foul of anti-aircraft fire and failed to return to Westerland.

On 17 April the heavy cruiser *Suffolk* bombarded the seaplane base at Stavanger, badly damaging installations and destroying four seaplanes.

Initially the force was attacked by Heinkels of I./KG 26 which had taken off from Sola. Despite claims of two hits on the *Suffolk* she steamed on, apparently unharmed. For nearly seven hours the *Suffolk* was attacked by Ju 88s of II./KG 30, sustaining heavy bomb damage. Had it not been for a fortuitous encounter by a dozen Blenheims, she may well have been sunk. The RAF bombers of 107 Squadron were on their way to attack Stavanger-Sola, from their temporary base at Lossiemouth. Seeing the plight of the British cruiser, the Blenheims broke up the formation, forcing them to return to Westerland. The *Suffolk* limped back into Scapa Flow on the morning of the next day with her quarterdeck awash.

On the afternoon of 19 April, near Namsos, convoys FP 1 and FP 1 (B), consisting of four French troopships, carrying troops of the 5 Chasseurs Alpins and escorted by the French cruiser *Emile Bertin* (Rear Admiral Derrien) and six French destroyers, rendezvoused with the British cruiser *Cairo*. Although the troops were successfully cleared, the *Emile Bertin* was hit by bombs from Ju 88s of II./KG 30 and was forced to retire to Scapa Flow. On 21 April aircraft of II./KG 30 sank two anti-submarine trawlers at Aandalsnes. A combination of some two dozen aircraft from KG 30 and III./LG 1 were in action on 23 April, at the Aandalsnes area, to attack shipping in fjords. The reported sinking of a Norwegian steamer was somewhat balanced by the loss of one of LG 1's aircraft.

On 10 May 1940, the day Germany began the invasion of Holland, Belgium and Luxembourg, pilot Unteroffizier Peter Wilhelm Stahl joined KG 30, under the command of *Gerschwaderkommodore* (equivalent to Wing Leader) Oberstleutnant Löbel. Stahl reported to II. *Gruppe* at Oldenburg, with the crew he had trained with at Barth; they were: navigator/bomb aimer Unteroffizier Gross, radio operator Unteroffizier Harras and ventral gunner Gefreiter Arndt. The day after their arrival they were detailed to 5 *Staffel* of II. *Gruppe*. During the first day of the invasion of the Low Countries KG 30 lost eight of its aircraft, four from I./KG 30, one from II./KG 30 and three from III./KG 30.

Meanwhile, during an attack on shipping near Narvik by Ju 88s of II./KG 30, on 18 May, the battleship *Resolution* was hit by a 1,000-kg bomb which penetrated three of her decks. On 26 May the anti-aircraft cruiser *Curlew* was bombed and sunk by Ju 88s of KG 30, off Skaanland. The *Curlew* had originally been intended to be the flagship of Lord Cork (Admiral of the Fleet); instead he flew his flag in the anti-aircraft cruiser *Cairo*. Just before midnight on 27-28 May, *Cairo* and *Coventry* (Rear Admiral Vivian), the destroyers *Fame*, *Firedrake*, *Havelock*, *Walker* and *Whirlwind* and the sloop *Stork*, steamed into Rombaksfjord to execute a close bombardment from both sides of the Narvik peninsula. At midnight troops of the Foreign Legion and 6 Norwegian Division began crossing Rombaksfjord to a peninsula, just north of the town. At the same time, supported by the cruiser *Southampton*, the Polish brigade began its offensive across the hills of the Ankenes sector in the south. At 04.00 the *Cairo* was hit by a bomb.

Dunkirk, where the main evacuation of the British Expeditionary Force took place, had been spared from enemy bombardment for thirty-six hours, from 29 May, because of rain and a 300-foot cloud base. However, on 31 May, at 15.32, formations of *Luftflotte* 2 reappeared, this time strengthened by Ju 88s of KG 30 from Holland and LG 1 from Düsseldorf. The evacuation suffered continuous aerial bombardment, resulting in the sinking of the passenger ship *Queen of the Channel* on 28 May, the destroyer *Grenade* and the passenger ships *Lorina*, *Fenella*, and *King Orry* on 29 May and the *Normannia* the following day.

1 June brought no respite to the aerial attack; the destroyer leader *Keith*, flying the flag of Admiral W. F. Wake-Walker, and the destroyer *Basilisk* were sunk, along with the minesweeper *Skipjack*, which was carrying a great number of troops. Renewed attacks resulted in the destroyer *Havant* and the French destroyer *Foudroyant* being sunk and the personnel vessel *Prague*, which was carrying 3,000 French troops, being seriously damaged. The *Brighton Queen* and the *Scotia*, both crammed with French troops, also went to the bottom; many other ships were damaged.

During the summer campaign of 1940 KG 30 was used in other theatres of war, including a massed raid upon Paris on 3 June. After the German breakthrough in June, *Luftflotte* 2, under General der Flieger Albert Kesselring, was given the responsibility of harassing the Allied evacuation from France's Atlantic ports.

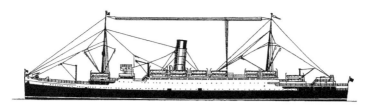

IV

THE FINAL VOYAGE

At Liverpool docks, on the morning of 13 June 1940, the crew began to pay off the *Lancastria*, signing off articles, picking up their discharge books and collecting their wages. The troopship was scheduled for a routine overhaul. Captain Rudolph Sharp had already left for his home in Liverpool, leaving his duties, as was customary, to his chief officer Harry Grattidge. Grattidge's duties were many and varied as the ship was prepared for cursory dry docking procedures. At Glasgow Captain Sharp had requested the removal of 1,407 tons of surplus oil fuel, which was being carried in deep tanks at the bottom of No. 3 hold. It was a request for which time was not allowed and which was later to become a fatal oversight.

Meanwhile, excited crew members filtered down the gangway to begin journeys home for long-awaited leave with loved ones. Grattidge's time would come, but first he had to attend to a pile of paperwork and sign the General Manager's report. He planned a three-week leave at his home in the Lake District. He did manage to slip uptown for a brief lunch at the Adelphi before strolling back to the Cunard offices at Pier Head, where he had left some documents for safe keeping. Here too he expected to pick up his railway warrant for the subsequent journey north.

Cunard's marine superintendent was Captain Davies, an energetic and efficient Welshman. As soon as Grattidge saw him approaching he knew something was wrong. Davies instructed him to hail a taxi and return to the ship immediately. From there he was to recall the crew: the *Lancastria* was urgently needed at Plymouth and would be sailing at midnight.

As soon as Grattidge arrived back on board he telephoned Captain Sharp, informing him of the change of plan. Sharp instructed him to call back the crew and assured Grattidge that he would be back aboard before sailing. However, the first instruction, to recall the crew, was not an easy procedure. By now most were either on trains or awaiting their arrival at Lime Street and Central stations; others were doing the same at

Liverpool's bus terminal. Tannoys crackled out inaudible messages requesting crew members to report to the station master's office. For those living farther afield, telegrams were sent, stating: "You are urgently requested to return to the ship immediately. Acknowledge. Master.' Few had the luxury of owning a telephone, but those that did were contacted from a local post office.

While all this was taking place the ship, which was berthed at Gladstone Dock, had to be prepared for sea. Food, water and oil fuel had to be loaded or pumped aboard. Chief Engineer James Dunbar organised his staff; boilers had to be brought back on line and engines rotated as the turbines were warmed through in readiness for the forthcoming voyage. There were a hundred and one jobs to do and each department buzzed with activity. Watchkeeping rotas were, for the moment, suspended until enough crew members were back on board to reintroduce the system. Not knowing their destination after reaching Plymouth, it was imperative to fill fuel and water tanks to capacity. Slowly, but surely, all but three of the disgruntled crew filed back aboard, wondering what on earth was going on. What could be so important to warrant such a dramatic change of plan?

Michael Sheehan had just been paid off a ship in Avonmouth after a recent trip to Montreal. He had returned to Liverpool with the intention of joining a Canadian Pacific Line ship, but in a public house near the docks the Cunard shipping master had entered, asking for crew to join the *Lancastria*. Michael volunteered, signing on as a quartermaster and boarding the ship as soon as she entered Sandon Lock. He had just located his cabin and dumped his gear when he was detailed to the twelve-to-four watch. He was to relieve his watch mate at the wheel immediately, as it was 2 p.m.

The oldest member of the crew was seventy-four-year-old deck hand Donald Sutherland; and the youngest was deck boy T. O'Connor, who was making his first trip to sea at the tender age of fourteen. The *Lancastria* sailed from Liverpool on schedule just before midnight on 13 June in the company of the *Franconia*, which had also been called into immediate unexpected service. The two Cunarders arrived at Plymouth on the morning of 15 June, after a thirty-hour voyage, and dropped anchor. On their passage along the west coast they had passed a fleet of Isle of Man packet-boats, Irish cross-channel steamers and several freighters, all steaming in the same direction.

Staying on board the *Lancastria*, Sharp and Grattidge were visited by officials from the Ministry of Shipping. Their purpose was to give them sailing orders and to inspect the four accommodation decks. By design, the boat and promenade decks were used solely for utility purposes, while B, C, D and E decks provided cabin accommodation, insufficiently spacious for large numbers of troops, but the inspectors found that the holds could provide extra space for many more men.

On *Lancastria*'s A deck, referred to on board as the promenade deck, which began forward and abaft of the 'island'-type bridge, were four lifeboats, two either side of her foremast. Behind the bridge, and one deck higher, was the boat deck. Here another twenty-four lifeboats and two motor barges were stowed, two to each Welin davit. The two barges were stowed abreast and inboard of the first four, nested, lifeboats. A single funnel, which was positioned centrally, was directly in line with the second two pairs of lifeboats, while the after mast protruded from the boat deck between the sixth set of four lifeboats. The two masts and funnel had a slight but pleasing rake. Below the boat deck, A deck continued a short way aft, housing four more lifeboats and two swimming pools, which were currently empty of water and roped off. Aft of A deck was the docking bridge. B deck was open astern of the after mast, as far as the stern of the ship. Its accommodation area continued as far forward as the for'd end of the boat deck.

The majority of the *Lancastria*'s first-class cabins, with en suite baths, were on B deck. The public rooms were on A deck and were currently bereft of their customary furniture and fittings. They comprised a garden lounge, dance floor, gymnasium, smoke room, writing room, cocktail bar and café. Most of these rooms were divided by vestibules, which led off from a large wood-panelled foyer lounge. Here a veneered stairwell embraced double companionways which descended individually to all lower decks. The first-class dining saloon was on D deck and, in the ship's days of glory, housed thirty-eight tables of various sizes. Now it was set out for troop work and was much more crammed and Spartan. The marble pillars, which appeared to support the deck above, were permanent fixtures and gave some idea of the original grandeur of the ship. A stripped liner adapted for troopship work invariably lacked the atmosphere and lustre that permitted its peacetime passengers to escape into the make believe world it was originally designed for. Stewards, who had waited on their every whim, cooks, who had provided exquisite food at any time of the day and musicians and artists, who had provided almost continuous entertainment, were all a thing of the past. In its place the ship had been transformed into little more than a floating canteen and doss-house, providing the basic requirements for its non-paying passengers, who were either going to or from a war zone.

Acting on sudden orders the *Lancastria* weighed anchor and proceeded from Plymouth Sound an hour before midnight on 15 June; her destination – Brest. She was accompanied once more by the 20,341-ton *Franconia*. The passage over to the French coast was uneventful, even the sea was flat calm.

38 (above). *Franconia* boasting Cunard's white cruising livery and anchored at Liverpool.

39 (opposite). Map showing the probable route of the *Lancastria* and *Franconia* from Plymouth to France.

At daybreak, some way off Brest, the coast was hidden from view by clouds of black smoke, which were drifting lethargically from demolished oil refineries and storage tanks, across the coastline and out across the English Channel. Captain Sharp received instructions to proceed to Quiberon Bay, signalled by the destroyer *Wolverine*. Throughout the fine afternoon of 16 June the two ships shaped course southwards, still in sight of the French coast. Nearing their destination and with the day beginning to draw to a close, the *Franconia* was led into the twisting channel, which started about ten miles north of Belle Ile, by a trawler and passed through the boom defence, while the *Lancastria* steamed a little way astern. Suddenly, and without warning, the leading ship was attacked by a lone Ju 88 bomber, which dropped a stick of bombs so near to the *Franconia*'s stern that she was physically lifted out of the water.

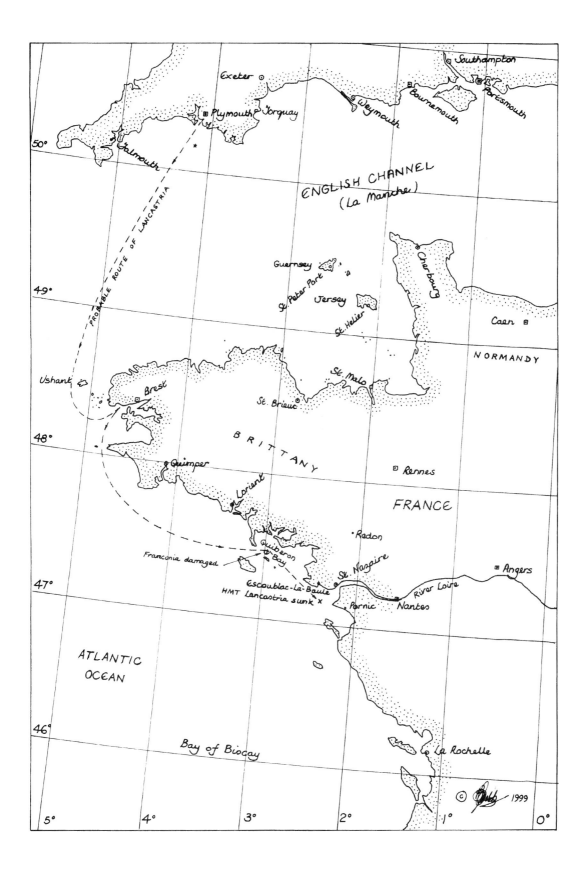

40. Another view of the *Franconia*; she was near-missed by a Ju 88 as she entered the twisting channel leading to Quiberon Bay. She took no further part in the evacuation. This photograph was taken on 1 March 1948, as she entered Valletta harbour carrying a large number of troops.

Although the *Lancastria* was the larger of the two Cunarders, the German pilot had selected the *Franconia* as his prime target. The proximity and force of the bombs, although they had actually missed the ship, nevertheless sprung some of her shell plates and put an engine out of alignment. This was serious damage, and the *Franconia*'s master was left with no alternative but to drop anchor and await damage reports. The decision was made to return home (she arrived back in Liverpool with water lapping over her engine room plates). The *Lancastria* steamed on into Quiberon Bay alone, dropped anchor around 18.00 hours and awaited further orders.

Captain Sharp did not have to wait long; acting on fresh instructions he weighed anchor around midnight and, under the cover of darkness, proceeded to Charpentier Roads, near Saint-Nazaire, arriving at 06.00 on 17 June. The *Lancastria* anchored in approximately 12 fathoms of water (72 feet or 22 metres) at lowest tide. All morning the sky throbbed to the distant sound of enemy aircraft. Shortly after her arrival the *Lancastria* was boarded by a naval transport officer (NTO) who informed Sharp that he must take as many troops as possible, without regard to the limits laid down by international law. When Chief Officer Grattidge asked the NTO if this was another capitulation, the officer replied: "Don't even mention the word. It's merely a temporary movement of troops." It was hardly a convincing statement.

62

Grattidge recognised the two destroyers which tied up alongside to begin embarkation. He had worked with them in Norway during the evacuation earlier in the month. An officer on board one of them asked Grattidge if he could spare a hawser, as most of his were unsafe to use. The reply was affirmative, adding that he would require a receipt! The naval officer broke into laughter, replying "you can have a receipt, but you'll be lucky if you get it home!"

From 08.00 ships of all sizes transported personnel from Saint-Nazaire to the *Lancastria*. By the early afternoon she had embarked nearly 6,000 personnel, including a small number of civilian men, women and children. Captain Sharp, with his ship full to capacity, awaited completion of the embarkation of other ships and further orders. He assumed that his ship was to sail in convoy, escorted by warships of the Royal Navy.

41. Groups of troops line the quay and the inner (north) caisson of *Normandie* dock at Saint-Nazaire, awaiting embarkation on board the *Highlander*. The ships in the background are inside the port in Penhouet Basin, the larger part of the docks at that time.

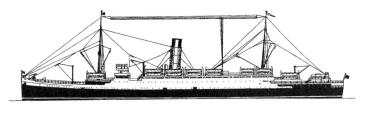

V

LAST CHANCE TO EVACUATE

Meanwhile, General Lord Alanbrooke, who had handled his men with great skill at Dunkirk, had handed his 2 Corps to a very junior Major General Bernard Law Montgomery before departing from French soil by ship on 30 May. He was sent back to France in mid-June, by General Sir John Dill, Chief of the Imperial General Staff (CIGS), to make the necessary arrangements for the evacuation of approximately 150,000 troops and the retrieval of large stocks of vehicles and equipment that had been accumulated since September 1939, when war had first been declared. General Brooke met Marshal Maxime Weygand on 14 June at his new military headquarters in Briare, on the upper reaches of the River Loire. The tired French commander informed Brooke that 'the French Army had ceased to be able to offer organised resistance and was disintegrating.' During the evening of the same day Major Macartney, from Quartermaster General (Movements) War Office, also reported to Brooke, who by now had moved to Le Mans, to outline the order of priority for shipment of stores etc., and to provide an outline plan for the evacuation of troops and personnel. During the early hours of 15 June Lieutenant General J. H. Marshall-Cornwall met with Brooke to discuss the current situation; Brooke placed all British troops (Norman Force), working with the 10 French Army, under his command. He had been given orders to co-operate with that Army until the opportunity arose to disengage his troops and withdraw them to Cherbourg for evacuation.

The withdrawal of British Expeditionary Forces (BEF) from Cherbourg began on 15 June. Flights of the Canadian Division, which had arrived at the assembly area, were sent back to Brest for embarkation, corps troops were re-embarked at Saint-Malo and various lines of communication (L of C), base details and transportation troops were moved nearer to the west coast of France in readiness to evacuate back to Britain. The latest position of the German Army Group B was, in relation to the front of the 10 French Army, still unclear. Low cloud and poor visibility had prevented aerial reconnaissance and the lack of ground

64

troops between Alençon and Tours meant that an examination of that area was also not possible. It was generally thought that there was little enemy action west of Rouen. However, in and around the Conches-en-Ouche area, it was known that the 157 Infantry Brigade was engaged in battle with German infantry. Furthermore, a British bomber pilot had witnessed a German column of all arms moving south near Evreux, where he been compelled to make a forced landing after running into heavy anti-aircraft fire. This report confirmed previous information about the German Army Group B's movement south, towards Chartres. Major General Edward Barrington de Fonblanque, three officers and two clerks naturally felt exposed, due to a lack of troops in that area and wisely moved his headquarters back to Vitré, twenty miles west of Laval, with the General Officer commanding the L of C Area and part of his staff (Brooke was entirely dependant on L of C Signals for his communications).

At around noon Brooke was contacted by the CIGS informing him of Churchill's concern over the withdrawal of the 52 Division (not including the troops with the 10 French Army). The Prime Minister wanted the embarkation arrangements cancelled, as he feared a disintegration of morale within the French Army if it was implemented. Brooke explained that his plans had already been approved and to change the 52's embarkation arrangements from Cherbourg could jeopardise their eventual re-embarkation. The CIGS replied that Churchill did not want the withdrawal to proceed without the Government's approval.

Meanwhile, Brooke was becoming increasingly alarmed by the lack of knowledge concerning the whereabouts of the German Army near Le Mans. If the enemy penetrated towards Laval and Rennes, it would seriously endanger the safety of both himself, his immediate staff and the remaining members of the BEF. At 21.50 Brooke spoke once more with the CIGS, informing him of the situation as he perceived it and pressing once more for the evacuation of the 52 Division. The required shipping was now available at Cherbourg. An hour-and-a-half later the CIGS gave Brooke permission to embark one field regiment, one field company and other details of the 52 Division who were not deemed necessary for the support of the remaining men of the Division. Later that night, with the embarkation orders already issued, another battalion and a troop of anti-tank guns, from the 52 Division, were put under the command of General Marshall-Cornwall, to protect the southern part of the Cherbourg peninsula in and around Saint-Sauveur-le-Vicomte.

On 16 June telephone conversations continued between Brooke and the CIGS. Once again no aerial reconnaissance was possible due to poor weather conditions. However, reports from the Norman Force and Motor Contact officers did reveal that the enemy was in contact with the 10 French Army along its front, but the only serious confrontation was against the 157 Infantry Brigade. Captured enemy documents revealed that it was German Army Group B's intention to attack Cherbourg and Brest on 16 June.

During the afternoon Brooke moved south-west to establish new headquarters at Redon, about 25 miles north of Saint-Nazaire. Here, he again contacted the CIGS, and was told to keep the Norman Force with the 10 French Army until its disintegration. Then, and only then, Marshall-Cornwall was to withdraw his force for embarkation from Cherbourg or, if that were impossible, another convenient port. Meanwhile, Brooke organised the transportation of supplies and ammunition to Cherbourg, in readiness for the Norman Force's expected withdrawal. Once started, this would be a difficult procedure to reverse. That same evening Brooke conversed with Major General Drew, Commander of the 52 Division, and learned that one of Drew's brigades had already embarked and that the second brigade would follow suit on 17 June.

On the morning of 17 June Brooke received the half-expected news from Marshall-Cornwall; the 10 French Army was in full retreat towards Laval and Rennes, and he was withdrawing his remaining troops to Cherbourg for embarkation. Shortly after, Brooke ordered Air Commodore Cole-Hamilton, who commanded the Air Component, to move, with two fighter squadrons and his one flight of reconnaissance aircraft, to the Channel Islands. From there he was to co-operate with the Norman Force to carry out reconnaissance duties and protect the embarkation areas in and around Cherbourg. The remaining fighter squadron was to operate from Brest, carrying out similar duties in that area.

At 11.30 Brooke explained his plan to Air Marshal Barratt, also discussing the embarkation arrangements from La Rochelle for his men, who were defending Nantes and Saint-Nazaire during the evacuation. The CIGS telephoned Brooke at 13.00 stating that the BBC had reported that the Pétain Government had requested an armistice. Brooke then spoke with the senior naval officer Captain Allen, RN, and General de Fontblanque to explain the recent decisions and the current situation. He then ordered them to make every possible effort to embark as many men as possible along with guns, equipment and vehicles. By 15.30 Brooke had discovered that all telecommunications with London had been severed at Rennes and that he had similar problems with all the ports in France, with the exception of Nantes. At 16.15 he left Redon and proceeded to the outskirts of Saint-Nazaire, with his staff, the General Officer commanding the L of C and Captain Allen.

———

Sergeant Strudwick was in charge of a hundred vehicles and drivers belonging to the British air forces in headquarters at Coulommiers, about thirty miles east of Paris. His unit, codenamed 'Panther', was dispersed in nearby villages. Such was their plight that they slept in their lorries and ate in local cafés. Every day the café owners were paid by the accounts officer for the food and drink supplied to the troops.

In early June the sections were called in to headquarters, where they received orders to load the various departments' equipment and drive to Olivet, via Fontainebleau, where their new headquarters were to operate. The journey was extremely slow, frustrated by traffic that was heading in the same direction, south, away from the advancing German army. The roads were cluttered with all forms of wheeled transport from bicycles to farm carts, all piled high with treasured belongings and the necessities of life. Sergeant Strudwick recalls:

> ...Some of the sights were heartbreaking, I remember seeing a farmer in tears, his horse pulling his wagon had collapsed in the road and was obviously finished. Some pitied him, some cursed him for blocking the way. During our stay at Olivet every day and night the endless traffic groaned slowly on. A man and a woman approached me, he was pushing a small motor cycle, the woman a pram with a small child in it. They had run out of petrol. I filled his tank, they then tied the pram to the motor cycle and with both adults on the motor cycle and towing the pram they joined the trek south. I noticed, as they pulled away, that the pram tyres were already worn down to the rims...

On 10 June the RAF's headquarters were moved to 21 Aircraft Depot at Nantes, while Sergeant Strudwick remained at Olivet in charge of the rear party of motor transport. He was instructed to wait for the sections that had been detailed for evacuation duties and in the meantime to offer fuelling facilities to other vehicles passing through. During the afternoon of 14 June, acting on the orders of Wing Commander Macfadyen, who was the officer in charge of the rear party, Sergeant Strudwick assembled all motor transport and moved off at dusk towards Nantes. The twenty-four hour journey was repeatedly hampered by air raids, accidents and even security checks by the French police. Strudwick continues his story:

> ...During the evening of the following day, 15 June, our mixed convoy arrived at Nantes. Here [there] was disorder; canteens and NAAFI store sheds had been evacuated and thrown open. Soldiers and airmen alike were drinking whiskey and gin neat from the bottles which were theirs for the taking, from the wide open tents and sheds. I tried to talk sense and persuade my men not to indulge, as I had received instructions to assemble all available lorries and drivers at dawn, at a certain point, to ferry men into Saint-Nazaire. I gathered from this that we were to leave the country...

With the exception of one driver, who was so drunk that he could not stand, despite various shock methods to sober him, Strudwick led his drivers to the assembly point where he loaded his dozen or so vehicles with airmen and troops. The bright sunny morning of 16 June was soon darkened by black smoke, which billowed from sabotaged petrol and fuel depots. As they reached the outskirts of Saint-Nazaire they were turned off the road, by military police, onto an airfield which was being used as a reception area. This was as far as road vehicles were allowed to go, due to heavy congestion at the port; the remainder of the journey was to be carried out on foot. In the RAF's case, the men were required to march with their standard active service kit: full pack, kit bag, two blankets and a ground sheet. After a cup of tea, corned beef and biscuits, which was provided at a hastily rigged cookhouse in the corner of a disused hangar, a party of about a hundred set off towards the port that afternoon. They arrived outside locked gates, only to be told that the gates would not be reopened until the following morning. The tired men slept on the roads and pavements, some placing their helmets over their faces to protect them from the air raids which persisted intermittently throughout the night.

———

Rumours were rife, and some placed the Germans as near as Le Mans, barely 150 miles from the port. At Chateau Bourgon, an airfield on the outskirts of Nantes, which was home to the French aircraft manufacturer Potez, 98 Squadron and 22 Aircraft Depot prepared to leave. 98 Squadron were the reserve and support group for other Fairey Battle squadrons deployed in France. On 15 June all the squadron aircraft were flown back to Britain, including a number of training aircraft, which operated from a nearby satellite airfield. Each aircraft was able to carry one ground crew besides its normal operational crew. In the evening, all remaining junior ranks of 98 Squadron were assembled in a NAAFI tent, where the Royal Army Service Corps (RASC) allowed them to help themselves to the remaining stocks of chocolates and sweets.

They were then allocated to a three-ton Albion truck, complete with solid tyres. With more than thirty RAF personnel and kit, it was hardly surprising that few could sit during the bumpy journey to Saint-Nazaire docks. When they arrived, there were no ships ready to take them, so they were re-directed to an airfield which was under construction on the outskirts of the city. The airfield had been dug for mole drains and the latticed ditches served as convenient slit trenches, which many used for cover from the sporadic night air attacks.

––––––

Possibly one of the longest journeys made was that of the employees and families of Avions Fairey in Gosselies, Belgium, near Charleroi and 30 miles south of Brussels. One family, M. and Mdm. Legroux, their 13-year-old daughter Emilie and 11-year-old son Roger, were among a sizeable group that were forced to move southward three days after Germany invaded Belgium on 10 May. The factory was damaged during the first hours of hostilities and the whole workforce started to clear and pack papers, plans, documents and a partly-built Hurricane, which was being built under licence. Everything was then loaded onto trucks, before starting the long journey to Bordeaux. They reached their destination on 23 May and were accommodated in the outskirts of the city. Mr E. O. Tips, the managing director, was already in England, while his family remained in Bordeaux with the others. Meanwhile, the men worked in a local aircraft company. As the Germans advanced deeper into France the employees and their families received instructions to proceed to England. On 15 June they travelled to Nantes, some by train and some by road, where the documents and material saved from Avion Fairey, and the single men, were shipped to England safely in an old French coal ship. The married couples and children were to travel to Saint-Nazaire for passage to the same destination, but on another ship.

––––––

Food was scarce, and many of the major roads were congested with masses of Dutch, Belgian and French refugees, all trudging away from the advancing Germans, trying to avoid capture. Daily the refugees and army personnel were bombed and strafed by German aircraft. Some of the soldiers of the Royal Army Ordnance Corps (RAOC) were reduced to eating iron rations, scrounging bread from other army lads and French locals. As the soldiers left Nantes each was given five rounds of ammunition, a token gesture that was better than nothing.

Six gunners of 159 Battery, 53 City of London HAA Regiment, Royal Artillery (RA) also joined the group. Their headquarters had been set up in the lovely grounds of Chateau Lombarderie, on the outskirts of Nantes, in the middle of May. Early in June their Regiment had moved south to Marseilles, leaving the six gunners as a rear party.

———

In Rouen, Private Sidney Dunmall and other members of the Royal Army Pay Corps (RAPC) had thoroughly enjoyed their short stay. Cinemas, theatres and interesting shops had given them plenty to explore and do. A tram ride even enabled them to extend their perimeters to the French countryside, when free time allowed. However, this peaceful existence was soon to change. By the middle of May columns of refugees filtered through the city day and night. Along the River Seine French engineers set explosive charges, ready to destroy the bridges, while other French soldiers disarmed Belgian soldiers. There was even the bizarre arrival of a Brussels fire engine with the crew still wearing their uniforms, as if ready to attend a fire.

By the beginning of June the RAPC had been instructed to pack their equipment and march to Sotteville-lès-Rouen, where officers eventually persuaded the stationmaster to allow them to board an empty cattle train. Each truck was clearly labelled with the same notice, stating '40 men or eight horses'! As they approached Rennes, the engine driver obeyed a semaphore signal and brought his train to a halt. It was conveniently near an *estaminet* (a small French café, which also sells alcoholic drink and refreshments). A number of troops scurried up the hillside and entered the building, purchasing bottles of champagne, wine and spirits from an elderly couple that ran the business. As they started back towards the train they were cursed by an irate CO and urgent blasts from the steam train's whistle.

Breathless, Sidney sat on the straw-covered floor and fumbled with the restraining wire and cork of a bottle of champagne he had just purchased. He was soon to discover that his choice was ill-judged; the heat of the day and the bumpy return to the train was to prove a deadly combination. The cork accelerated skywards striking the roof of the truck, closely followed by the entire contents of the bottle, showering everyone in the vicinity. A nearby friend saw the despair on Sidney's face, as he stared at the empty bottle in disbelief. He invited him to take a swig from his bottle; the strength of the contents proved quite a shock for the young soldier – it was green chartreuse!

The train eventually puffed into Pornichet where the RAPC were taken to their new headquarters in a large private house. Their stay was to be short. Barely a week later they too were assembled, briefed and marched to Saint-Nazaire, joining hundreds of other troops from the infantry camp at Pornichet. Their march ended at Saint-Nazaire sea front, where they spent the night. As they peacefully slumbered on a grass verge, using their respirators on top of their steel helmets as pillows, they were soon awakened by a nearby ack-ack battery, which blazed away at unseen enemy aircraft approaching Saint-Nazaire. They discovered some slit trenches, where they spent the rest of the night. As day broke they were greeted with early morning mist and drizzling rain. They were then assembled and marched to a busy quayside to await embarkation to a large ship which was barely visible through the haze.

————

Sapper Leslie Bailey, RE, had joined 663 Artisan Works Company in January 1940 and was shipped to Brittany shortly after. Their job was to build Nissen huts for BEF troops in the district of La Baule. Their commanding officer, Captain Morgan, allowed them to build one for their own use, providing that they built it in their own time. This was just the incentive they needed; in no time at all everyone was housed in a new hut complete with running water and hot showers. Several rented French radio sets created a homely atmosphere. Leslie was looking forward to some leave at the end of June, when he was to marry Marie Horrill, a pretty girl he had met in Plymouth towards the end of 1938.

As the Germans pushed further south into the heart of France orders were received to destroy non-essential equipment and proceed to Saint-Nazaire. The radios were the first to go, smashed beyond use. Once ready to leave for the port, the 250-man unit were more than surprised to discover that their six trucks had been stolen by another regiment! With no other alternative, they hitched lifts to the outskirts of the port. One amusing mishap took place on Leslie's truck as it sped along the road. A glowing cigarette end had ignited the camouflaged awning which covered the truck. The driver quickly stopped the vehicle and the blazing cover was discarded; luckily no one was injured. The unit eventually reached Saint-Nazaire, where they regrouped and awaited orders.

————

One group of soldiers who were not so lucky to hitch a ride was a detachment of 2 Battalion Sherwood Foresters, belonging to 5 Company. They too had been stationed at Rouen for some time. Shortly after the successful evacuation of Dunkirk they were formed up, in full marching order, and told that they were moving out, by foot, to an unknown destination. That destination turned out to be Saint-Nazaire, a journey of just over 200 miles. Nearing the end of their long march they came across a farm where they took the opportunity to wash and freshen up. G. Skelton and three of his pals asked their company sergeant major if they could go to a nearby village for a few drinks. The CSM was a popular man and granted them permission, providing that they promised not to be late.

Skelton had had a windfall a few days earlier, when he won several games of Housey Housey (Bingo). Knowing that French currency would soon be of no use, they proceeded to 'paint the town' and have a good drink. The following morning, 16 June, they began the final stretch of the journey, very much the worse for wear. They reached Saint-Nazaire at around noon. It was a beautiful sunny day. They reached the sea front and walked down to the beach, joining many other troops who were, similarly, awaiting embarkation.

———

In the meantime Lieutenant Colonel E. Studdy, who was the commanding officer of 1 Heavy Repair Shop (Motor Transport) Overseas, RASC, attended a confidential conference at Base HQ, St Étienne de Montluc, Nantes, on the morning of 15 June. The base commandant informed all OCs (officers commanding) that they had been given 48 hours to leave France and that all vital equipment was to be prepared for evacuation without delay.

Three hours later, all ranks were paraded and informed of the situation, stressing the need for secrecy and urgency. Work began immediately; machine tools were lifted, stores packed and suitable vehicles, under repair in the workshops or awaiting repair in a nearby park, were made roadworthy for troop carrying. An earlier attempt to secure a suitable ship to transport the equipment back to England proved fruitless. However, the 4,542-ton steamship *Marslew*, which was already at Saint-Nazaire, became available to take a limited amount of HRS' equipment. Extra work, dismantling generator sets and heavy machine tools was exacerbated by the 5-ton limitation of the dock's cranage. 'Happy', one of the seven dwarfs, was on the move; for it was this cartoon character that was depicted on all 1 HRS' trucks, with the motto 'whistle while you work'! Undoubtedly this was the best tool in the shop.

42. Motto and badge of 1 HRS (MT) RASC. It was painted on the sides of their lorries.

Lieutenant Blythe, who had overseen the first convoy loaded with five lathes, three drilling machines and a quantity of light equipment, reported back from the ship at 21.00, stating that there was plenty of room on board and that an air raid was currently in progress. Back at the base, work stopped for six hours due to darkness and fatigue.

At 04.00 on 16 June work was resumed. An hour later orders were given to render every defective vehicle in the park totally unserviceable: cylinder heads and blocks, gearboxes and crankcases were smashed, chassis', frames and axles were flame cut with oxy-acetylene torches and all unshippable equipment destroyed. Unfortunately, a brand new Humber staff car was also put to the hammer by mistake; a certain staff sergeant was far from amused! A message was also received that twenty-four 3-ton lorries would report to St Étienne de Montluc at 10.00 to transport personnel of 1 HRS and 50 Company, Auxiliary Military Pioneer Corps (AMPC) to Saint-Nazaire for embarkation. Meanwhile, the second convoy of equipment left for the port; this included auxiliary power sets, a lathe transformer, a switchboard, hand tools, fitters' kits and cases of stores. Boxed electrical gear had to be left behind because of the necessity to use every available vehicle to transport an even more important commodity – men.

Hours before the final move the quartermaster's stores were destroyed with acid, the shunting engine was steamed at speed into buffers, the 5-ton transportable crane, Lister truck and other forms of machinery were also destroyed. The convoy left just minutes after the scheduled departure time and barely twenty-one hours after they had received orders to move out. They arrived at Saint-Nazaire aerodrome just after noon, amidst considerable chaos, and were told to wait until given orders to proceed to the docks. By mid-afternoon it became apparent that there was little or no organisation, and many units chose to ignore the order to wait and proceeded towards the docks in advance of their orders. During an aerial attack, Lieutenant Colonel Studdy went down to the dockside to weigh up the situation. He soon discovered that there was no communication between the aerodrome and the docks, which was swarming with troops. Studdy rectified the situation by making out a timetable, to prevent other units going out of turn.

By 02.30, on 17 June, Studdy had assembled his men from 1 HRS and men from the AMPC, only to be held up by about 500 heavily laden RAF personnel. Fred Coe carried a Bren gun on one shoulder and a rifle on the other while Tom Hutchison and others, all of 1 HRS, took it in turns to carry the Bren gun tripod, tools and ammunition on a stretcher. During the 5-mile march Studdy's men were repeatedly delayed about every half mile; the RAF men were reduced to a crawl, but refused to let the army contingent pass. As they entered Saint-Nazaire some French locals opened the windows of their adjoining homes, turning up radios that were currently receiving a recording of the Marseillaise, no doubt concluding the announcement of the armistice. The march had taken two hours to complete, whereupon the men were led to a pier, maintaining a 200-yard gap between each company. A mounted guard prevented overcrowding and double-banking.

———

Private John Lees West, RAPC, had transferred from the 164 Field Ambulance, Royal Army Medical Corps (RAMC) in March 1940. After a spell of home leave he was posted to the Command Pay Office at Rouen. Shortly after the evacuation of Dunkirk they were moved to Pornichet, a small resort not far from Saint-Nazaire. On 15 June he had taken a walk to Pouliguen, near La Baule. On arrival he was approached by two NCOs (non-commissioned officers) and told to report back to barracks. When he arrived, he was confronted by chaos and told to pack as lightly as possible. They left the hotel under a flurry of blasphemy from the French, who naturally thought they were being deserted for good. On reaching the outskirts of the town, they bedded down as best they could.

Next morning they were marched two abreast along a muddy high-hedged road towards Saint-Nazaire. Occasional aerial attacks forced them to take cover in a convenient ditch which flanked the road. They eventually reached the port blistered but unscathed, whereupon they were told that they would not be able to board their transport until the following morning. They too were forced to spend an uncomfortable night under the regular attention of enemy aircraft.

———

On Saturday afternoon, 15 June, Second Lieutenant W. B. Forster, who was commanding 3 section of the 29 Railway Survey Company, Royal Engineers (RE) at St Gildas, where survey work had just been completed, was informed by a sergeant from 154 Railway Operation Company that he was standing by to evacuate. Forster consulted Major Simpson of 12 Company AMPC (OC Troops) to learn that he too was under two hours' notice to move. Petrol and oil reserves were to be destroyed by his men. Forster hastened back to camp and took driver O'Connor with a van to a bowser, where they loaded 80 gallons of petrol in case they ran short.

Meanwhile, Second Lieutenant F. A. R. Bessant arrived from Rennes, informing Forster that they were to take orders from OC 159 Railway Construction Company or OC Troops. Unable to find the 159 Company Forster ordered the destruction of all secret papers and had all kit loaded into a car and a lorry. In the early hours of the following morning Forster received a message from Major Simpson, which stated that Simpson and 12 Company AMPC were to stay and defend. He advised Forster to report to Savenay or Saint-Nazaire before 07.00. After a couple of hours' sleep Forster and his men set off to Savenay, where he reported to Lieutenant Colonel V. C. Lester an hour before the deadline. After breakfast they joined Lester's convoy and reached the reception area at Saint-Nazaire four hours later. Here they met 159 Railway Construction Company and Forster decided to join them. The officer's kit was driven to the quayside and placed under guard. Several air raids had taken place during the day, but no bombing was heard. After marching in sections to the docks, it was eventually decided to spend the night on the quay. Three sections bedded down on some large wooden crates, which contained new Caterpillar tractors.

At 01.30 on 17 June there was another air raid. No bombs were dropped, but Sapper Hailstone was hit in the eye by a piece of shrapnel. The eye was subsequently bathed and bandaged.

———

Wing Commander Douglas Macfadyen was in charge of nine officers and just over 200 other ranks of the BAFF's headquarters at Nantes. Acting on instructions he ensured that his men were embussed early on 16 June before he went on ahead, towards Saint-Nazaire, to make necessary arrangements. He arrived at a partially completed aerodrome, which was being used as a convenient assembly point where soldiers and airmen awaited instructions to proceed to Saint-Nazaire. Here he was instructed, by an army major, to assemble his men in a hanger, which was in the process of being cleared by another group of RAF personnel who had rested there the previous night. Macfadyen's group of men arrived at 09.00 amidst the growing chaos of large disorganised groups of RAF and army personnel. By noon the assembly area within the airfield had swollen to over 10,000 men, with a three-mile traffic jam tailing back towards Nantes.

Macfadyen was becoming increasingly anxious about the welfare of his men; repeated enquiries to the army officer in charge, as to what was going on, brought little respite. His apprehension grew when German aircraft flew over the area, highlighting the dangers of accumulating so many men in one place. In accordance with instructions he dispersed his party around the airfield, but was surprised to observe a reluctance to do the same by a majority of other military units. Macfadyen had been told that a few military groups had seen the congestion and lack of organisation, and had ignored military procedure and marched straight on towards the docks (which were themselves becoming congested).

At around 17.00, after strong protest, he and his men were finally given permission to proceed to Saint-Nazaire in readiness for embark-ation. They arrived near the port only to be faced with more delays, as a quarter of a mile long queue shuffled its way towards the dock entrance. By 22.00 Macfadyen had received information that the French admiral, commanding the port, had forbidden further embarkation in view of the danger of lights being shown to enemy airmen. Furthermore, the port would not reopen until 04.30 the next day. It was difficult to understand why such a decision had been made; the moon was nearly full and the sea flat calm; therefore no lights was necessary. Throughout the night enemy aircraft frequented the area, too distant to be endangered by the inadequate AA defences which, all too readily, engaged the threat, lighting the sky with their spectacular onion-shaped arcs of equi-spaced tracer.

————

During the night the 9,716-ton hospital ship MV *Somersetshire* berthed alongside the quay with lights ablaze, illuminating her white hull. A wide green band and bright red crosses proclaimed her neutrality. An officer on board hailed the commanding officer of the groups on the dockside. Major Hart, who answered the call, was asked how many men he had with him. "About two hundred" he replied. The ship's officer offered him and his men passage to Blighty, providing that they left their arms behind on the quayside. Hart thought for a moment and reluctantly refused the offer. The *Somersetshire,* one of the few ships in the Loire basin until the arrival of the *Lancastria,* sailed for home the next morning with patients and staff from 4 British Army Hospital, and plenty of room to spare. For Major Hart and many other British troops the decision not to join them was to prove a costly but unpredictable mistake.

43. Troops boarding HMS *Highlander* from the quayside, most of whom are carrying their rifles.

44. HMS *Highlander* fully loaded and on her way out to the *Lancastria*.

VI

EMBARKATION

During the early hours of 17 June troops, RAF personnel, civilian workers and their families made their way towards Saint-Nazaire docks in preparation for embarkation to the *Lancastria*. She lay at anchor in the Charpentier Roads, about nine miles from the French port and just over five miles from land. The gates at the entrance to the docks were opened and the troops that had spent a restless night outside were allowed in. RAF personnel were one of the first groups to board a French tug at around 06.00. The embarkation was laboriously slow, taking one and half hours, due to the large amount of kit that they carried. In contrast, the personnel of 1 Heavy Repair Shop (HRS) RASC accomplished the same manoeuvre in a third of the time. All the ships being used for embarkation to the large troopship were outside the docks, alongside a stone-built jetty, at Saint-Nazaire. Meanwhile, after the naval transport officers had disembarked from the *Lancastria*, a hurried boat drill was carried out under the watchful eye of Chief Officer Grattidge.

Lounge Steward L. R. Welsh had been detailed, by Chief Steward Fred Beattie, to count each person, as they came on board into the port side of the ship, with a small hand counter. After a while he was relieved of his duties because the lounge he usually looked after was in turmoil. It had been reserved for warrant officers and sergeants, who were all swarming around the bar shouting for drinks. Welsh struggled through the mass of soldiers, asking them to queue outside the cocktail bar, which he then opened and started to sell soft and alcoholic drinks.

The *Havelock* (ex-*Jutahy*) and *Highlander* (ex-*Jaguaribe*) were two of six 1,340-ton destroyers originally ordered by the Brazilian Navy, which were building in the United Kingdom at the outbreak of war and were acquired by the Royal Navy shortly after. These two new ships, which had worked alongside the *Lancastria* in Norway earlier in the month, began embarking around 600 troops at a time into each ship, to speed up the

45. Scene on the foredeck of the *Highlander* as troops begin to board. A and B turrets and the open bridge are clearly visible in the background.

process. As the morning wore on, repeated journeys were carried out by tugs, trawlers, tenders and destroyers; craft of many shapes and sizes, both French and British. All were packed solid with their human cargoes. They included the small river-ferry boats *Saint-Brévin, Saint-Christophe* and *Portland*, the trawler *Paul-Leferme*, the pilot schooner *La Lambarde* and the large tugs *Minotaure, Titan* and *Ursus* (each capable of carrying 1,000, 400 and 400 people respectively). To begin with the weather was not good; there were low clouds, intermittent rain and a cool wind.

At around 07.00 a convoy of ships from Newport, South Wales, anchored in Quiberon Bay. The ships in the convoy were: *Robert L. Holt, City of Lancaster, John Holt* (with Captain H. Fuller as Commodore and Admiral J. Burgess-Watson, DSO, as Naval Commander), *David Livingstone, Glenlea* and *Fabian*, escorted by the HM trawlers *Agate* (ex-*Mavis Rose*) and *Cambridgeshire*. Later that morning they discovered the true nature of their voyage and were ordered to sail to Saint-Nazaire to embark troops. As the *John Holt* was not a troopship, Captain Fuller ordered all available hands to construct gangways to the 'tween-decks, enabling easier access to these useful areas of deck space.

On arrival at Saint-Nazaire Roads the convoy was told to anchor, from a signal station ashore. As the captains obeyed this instruction the

Dundrum Castle (which had been diverted from Dunkirk with a full cargo of wool from South Africa) and the *Marslew* (which was carrying 1 HRS' military stores) came out of Saint-Nazaire's dock carrying troops, while the *Baharistan*, *Floristan*, *Glenaffric* and *Clan Ferguson* went in. Captain Fuller was surprised to see so many ships at anchor, with others sailing out into the open sea. A mile further out from the *John Holt* lay the *Lancastria*, far too big to consider entry past the South Channel of the Loire estuary.

Another ship that would play an important part in the ensuing events was the *Ulster Prince*. She had sailed, in convoy, from Gourock with three other channel steamers (*Ulster Monarch*, *Royal Scotsman* and *Royal Ulsterman*), bound for Nantes. However, on reaching Quiberon Bay their destinations had been altered. The *Ulster Prince* and *Royal Scotsman* were diverted to Lorient, where the former disembarked around four hundred French troops, while the other two ships returned to Brest. From Lorient the *Ulster Prince* (Captain Williams) was given fresh orders to proceed to Saint-Nazaire.

———

At about 07.30 a sizeable contingent of RAF personnel arrived alongside the *Lancastria*. Once on board they were allocated to either E deck or No. 2 hold. Senior NCOs were given cabins. Leading aircraftman C. W. Cornish settled into a corner of the hold before going in search of breakfast. After queuing for some time he did eventually reach the serving hatch, only to be denied food due to an ARP (air raid precaution) alarm. The serving hatch was slammed down and the ship's crew went to their allotted fire stations. Realising that the chances of obtaining any food were remote while repeated ARP alarms were being sounded, Cornish made his way onto the main deck, where he watched the process of embarkation with interest.

———

Meanwhile, the party of Avions Fairey's families, which now numbered forty-five, stood on the quayside discussing what to do. Fourteen of them decided to make for the interior of France, refusing to risk the voyage. The remaining thirty-one, including M. and Mdm. Legroux and their two children, boarded the *Lancastria*.

———

Private J. H. Drummond, RAOC, boarded the ship much later and was also allocated to a hold well below the water line. There were a few RAF personnel and army lads already there. Drummond quickly assessed the situation and grabbed one of the few palliasses which were stacked in one corner of the hold and settled down for a short nap. Hardly closing his eyes he was confronted by an army lad who informed him that they were serving food in the crew's dining room. Once located, they both settled down to their first proper meal for weeks, consisting of roast beef, cabbage and potatoes. Before returning to the hold, they found a row of bathrooms and even had a hot relaxing bath.

————

Squadron Leader E. M. C. Shipp, MBE, was in the RAF Voluntary Reserve and had been in charge of the mechanical transport section of the British Air Fighting Force headquarters in France since the beginning of 1940. He had been taken out to the *Lancastria* by tug, arriving on board at about 08.00. He, and fellow officer Bob Doig, soon located the dining saloon and, on the way in, picked up a life jacket each. After a good breakfast they grabbed their meagre belongings and donned their life jackets to save carrying them. They had not walked far before some wag remarked "All dressed up and nowhere to go", to which Shipp casually replied "You never know, they might come in handy!" It never crossed his mind how true this last statement would prove to be.

————

Captain Clement Stott detailed his senior NCO, Sergeant Bygraves, to take a roll-call of the fifty AMPC troops of 67 Company under his command. Just then a body of troops marched past them towards the quay; they were followed by three hundred or so RAF men. All were allowed to board the awaiting ships before them.

————

Colonel Wilson and Lieutenant Colonel Griggs boarded a tug along with the Royal Engineers (RE) under their command. Once on board the *Lancastria*, Colonel Wilson was made officer commanding (OC) troops while Griggs was persuaded to be the ship's adjutant. They found a suitable office and quickly assessed the configuration of personnel already embarked. Besides large contingents of RAF personnel, AMPC, RAOC, RE, RAPC and RAMC men, there were odds and ends from many other regiments, as well as a number of civilians. While performing his duties during the morning, Griggs noticed two or three Hurricanes flying around the ship, a reassuring sight. He was fortunate to dine with some civilians and Salvation Army people, albeit on a cold salad.

————

At around 08.30 Lieutenant Colonel Studdy, who had boarded with his men of 1 HRS, was approached by Chief Officer Grattidge, who asked him to mount all the available automatic weapons on the boat deck. RASC officer Captain D. Abbott was handed the responsibility and, half-an-hour later, he reported to Studdy, informing him that of the seventeen automatic weapons sent up to the boat deck, only three Bren guns, from his own company, were complete with tripods, spare barrels and ammunition. The remainder were in pretty poor condition. Meanwhile, the ship's master-at-arms was training Tom Hutchison and Alan Moore, both of 1 HRS, RASC, in the use of the ship's 3-inch high-angle anti-aircraft gun. Studdy had already spoken to Grattidge, enquiring if there was an infantry officer on board with greater knowledge of this type of gun, but it appears that no such person was located. A Lewis gun was manned by the Royal Air Force (see Appendix 3 for list of 1 HRS gunners who were on duty during the time of the attack).

Staff Sergeant Major A. Picken, RASC, thought he had exploited his twenty years of army experience to the full when he was allocated cabin 123 on B deck. Unfortunately, when he found the cabin, the two bunks were already occupied. After dumping his pack he went in search of food. Descending to D deck, he fortuitously found the sergeant's mess and was served a four-course meal by uniformed stewards. On return to his cabin he told the other two occupants about the good meal that he had just consumed. They took their tin hats and left in search of the same spoils. It was the last Picken saw of them.

G. Skelton and his best pal Joe Saxton belonged to 5 Company, Sherwood Foresters. They had to wait some time before they were able to board a ship and proceed out to the *Lancastria*. During their journey to the troopship Joe asked his friend if he could look at the photograph of his girlfriend Lily, which was in Skelton's possession because Joe did not possess a wallet. He had given it to Skelton for safe keeping until they reached home. Joe took a good look at the picture and said "Well sweetheart, it won't be long now. We shall soon be together." It was a promise that was never kept.

Once on board, they found a vacant corner on the upper deck and ventured into the accommodation. There they purchased four bottles of IPA from one of the lounges and returned to their little space, drinking the ale whilst they leaned on the ship's hand rails. Knowing the difficulty of retracing their footsteps to return the empty bottles, due to the mass of people already on board, they threw the empties overboard. It was only then that they realised the distance to the water below.

———

As Grattidge threaded his way back along the upper deck towards the bridge he saw what he first thought to be two local children, perhaps ten-year-olds, both with the same grey eyes and golden hair. A French tug had brought them to the *Lancastria* from Saint-Nazaire, together with a few other civilians. They were dishevelled and dirty. Both children clutched a dog to their side; one was a superb golden retriever, the other a bedraggled mongrel.

Grattidge had had a bad experience at Gourock a few days earlier, when he had become involved in a bitter argument about quarantine regulations after troops of the Green Howards had broken the rules and brought dogs back from Norway. He was determined not to repeat the experience. However, after getting an elderly English lady to act as translator, the order to abandon the dogs was met with terrible tears. The lady explained that the children were not French but Belgian, and had brought the dogs all the way from Gosselies, just ahead of the German army; they were inseparable. After a brief silence, and unable to face little boys' tearful eyes, the chief officer knew he was beaten. He decided that sometimes there was only one thing that you could do with a regulation, and that was to break it!

———

One of the last contingents to board the ship was the Pay Corps. All life jackets had long since been issued (there being about 2,000 on board), leaving a great number of people without them. The only space left was on the open deck where they were instructed to lie down. John West did not fancy this option, as there were few places to take cover. He therefore made his way below deck, near the centre of the ship, where he propped himself up against a solid stanchion, ensuring some kind of protection should they be attacked by enemy aircraft.

———

Undoubtedly one of the strangest objects to be taken out to the troopship was Corporal G. Youngs' most treasured possession; a brand new French bicycle with which he had been issued for use in Reims, Troyes and Blois, in the course of his duties with the RASC. His commanding officer, Major N. F. Hart, had told him that he could keep it, providing that he could get it back to England safely. Youngs guarded the new machine with his life and, with his kit bag firmly tied to the saddle, he struggled aboard a small tender around noon. He was far from popular, many complaining about the space the machine occupied, with the kit bag protruding each side of the saddle. On boarding the *Lancastria* he was met with streams of abuse from crew members, but they reluctantly helped him to haul the machine aboard. Being detailed to the upper deck, his struggles were far from over. He eventually managed to reach the open deck amidst much cursing and swearing.

———

At around quarter past eleven *Lancastria*'s third engineer, Frank Brogden, began his 12 to 4 watch. One of his first jobs was to increase air circulation in the accommodation by speeding up the ventilation fans. By now the clouds had dispersed and the sun shone. Later, during one of the first aerial attacks, he was asked to go down to the engine room platform to assist in manoeuvring duties, should he be required by the deck staff. Also on duty (in the engine and boiler rooms) was the engineer in charge, two junior engineers, two greasers, two trimmers, a fireman and a stoker.

———

By lunchtime the decks of the *Lancastria* were crammed with soldiers, mostly overdressed in their khaki uniforms and sweating in the rising temperature. Grattidge weaved his way through kitbags, rifles, tin hats and men to review the situation. He checked with Thomas, the purser, and Fred Beattie, the chief steward, who had been overseeing the head-count all morning at the gunport doors, both port and starboard, as the troops swarmed aboard. Grattidge was horrified to discover that over 5,000 troops had already boarded, considerably more than the 2,600 men evacuated from Norway; he returned to the bridge.

Meanwhile Michael Sheehan, who was on watch in the wheelhouse at around 14.00, overheard a conversation that was taking place outside the starboard wheelhouse door, between a senior army officer, Captain Sharp and Chief Officer Grattidge. It concerned the number of personnel already aboard the ship. Knowing the latest figures, Sharp argued that the ship was already crammed well over capacity and, if he took on any more, where could he possibly accommodate them?

Twenty-one-year-old Michael 'Jesse' Fenton, Sherwood Foresters, stood on the main deck, where he was joined by the ship's chief officer as a French lighter manoeuvred alongside. He heard Grattidge shout out

"Attendre!" (wait). Captain Sharp yelled from the bridge "What's up Harry?" He replied, "As you know, we are already jam-packed Sir. We cannot possibly take any more!" Sharp paused, possibly influenced by the previous discussion with the army officer, and then shouted back "just take these and that'll be it."

As these last were embarked Grattidge noticed another small French lighter and the *Highlander*, both manoeuvring to get alongside, ready to offload over six hundred more soldiers. Obeying Sharp's last order, he refused them permission to board. A deluge of unprintable abuse followed from Lieutenant Commander W. A. Dallmeyer's bridge. He then steamed off towards the Orient Steam Navigation Company's 20,001-ton twin-funnelled troopship *Oronsay*, which had just dropped anchor some four cables off *Lancastria*'s starboard beam (about half a mile away). Sapper Edgar Blant, RE, who was on board the repulsed French lighter, had been standing on the gunwale, poised and ready to board. He soon realised that the decision, which was completely out of his control, had undoubtedly saved his life.

46. *Highlander* closes the damaged *Oronsay* in readiness to embark the troops she had originally taken to the *Lancastria*, after being refused permission to board. Note the gun mounted on the stern.

VII

EAGLES HIGH

Pilot Peter Stahl's first operational flight with II./KG 30 had taken place on 15 June 1940, when II. *Gruppe* had carried out an evening attack on the port of Cherbourg. The following day he piloted one of five Ju 88s sent in to attack bridges over the rivers Cher and Loire at Tours, which were successfully destroyed. Two of the aircraft were shot down by French anti-aircraft defences.

On 17 June, II. *Gruppe* was ordered to attack a large concentration of enemy ships in the Loire estuary. Flying in loose formation, 14 Ju 88s of II./KG 30, all displaying the Kampfgeswader's 'diving eagle' insignia on the forward section of their fuselages, took off from a Belgian airfield at Le Coulot, near Louvain (or Louven, as it is now known) at 14.00.

The scheduled two-hour flight took them over the old battlefields of the Great War, while lines of refugees ambled southwards, away from the advancing German army. The 400-mile flight brought them over the Loire estuary at around 16.00. Each aircraft was carrying four 250 kg bombs. As Stahl circled the French coast, in readiness to attack, a Ju 88 from another Gruppe of KG 30 was shot down, belching smoke from its port engine. He could see two troopships, with freighters and ships of all sizes scattered around the broad river estuary.

Stahl was warned of an approaching French Morane fighter, about 500 yards from him. With this in mind he set his sights on a large ship, without using his dive brakes, which would slow him down. He pushed the throttle controls to their stops and increased speed to 420 miles per hour. At the last moment he released his bombs. In the heat of battle, and under heavy anti-aircraft fire, Stahl flattened his dive to lose the pursuing fighter, which seemed unable to catch up. He was aware that he had to level off as he neared the ground. So, to throw off the fighter's aim, should he get close enough to open fire, Stahl started to twist and turn his aircraft. After several unsuccessful attempts to shoot Stahl's aircraft out of the sky and, no doubt, running short of fuel, the French pilot gave up the chase and turned for home.

II./KG 30's mission, which formed part of the deadly attack on the ill-fated troopship *Lancastria*, was carried out without loss even though Unteroffizier Geffgen's aircraft was riddled with more than seventy 7.5 mm bullet holes, fired from a French Morane fighter. He did manage to reach Belgium with his landing gear and bomb release mechanisms inoperable. Despite this, he landed his aircraft successfully on its belly, using the two engines and four bombs as skids! Neither the plane or the bombs exploded. Nevertheless, this was not a recognised or recommended code of practice, even in emergencies.

———

47 (right). Captain Rudolf Sharp, OBE, RD, RNVR, who survived the sinking of the *Lancastria* but was lost in the *Laconia* on 12 September 1942, when she was torpedoed by *U-156*.

Captain Sharp and Chief Officer Grattidge were stood on the bridge when the first aerial attacks began. Initially, it seemed that the KG 30's pilots had singled out the *Oronsay*, possibly because she had two funnels as opposed to *Lancastria*'s one. At first the attacks proved negative, a factor that was probably due to Captain A. E. Nicholls' astute order to weigh anchor and regain the advantage of being able to manoeuvre his ship.

While the air raid was reaching its present climax, Sharp was faced with a much more complex decision. A signal had been received from a nearby destroyer suggesting, that if the *Lancastria* was full to capacity, she should get under way. All through this particular raid, with bombs exploding and dropping ever nearer the *Oronsay*, Grattidge could see his captain pondering over the signal. Sharp was a solemn, heavily built man who, like many, disliked war and its implications. He knew he had total responsibility for all on board, and the tension showed in his face. He was also aware that his ship was inadequately protected against aerial attack and was hardly a match for any well-aimed bomb or torpedo. He also knew that the SS *Elpis* had been sunk by a U-boat, some 120 miles west of Ushant; even though it was being closed by the destroyers *Harvester* and *Punjabi*. Trying to gain some sort of assurance and lacking suitably detailed charts for these waters, Sharp sent the following signal back to the destroyer 'Can you route us if we proceed?' But the destroyer's commanding officer diplomatically declined to answer.

It was then that Sharp confided in Grattidge. "I think that we'll do better to wait for the *Oronsay* and go together. What do you think?" Grattidge thought for a minute or two and agreed with his captain, replying "I think we should stay, Sir," and a signal was sent back to the destroyer accordingly. After the sinking of the *Lancastria*, some argued that the decision to remain at anchor off Saint-Nazaire should not have been made by one man, but as Grattidge's testimony makes clear, this was not the case. It was the jointly-made, careful decision of two experienced officers.

At 13.48 the *Oronsay* was bombed on the bridge, wrecking her compass and steering controls and damaging the smaller port for'd lifeboat and davit. Luckily no one was killed, although the staff commander, I. E. G. Goldsworthy, and seven crew members were injured. Even Captain Nicholls did not escape injury entirely, suffering from hearing difficulties in later life as a result of the explosion. Expecting similar attention in the near future, Sharp gave the order to turn out *Lancastria*'s lifeboats, ready for lowering; while Nicholls was left with no other alternative but to anchor once more. There was a light north-westerly wind with a slight sea and swell. The sky was cloudy with bright periods. The *Lancastria*, still at anchor, was heading west-north-west with the sun in that quarter.

48. View of the demolished bridge of the *Oronsay* and the port for'd lifeboat, which is hanging precariously from its davits.

The attack had also been witnessed by J. Mansfield and Frank Spooner, both attached to 1 Base Supply Depot, RASC. They had just sat down on the upper deck of the *Lancastria*, near the bows, where they had laid their kitbags and leisurely rested against them. Almost at once they heard the roar of an aeroplane and saw it soar past mast-high, about 100 yards from their starboard side towards the *Oronsay*, which appeared to be moving. They saw several bombs strike her bridge and watched the enemy plane curve away, unscathed, from sight.

RAF Hurricanes appeared from time to time, but as they had flown from English shore bases, their patrols were limited because of the necessity to conserve enough fuel for the return flight.

VIII

THE *LANCASTRIA* BECOMES THE PRIME TARGET

In the survivors' accounts which follow many different perspectives on
Lancastria's final moments are preserved. They vary slightly in detail, as
eyewitness accounts always do, but they confirm that several aircraft made
attacks on the ship and that four bombs hit their target, each in the
vicinity of Nos. 2, 3 and 4 holds and the centre of the ship. The ship
began to sink by the head with remarkable speed and was only slowed
down by the fact that the *Lancastria*'s forefoot came to rest on the bed of
the river estuary.

From 14.00 the crew of the *Lancastria* had been going to and
from their ARP stations at fairly regular intervals. But it was not until
15.43 that the officer of the watch sounded the ARP alarm for the last
time, signalling the arrival of more Ju 88s. The alarm was blown on mouth
whistles and electrically operated gongs which clanged below decks,
warning everyone to take cover, an impossible task for most on the upper
decks. Two minutes later two bombs just missed the *Lancastria* on the port
side in line with the after part of the boat deck. The *Lancastria* had been
singled out as the enemy's new target.

———

Sergeant Strudwick, who was asleep in Cabin 118 on B deck, describes
what he saw:

> ...Sergeant Foster and I soon fell asleep until I was awakened by the
> ringing of a bell, which in my drowsiness I at first mistook for an alarm
> clock. When my senses cleared, I realised that the bell was too loud for an
> alarm clock and must be the ship's bell for action stations. I hopped off
> my bunk and put my head out of our port hole, on the port side of the
> ship, and saw two huge circles of water settling down. I immediately drew
> the conclusion that we were being bombed and the two circles on the
> water were near-misses...

At the same time I. Macpherson's friend (both RAF) rushed into his
cabin to say that a couple of bombs had fallen to port, only fifty yards

away from the ship. They were undoubtedly the same two bombs that Strudwick reported seeing the splashes of seconds later.

———

Lance Corporal Charles 'Fred' Coe manned a Bren gun on the for'd port side of the upper deck, alongside No. 2 hatch. Corporal Geoff Touzel acted as his number two, attaching fresh magazines as and when required, while Lance Corporal Fred 'Gandy' Bolton and others refilled them with twenty-eight .303-inch rounds (they could take thirty-five rounds, but experience had taught them that this invited jamming, due to a weak spring mechanism, which was supposed to hold the rounds in place, but not always). A team of Royal Engineers manned a similar gun opposite them, on the starboard side. The first attack on the *Lancastria* came from the port quarter out of the sun. Fred Coe cursed his luck: he could not see anything. Corporal Old, another member of his group, went below to get some sunglasses and, in the pell-mell of battle, two bombs exploded close to the ship's port side, in line with the after boat deck, soaking Fred and his gun crew in the process.

Minutes later a second aircraft flew in low from the bows, sweeping towards the stern of the ship. As it came in Fred squeezed the trigger and opened fire, but the next thing he remembered was that there was a terrific explosion; a bomb had plunged straight through No. 2 hatch cover and into No. 2 hold with devastating effect. The Royal Engineers stationed opposite 'Gandy' Bolton and some of the other magazine loaders had been killed by enemy machine-gun fire. In the track of the aircraft's gunfire the flush teak deck had been transformed into long jagged splinters.

———

Quartermaster Michael Sheehan had been summoned by the first officer to put the 4 to 8 watch on the shake at around 15.40, a standard procedure in any type of ship. He had just descended through the whale-back scuttle hatch, situated on the foredeck for'd of No. 1 hatch cover, and reached the crew's quarters on C deck when the bombs from the second aircraft hit the *Lancastria*. The resulting explosions threw him up the far end of the working alleyway, near the companionway he had just descended. At the foot of the companionway lay a crew member, who had been wounded in the attack. People were trampling over him in the rush to get up on deck; Michael assisted the wounded man onto the foredeck before returning to the bridge.

———

49. A dramatic view of a Ju 88 bomber in a steep dive. Its four bombs are ready to drop – a sight that Fred Coe, George Crew and many others who were on deck will probably never forget.

Meanwhile, Fred Coe and Geoff Touzel looked about them, while the ship rocked from port to starboard. The ship began to sink by the head so quickly that they were soon up to their knees in water. Nearby, a second lieutenant and four men cried out "We have no life jackets and we can't swim." The two gunners quickly broke up some Bren and Lewis gun boxes and left them to it. They then swam over the guard rails and struck out away from the main group of survivors, who were being machine-gunned from the air. After about an hour in the water they were hauled over the gunwale of one of the *Highlander*'s lifeboats. As soon as the lifeboat was full it returned to the destroyer, where the survivors boarded the ship using the scrambling nets provided. Towels, cigarettes and neat 'Pusser's' rum were issued in plenty. However, attempts to remove the black fuel oil with cold water proved fruitless.

———

George Crew had settled down near the starboard side of No. 2 hatch. He saw the second Ju 88 bomber flying directly above the ship from the bow to the stern, about 200-300 feet above sea level. He stood on the deck and managed to fire two shots, at the glass front of the cockpit, with his .303-inch rifle. At the same time he saw the aircraft drop its bombs; one, which he thought was coming straight at him, went into No. 2 hold and exploded. All around him people and equipment were covered in grey dust. George's uniform hung in tatters and one of his boots had been ripped off by the blast. A Bren gun crew nearby had been killed, so he stood behind the unmanned tripod and unleashed a number of rounds into a third aircraft, but with no visible effect. The enemy guns on this third plane remained silent and no bombs were dropped.

Nearby George saw an army officer propped up, with his face burnt and covered in dust. He bent down to speak to him. The officer muttered "How's my boys?" George replied "They're okay sir, they're launching a lifeboat." It was not until the officer asked about his wife that he realised that he must have been talking about his own family. George said "I'll have a look for a life jacket," but his search proved fruitless. By the time he returned to the deck, where he had last seen the officer, it was awash, and there was no sign of the unfortunate man. He was left with no alternative but to abandon ship.

————

Chief Officer Grattidge, who had been unable to get leave since the outbreak of war, had retired to his cabin below the bridge. He could normally grab a few minutes sleep with ease, a knack made easier by the demands of war – but something unnerved him on this occasion; perhaps a sixth sense. He looked at his watch, it was 15.40. Still sleep evaded him. His watch, which was on the arm on which he was resting his head, seemed to tick with loud and ominous tones. He took another look at the time, it was 15.44. In his own words he continues:

> ... At close range the air raid warning blew up over the harbour. I leapt from the bunk – 15.45; no chance of sleep now. For perhaps one full minute I stood there in the cabin, actually listening to the longest and most fearful silence I have ever heard. Then the bomb noise again, coming nearer and so fast that it ripped at your eardrums, the chilling banshee scream of bombs howling from the sky. Four times the *Lancastria* bucked and shuddered like an animal in pain. I ran topside to the bridge. "By heaven, Sir, this is bad..." 15.48...
> "How many [are] down No. 2 hold?" Sharp shouted.
> "About eight hundred RAF [personnel], Sir. Why?"
> "I think that first one struck there and blew away their exit. God look at those flames..."
> For a moment it was impossible to see anything. One bomb, which we thought was an incendiary, had gone down the funnel ... [it hadn't, but it was close to it]. Vast clouds of inky smoke came pumping over us. The smell of oil caught me in the pit of the stomach – one bomb at least

must have burst down No. 3 hold, releasing about 500 tons of fuel oil. That might mean a running fire, the most difficult of blazes to control aboard a ship. Over and over again I could hear the signalman repeating "Hello ... hello ... engine room," but there was no reply. No answering ring came over the bridge telegraph. All contact with the engine room had been cut off.

Then the smoke drifted and parted, and we saw the most terrible sight the *Lancastria* could offer; the mess of blood and oil and splintered woodwork that littered the deck and the furious core of water that came roaring from the bottom of the ship in No. 4 hold. I knew now where the fourth bomb had gone...

––––––

Captain Sharp had also rushed from his cabin and reached the wheelhouse seconds before his chief officer. After the explosions had subsided and the smoke had cleared Grattidge's eyes met those of his captain. There was no need for an order; Grattidge grabbed the megaphone and shouted "Clear away the boats now ... your attention please ... clear away the boats." Over the weatherboard of the bridge he could see the ship's crew frantically trying to reach the lifeboats, pushing and shoving their way past hundreds of tightly-packed soldiers. Some soldiers scrambled into an inboard lifeboat, which was cradled on deck, and sat there, seemingly hoping that it would launch itself. In the confusion that followed, Grattidge noticed another soldier slashing at the rope fall of a lifeboat with his army jack knife, as the boat hung motionless and suspended. He shouted to the soldier, knowing full well what would follow if the rope was cut, but the soldier did not hear him. As he severed the last strands of the fall one end of the lifeboat dropped vertically and swung outboard, spilling the passengers into the sea.

The *Lancastria*, which was now bow down, started to list to starboard. Feeling that there was only one chance to right her, Grattidge lifted the loudhailer once more, shouting "All hands to the port side ... all hands to the port side ... clear away the port boats." Slowly, as more men moved to port side, the ship righted itself, gaining precious time. Then she began to settle to the port side, but this time there would be no chance of restoring her balance. Thousands of passengers and crew lined up on deck in readiness to abandon ship. Grattidge could see that many were still wearing their army boots and ordered them to take them off. Just then the German planes came in once again, this time skimming the surface of the sea and spraying the ship with machine-gun fire. The bullets spattered and ricocheted in and around the bridge, killing the first officer, Richard Roberts, and the boatswain, William Hayden. The ship's list was worsening by the minute. People began to leave in greater numbers and some undressed before they dived in. Grattidge noticed several nuns, who had boarded earlier from a French tug, also jumping into the sea.

———

After witnessing the hit on the *Oronsay* from the bridge, J. Mansfield felt very insecure because he could not swim. As there were an insufficient number of life jackets on board, and he had not found one, he and 21-year-old Frank (Francis Percy) Spooner now went below in search of some. They eventually reached a cross alleyway where a ship's officer was courageously offering his life jacket to a couple of young soldiers; on hearing their refusal Mansfield seized his chance, saying "Thanks mate! I'll have it." As he was the non-swimmer he tied it around himself and both returned to their places on the open deck. Mansfield continues the story:

> ... about 14.00 action started up once more, with more aircraft on the go this time, or so it seemed. A couple of bombs narrowly missed the ship at different times. A call then came for us to hand over any ammunition we had as the Bren gun which had sustained anti-aircraft fire for quite a long period, from the prow of the ship, was running low on ammunition and needed more. I was down at my kit on my knees taking clips of ammunition from the pouches when a rush of people looking for whatever cover there might be signalled another attack, and I went with the push and threw myself flat on the deck. [Frank did the same].
>
> A split second later [all] hell broke loose as [a] bomb hit us, only yards away. A fiery cloud of red-hot flame engulfed us, the deck below us shuddered and bumped as if in an earthquake and there was a feeling as though red-hot ashes were being scattered across us from some gigantic furnace door. This, with the thunder of the explosions, seemed to go on for some moments, and finally I opened my eyes (yes, they had been closed) to see blackness. I thought I had been buried under something, but when I took a look, blackness was going grey in one spot, and I realised it was black fumes from the explosion that enveloped us. I turned my head towards Frank and yelled above the noise, "are you alright Spooner?" and was pleased to hear [him say] "yes, are you alright Mansfield?"
>
> We got to our feet and weighed things up. Because of the number of people crowding [towards] the ship's rail to get off (the ship was sinking, we were on the starboard side) I looked across to the port side and saw no one going off from there and decided to investigate. I crossed the deck diagonally because the deck house covering the top of the

[companionway] was in the way. I looked over the port rail and saw the gaping hole in the port side taking in water so fast it was no wonder nobody was going over that side. I [took off my steel helmet and boots and] turned away to go back the way I had come, but a movement under my feet and a definite tilt of the deck to port told me not much time was left and I went straight across to the starboard rail (not diagonally as I had come) and found room to go over and a rope hanging from above for good measure...

Frank Spooner did not survive the ordeal and his body was never recovered. He is remembered on the Dunkirk Memorial at Nord, France (see Appendix 1).

————

At around 14.30 the Legroux family made their way to the dining saloon. Half-an-hour later, while starting to eat their meal, two alarms were sounded in quick succession. The family began to feel uneasy, with M. Legroux expressing regret that he had not followed the others back into France. After finishing their meal they returned to their cabin when, at 15.55 a third alarm sounded. They heard guns firing from above and were just putting on their life jackets when the ship shuddered from a violent explosion; the noise was deafening. A split second later another explosion was heard. M. Legroux opened the cabin door into the alleyway and, amidst screams and cries, led his family towards the boat deck. This normally-easy task was made much more difficult because of the mass of people and the steepness of the companionway.

Their efforts eventually bore fruit and they reached the boat deck amidst a seething mass of humanity. Many hundreds of soldiers were wearing life jackets, but a great many more were without them. M. Legroux helped his wife, his son Roger, his daughter Emilie and Mrs Tips into one of the lifeboats. It was the last they saw of him. Unfortunately they had got into the lifeboat which had the falls cut by the soldier, and they were tossed into the sea.

————

'Jesse' Fenton boarded the ship mid-morning and reached the upper deck with four of his companions, all Sherwood Foresters. Once settled Jesse opened a tin of 'Bully' beef and offered it around. Everyone declined, so he ate the lot himself. Little did he know it at the time, but that tin of corned beef saved his life. Shortly after, someone called out "They're serving chicken down below." His four friends went below, while Jesse declined the offer. Three of them he would never see again. Shortly after, enemy aircraft began to attack the ship and all those on deck were told to get below. Lance Corporal Green had spotted one of the planes straight away and began firing his Bren gun.

Jesse had just got below when he heard an almighty thump and felt the *Lancastria* list immediately to starboard, and then it listed to port. As he rushed back up on deck, behind others, an army lieutenant foolishly tried to stop them at gun point; he was flattened in the rush. Climbing over the high (starboard) side he saw his friend (one of the four who had gone below), Jackie Wright, who said "I can't swim Jesse. What shall I do?" Jesse replied "Strip off and grab anything that's floating." As he stripped he turned and saw Jackie stood there, fully clothed and with a dazed look on his face. There was nothing he could do, so he walked into the sea and grabbed two kitbags floating nearby. Looking about him he saw a latticed hatchboard, which he made a beeline for, but this proved to be unstable. Then he saw a large plank of wood to which he transferred and clung on. As he looked about him he saw two older men gurgling and choking in the thick black fuel oil which oozed from the ship: they quickly drowned.

———

Shortly after a crew member had entered Sergeant Strudwick's cabin to close the deadlight over the porthole he felt and heard a tremble and a thud followed by a strong smell of burning cordite. The *Lancastria* had been hit. He eventually made his way to the starboard side of the after open deck, where he climbed over the rails and sat on the ship's side placing the heels of his plimsolls in the recess of a porthole. His former companion, Sergeant Foster, had disappeared, but to his surprise, just along from him was his immediate superior, Flight Sergeant Drew. Both were wearing kapok life jackets and were fully clothed. Strudwick continues the story:

> ... I remember looking down into the water thick with men, most of them alive, but a few apparently dead. The sea was also littered with all sorts of floating debris, such as boxes, planks, kitbags, tin hats and packs. Nearly all these items must have been thrown overboard by the men...
>
> ... I decided it was time that we left the ship and started working my way down the ship's side using portholes and the ridges of overlapping [hull] plates as footholds. I slipped and found myself falling feet first towards the water. I instinctively held my life jacket down with both hands as I had been taught to do on pre-war troopships. I must have been lucky not to fall on anyone with the water round the ship so thick with men...

... I struck out with a steady breast stroke away from the ship to less congested waters and then turned on my back to see what I had just escaped from. This is a sight I shall never forget, a sinking troopship viewed from water level and at a distance of about fifty yards. The *Lancastria* was well down with her bows completely submerged and still listing away from me to port. The stern was well out of the water with her screws visible and pointing skywards...

... There were a lot of dead fish lying on the surface, killed by the bombs exploding in the water. As I swam away the hissing of the sinking ship grew faint and I turned on my back for another look at the doomed *Lancastria.* By now it appeared to have levelled out and all I could see was a shallow mound like a huge whale's back above the water, with a lot of men still standing on it. The mound was getting smaller as I watched; this was the last of the *Lancastria.* I turned and continued once more [towards a] smaller ship [probably *Highlander*]. The roar of a diving aircraft caught my ears. I looked up and saw [an] aircraft diving steeply towards yet another ship some distance further away than the one to which I was swimming. I saw two yellow bombs leave the aircraft and I watched them all the way down to the sea and then a thump and two large spouts of water. At the same time I felt a tingling sensation all over my body...

... This was repeated three or four times by aircraft before I reached my rescue ship...

———

Third Engineer Frank Brogden was still standing on the manoeuvring platform deep in the engine room when the ship was bombed. After receiving instructions, he and all the other duty staff and crew left the engine room through an escape hatch, which terminated on the boat deck. On their way up they came to the working alleyway, which was the main thoroughfare for the crew, where they instructed a couple of troops, who stood nearby, to join them. By the time they reached the deck it was only a few feet from the water. A large number of troops had already left the ship, some clinging on to rafts and lifeboats that had been successfully launched minutes before. Two more lifeboats were stuck in the davits; Frank and some of the other staff tried in vain to launch them. They stayed on the boat deck amidst the chaos of a lot of people running about in different directions shouting and screaming. Others were led down injured. Frank descended to the promenade deck, where he noticed that the heavy wooden hatch covers had been blown off No. 4 hatch. Oily water was rising up the vertical trunkway as the sea engulfed the port handrail. He scrambled towards a Sampson post and started to ascend back to the boat deck as the ship heeled over further to port. He and others slid off the slanting deck into the sea, quickly distancing themselves from the ship to avoid the expected suction.

———

William Rose, of the Sherwood Foresters, had been sat on No. 2 hatch when the *Lancastria* was near-missed. He took shelter under the promenade deck. Shortly after the ship shuddered when she was hit in No. 2 hold. William ran for'd to the hold. The hatch covers had been blown off and below, in the hold, he could see men swimming around in water. He and others threw ropes down to assist them; they even managed to get a few out, but time was against them. By now the ship was well down by the head and he could hear trapped men screaming and shouting below. He stood poised by the handrail uncertain what to do; the shouting made him hesitate, gnawing at his conscience. Then somebody pushed him over the side and he swam away from the ship.

———

A young RAF padre, holding a Bible, descended a rope into No. 2 hold to comfort some of the trapped men; he was unconcerned about his own safety and led the living to sing the hymn 'O God Our Help in Ages Past'. War brings out some astonishing acts of bravery, and this was but one of them.

———

Leslie Bailey had boarded the ship from a small French tender with the other Royal Engineers of 663 Artisan Works Company. He ended up on E deck where he managed to find a bathroom and had a wash and shave. He too had felt the shudder of a near miss. It was shortly followed by two deafening explosions which shook the ship. He felt the ship list to port and decided to go aloft. Men were clambering over others to get out, but he eventually managed to reach the boat deck where he was confronted with confusion as more and more men spilled onto the deck from the accommodation area.

Leslie assisted in lowering two lifeboats on the port side. Then, suddenly remembering that he could not swim, decided to get into the third boat. However, the lifeboat's descent was far from smooth as first one end dropped and then the other. Suddenly, when about ten feet from the water the after fall snapped spilling the people in the overcrowded boat into the oil-ridden sea. In the turmoil he shouted to a nearby swimmer "I can't swim!" The swimmer helped him onto an upturned lifeboat but his oily hands made it impossible to hang on. He looked about in desperation. To one side he could see the port handrails of the *Lancastria* dipping beneath the surface. Above, on the starboard side, he could see people sliding down the steep deck into the sea. Alongside him he saw a wooden ladder floating in the water, which he grabbed hold of; he was soon joined by three others.

———

Sapper Percy Brown, RE, also of 663 Artisan Works Company, had avoided injury during the bombing, but noticed that No. 2 hatch cover was missing. Lying beside the combing was a headless body. Perce decided to make his way midships, where he came across the popular sergeant, 'Wally' Unsworth. The sergeant had already mustered about ten other men and ordered Perce to assist them in dropping a rope to the bottom of another hold, which was several decks down, where over a hundred men were struggling in the rising water. All the companionways had been blown away by the blast and their only hope of salvation was by that single rope. They managed to get a few out, but others were not so lucky; three men managed to get hold of the rope and were slowly being hauled to safety from above. However, many more men grabbed hold of them and the added weight sealed their fate. As it became apparent that the ship would soon sink, Perce turned around and said "come on Sarge, it's nearly time we weren't here." "You go on, Sapper" he said "I can't swim." It was the last time Perce saw him. Sadly, Sergeant Unsworth did not make it (see Appendix 1).

———

It was G. Skelton's nineteenth birthday; he had been sitting on the deck talking to his friend Joe Saxton when a bomb exploded quite near them. It was like a flash of lightning and the ship shook violently. He turned towards his friend only to discover that he was missing. At the same time he noticed that his right shoulder was covered in blood. He then realised that he had been wounded, luckily not seriously. He was a non-swimmer without a life jacket, not a situation he relished. He eventually took the only option left to him, if he wished to survive, and jumped into the sea. Ignoring the advice of a fellow soldier before he jumped, Skelton remained fully dressed, boots and all, a decision that nearly cost him his life. Frantically trying to stay afloat he went under twice before he saw a large piece of timber just in front of him. It was comparable, in size, to a railway sleeper and, for once, his long nails proved an advantage as he dug them into the rough surface. Catching his breath he eventually scrambled on top and straddled his legs over each side. Here he heard the defiant voices of men, still standing on the *Lancastria*'s upturned hull, singing 'Roll out the barrel' and 'There'll always be an England', songs he would never enjoy again without a tear in his eye.

Lieutenant Colonel F. E. Griggs, RE, was just making his way back to the O/C troops' office. He had just entered the first-class dining room on D deck when a bomb crashed through the deckhead, piercing its way through to the decks below. The force of the blast threw him backwards into the central companionway. He decided to go below and investigate the extent of the damage but, when he reached the companionway, he was confronted by a mass of troops, all heading in the opposite direction towards the upper deck. It was impossible to go against the stream of men, so he decided to try to get back to the office, but was prevented from doing so because of the ever-increasing press of men. By now the alarm bells were ringing and the ship's siren was blasting out a continuous lament, all adding tension to the chaos within, though Colonel Griggs remembers that there was no real panic, just a sense of great urgency.

He eventually reached the boat deck, which by then was deserted. Inside the wireless room a radio officer was still tapping his Morse key, but loss of electrical power rendered his equipment useless. The radio officer then offered Griggs a glass of gin, which he quickly drank before deciding it was time to leave the stricken ship. By now the deck was listing at an angle of about forty-five degrees, with the port deck rails awash. He slid down the deck and entered the warm, calm water, still wearing his uniform, Sam Browne (army belt), shoes, tin hat and lifebelt. He distanced himself from the sinking ship as quickly as possible. However, he was not out of danger yet. One of the bombers had recircled and started to machine-gun the survivors in the water. Griggs made himself as small a target as possible by directing his body in a straight line away from the attacking aircraft. After a second attack he was relieved to see that the nearest splash was about three feet away. Surrounding him were quantities of small fish, all stunned or killed by the explosions.

Sergeant Tom Payne, RAF, had lost touch with his friend, Leading Aircraftman Jim Pike, as soon as he boarded the *Lancastria*. He was in the process of searching for him and had just descended to the next deck, when he heard a sickening dull thud. The blast of the explosion threw him the length of the alleyway. He struggled to his feet in a daze; his head was spinning. He stumbled forward and found himself gazing into the dining room. Everything was strangely quiet, a couple of chaps, who were standing beside him, stared towards a large gaping hole in the centre of the dining room deck. Clouds of smoke began to fill the room and Tom descended a nearby companionway still in search of his friend. From this deck he could see into one of the holds. A temporary wooden companionway had collapsed under the weight of men and now there was no exit. Their only chance of survival came from the upper deck; here ropes had been secured and thrown down to assist them. The struggling mass of men, all trying to reach the ropes, was sickening to watch.

Tom was reminded of the seriousness of the situation as the ship listed heavily to port. He rushed aloft and reached the upper deck. It was crammed with men, some partly dressed and some naked. The sight of these fine men, all waiting quietly and orderly for their turn to jump made him feel ashamed of his panic even though he, like others, was in a tight corner. To survive he realised that he would have to keep a level head. He reached the ship's starboard handrail, nearest the French coast, and briefly noticed the *Oronsay* about half a mile away. The sight below him was ghastly. Black fuel oil spread from the ship's port side as swarms of men swam about in the horrible mess. Men were jumping into the sea while others slid down ropes, skinning their hands in the process. By Tom's side a group of men picked up a latticed wooden raft and heaved it over the ship's side. Inevitably it landed on top of a number of men, killing several of them. At that moment he saw the German planes renew their attack and heard the rat-tat-tat of their machine-guns followed by the cries of men who had been hit. Black and bloody faces stared at the ship in search of help.

Tom slid down to the lower port side and entered the oil-ridden sea. He then swam towards the stern of the ship. Hearing screams, he looked up in time to see a lifeboat being up-ended and all the occupants hurtling down towards him. He only noticed one face, that of an agonised mother clutching her baby tightly to her chest. As the ship sank lower Tom rounded the stern and made towards the *Oronsay*. Another German plane swooped down and machine-gunned the survivors. In front of him a young lad was shot in the head; he was killed instantly.

Tom Payne poignantly continues the story in his own words:

> ... I swam on but stopped abruptly. Ahead were two men, neither could swim but they pounded the water as dogs do. It was evident that they [were] trying to help each other as neither uttered a sound. They got locked in each other's embrace and went down once. They surfaced and

their faces were deathly white. Silently they sank a second time. This time they did not surface. Two very brave men had given their all.

A lifeboat was quite near and I swam towards it. Suddenly a woman's agonised cry rang out "Baby here, baby here." As an echo I heard the small voice of a child repeating "Baby, baby." The lifeboat, however, was now full and pulled away from us and my blood froze as that poor mother sobbed out "My baby, my baby."

I looked over to see a man and a woman swimming along holding up out of the sea a tiny mite, a little girl, and I realised it was the same woman who had nearly landed on top of me when the lifeboat tipped up. The sight of this man plodding along in grim silence and the mother who cried out only for the child's safety warmed my heart and I struggled onwards beside them...

... Suddenly I found a piece of wood, not a very large piece, but it would do fine to put the baby on, I thought, and swimming over we pushed it under the baby. She looked quite comfortable and now I felt I must get away from those cries of distress and swam away...

———

The child was Jacqueline, the two-year-old daughter of Clifford Tillyer, an Avions Fairey technician, and his wife Vera. They had been eating a meal in one of the dining rooms when the ship was bombed. Clifford picked up little Jacqueline and all three made their way to the boat deck, shouting "There's a baby here, there's a baby here." Perhaps it was Jacqueline's little voice, echoing the same plea, which had the desired effect. Whatever it was, soldiers moved aside to let them through. Jacqueline and her mother were put into a lifeboat while Clifford reassured them that he would get into another boat. The soldiers would not hear of it and insisted that he stay with his family.

When the lifeboat reached the sea it filled with water (possibly the bung, used for draining the lifeboat during storage, had not been replaced, but this is not recorded). Clifford and Vera, both strong swimmers, swam away from the ship, supporting Jacqueline between them. They eventually placed her on the small plank of wood, which had been discovered by Sergeant Tom Payne (see previous account) until they were rescued. Vera's watch had stopped as soon as the lifeboat sank. The time was 16.07. Jacqueline still has the watch.

———

Private Bill McGinty, RAOC, had boarded the *Lancastria,* after four weeks of fighting a rearguard action from the Belgian border to the outskirts of Paris. Once on board he and two mates managed to get a shower and sit down to their first decent meal since arriving in France on 1 April. With roast beef and Yorkshire pudding still high on the agenda of conversation, they decided to get some fresh air on the upper deck. At around 16.00 the ship's air raid alarms sounded and, looking up, they could see the distant dots of enemy aircraft flying towards them in formation. He continues his story:

... To say that panic ensued is to put it mildly as the seething mass of humanity started to run, not knowing where to go or what to do. The planes were Junkers 88 dive-bombers which broke formation, flew west, and attacked the ship out of the sun.

The three of us literally fought our way back to the deck below to pick up rifles and helmets [before] returning to the wide [companionway], and as I placed my hand on the newel post, it felt as if I had pressed an electric button. With a blinding flash, the far side of the deck crashed through with a tumultuous roar of sparks, steam and choking cordite fumes, plunging us in to complete darkness.

We were thrown like dolls against the [side of the companionway] and in the inky, choking blackness could hear the screams of the dying and severely injured. Realising that we were still alive, our first instinct was to return, if possible, to that open deck.

We later learned that a large bomb had penetrated three decks above and eventually blown out the side of the ship below the waterline. Mortally hit, the gigantic liner shuddered in its death throes and started to roll slowly to one side then the other. Fighting for breath, I picked myself up, grabbed the handrail and started to climb, stepping over debris and bodies, only to find after a while that the handrail disappeared where it had been blown off.

I managed to slither to the opposite side but due to the list the [bulkhead] was no longer at right angles. It was like crawling on a vee with one leg on the [bulkhead] and the other on the [companionway]. After what seemed like an eternity, I rounded yet another corner and on looking up, saw great shafts of sunlight fighting to penetrate the thick clouds of acrid smoke and dust.

On finally reaching the tilting open deck we looked like bedraggled escapees from some Minstrel Show with blackened faces and bloodshot eyes. White lines ran down our cheeks where tears had washed away the soot. The scene which met us was the worst so far. Dead and dying were everywhere. Broken bodies with smashed timber and debris; some completely unrecognisable as human beings. One or two, with bloodied heads, were on their knees, their prayers drowned by the screams and shouts from those in agony, and those demented with terror...

... We managed to struggle to the twisted rails – the ship now settling down at a frightening angle – where many were standing as if transfixed. Either they could not swim, or were terrified by the height from which they had to jump into the sea. Many did, like ourselves, jump but unless you leapt out as far as possible there was the danger of hitting the side of the angled ship and sustaining more injury. I missed the side, hit the sea with a great 'thwack' and thought I would never surface.

The attack was still at its height; as I went down I opened my eyes and every few seconds could see, in the crystal clear water, lines of bullet and incendiary tracks whizzing past . . . aimed at killing as many survivors as possible, but also bidding to set alight tons of oil now spreading over the sea from the ruptured tanks, which also made swimming almost impossible.

With bursting lungs I surfaced, to swim past hundreds of bodies, dead and alive, and make my way to a large piece of timber in an effort to escape the sinking liner's vortex. Others had the same idea, and this support sank under the weight of numbers ... We watched in horror as panic-stricken troops jumped from the [upper] decks into already-packed boats. One lifeboat was halfway down the side [of the ship] when the [ropes] snapped, pitching its human cargo into the sea...

———

Undoubtedly one of the luckiest people to escape from the *Lancastria* was Private J. H. Drummond. He had just returned to No. 3 hold after a hot bath; from there he heard the resonant sounds of distant explosions. However, it was not until a young soldier had rushed down to inform them that the *Oronsay* had been bombed by aircraft that he knew their origin and target. Drummond grabbed his rifle and made for the upper deck, only to be ordered back below by a warrant officer. Shortly after, an explosion concussed his ears with indescribable pain; he jumped to his feet, only to be reassured that it was a near miss. He laid back down on the deck and lit a cigarette to calm his nerves. As he took a few puffs he entered into a discussion with another young soldier, who was sat nearby. Seconds later the for'd bulkhead erupted in a huge sheet of flame, blowing him upside down against the after bulkhead; at the same time he felt and smelt his hair burning, while his face reddened from flash burns. To make matters worse, and adding to the confusion, all the lights were extinguished, leaving the hold in total darkness. Near-asphyxiation followed, due to a temporary lack of oxygen, a result of the massive explosion.

Slowly air permeated the cordite and smoke-filled space and he was able to breathe again. He was completely disorientated. He struggled around in the darkness and debris; and then he heard someone grunting, sobbing and straining to get out. Feeling that he had no alternative but to help, he made his way towards the sound. As he reached it, he enquired if there was a way out. A voice replied "Please push me up." He felt for the man in front of him and pushed him upwards. Another voice called out from behind, assuring Drummond that there was a way out. He pulled the man in front of him and assisted him in the same way. He then tried to follow, but was faced by a huge flat piece of steel. After several attempts to surmount the obstacle he slumped back down onto the deck exhausted.

He had resigned himself to the inevitable when, from the stillness of the blackened hold, another man spoke enquiring "Is there any way out?" With renewed hope he replied "Yes, give me a push up." As he was elevated by his unknown helper he could feel the edge of the sheet of steel and saw a very faint glimmer of light far above him. He crawled towards it and reached a companionway. It was dimly lit from an adjacent alleyway. He soon realised that this was the light he had first seen and quickly made his way towards it. From there he saw another shaft of faint light and moved in the direction of its source; he was confronted by a cabin with the door smashed open. Inside was a mass of tangled electrical wire, no doubt a result of the explosion. Ignoring the risk of an electric shock, he dived headlong through the confusion of cables and entered another alleyway, where he caught sight of more light further along.

The two men he had assisted earlier had gone in the opposite direction; the last he saw of them they were trying to get through a porthole. What happened to the man who had assisted him was pure conjecture. As he rushed wildly towards the diffused light he could see that the ship was listing heavily to one side and that the water was steadily creeping up into the accommodation area from which he was now trying to escape. He then reached the spot from where the light emitted; it was a cross alleyway with the port side gunport doors opened and secured inboard. The deck was listing and barely above the water level outside. Beside one of the steel doors stood the warrant officer whom he had previously met; he was staring into the sea. He offered Drummond a cigarette and said "Better get in lad, there will be a lot of stuff on the top deck toppling over soon."

Hundreds of men were swimming away from the ship. So, with clothes blackened and ripped to shreds, but life jacket intact, he jumped in, remembering to hold his lifejacket down but forgetting that he had just lit his cigarette! When he surfaced he saw a lifeboat some way off. It appeared to be empty, so he decided to make for it, despite being a novice swimmer. His efforts eventually bore fruit and he hung on to one of the looped side ropes. From within the boat he could hear a heated argument about which way to go: back to the French coast or out to sea? The decision was carried in favour of the latter.

Shortly after, he was noticed by a young soldier and eventually hauled over the gunwale, where he was unceremoniously slung into the bottom of the very overcrowded boat. There was so little room that people sat upon him. It was the least of his worries, for the moment he was safe.

————

C. W. Cornish had returned to the hold after an unsuccessful search for food. He removed his tunic and boots and had just settled down for a nap, when he heard a roar and everything went pitch black. Coming to his senses he knew that his survival depended upon finding a way out. He groped around in the darkness until he saw a faint shaft of light filtering through the smoke from the hatch cover high above. By this time ropes and chains had been lowered from the upper deck and a few people attempted to climb them to reach safety. Unfortunately not all succeeded; he saw two men fall back into the hold, landing nearby. He grabbed a rope and ascended to C deck, where a seaman assisted him over the hatch combing. He was then directed for'd. It was not until then that he realised that he was quite naked except for his belt and socks (a result of the explosion)!

As he came out of the accommodation onto the upper deck he was surprised to see the whole bow section totally submerged. He dived into the sea and swam away from the ship, fortunately missing the slicks of oil that spilled from ruptured fuel tanks. He soon sighted one of the lifeboats and was hauled aboard. Already on board was an English family with their two-year-old daughter, the youngest survivor of the disaster (Jacqueline Tillyer).

————

RASC drivers J. Broadbent and Sid Keenan had found an unoccupied *Officers Only* washroom. They bolted the door and Broadbent ran a hot bath, while Sid took his time lathering his face; he then proceeded to have a long-overdue shave in front of a conveniently placed mirror, when the alarm bells rang. It was followed by a terrible crash, which caused the ship to shudder from the impact. By the time both men had reached the upper deck it was already a case of every man for himself. Men were jumping into a mass of people who were already in the sea.

————

Bill Slater and Sid Chenery were playing chess on a pocket-size travel set at the time of the attack. At first the *Lancastria* listed to port and the

50. *Lancastria* down by the head with her forefoot resting on the sea bed. The *Highlander* has been forced to manoeuvre into the open sea to avoid further bombing. The French lighter from which Edgar Blant had so nearly boarded the *Lancastria* is still alongside the *Oronsay*, which is anchored.

tables, chairs and a piano started to slide down the deck. They both ran up the sloping deck and opened the starboard door onto the promenade deck. Just then the ship righted itself and Bill went for'd and looked down to D deck where he could see five men in a mixture of water and fuel oil doing their best to stay on top. They were trapped in a space used for baggage on the starboard side, alongside No. 4 hatch. The force of the explosion in No. 4 hold must have broached the baggage space and holed some of the decks above it. A number of men had lowered a rope to pull them out, but every attempt was foiled by the fuel oil, making the rope too slippery to grip. Bill made a loop in the rope and they managed to haul one man out. They repeated the procedure as the remaining four trapped men rose with the flood of water. Bill was directing the operation when the other men dropped the rope and ran. Unable to pull the men free on his own and knee-deep in water, he was left with no alternative but to try to save himself.

He waded across the deck to a starboard lifeboat and climbed in. In ideal conditions the boat was supposed to hold 65 people. Bill estimated that there were about 120 in this one. The problem was that no one knew how to launch it. After about two minutes the *Lancastria* listed onto her port side for the last time, causing the lifeboat to strike the starboard side of the ship and spill the occupants into the sea. When Bill surfaced he found himself beneath the lifeboat, now floating at sea-level, but upside-down and still attached to the ship. It was obvious that, when the ship sank, it would take the lifeboat with it, unless they could sever the connection. Thankfully, a ship's officer swam over and uncoupled the boat from the ship. He then suggested that they should hang on as best they could to the lifeboat's keel. When the *Lancastria* finally rolled over and sank Bill was barely ten feet from the troopship's keel. However, the expected suction simply did not occur, at least not where he was. He then hung on until he was eventually rescued.

———

Captain Fuller, Commodore of the newly arrived convoy from Newport, who was on board the SS *John Holt*, witnessed the aerial attack and saw the *Lancastria* hit for'd at 15.48 (the time recorded by him). The troopship immediately disappeared behind an enormous cloud of black smoke. By 15.50 the smoke had cleared and she appeared to be listing to port and was down by the head; he also noticed that the starboard half of her signal yard had gone and that her starboard rigging was slack.

———

Aircraftman M. B. Andexser, who had been working on an air firing and bombing range at the small fishing village of Pornic, had boarded the *Lancastria* and, obeying instructions, entered one of the ship's holds along with many other RAF servicemen. He relates his story:

> It was not long before the bombs began to fall near our ship. Some bright lad said not to worry they are only small ones anyway, when it happened. I was lying down at the time and there was one almighty bang that seemed to lift me clean off the deck where I was, and as if I had been smacked in the ears by an unseen force. What followed in the complete black hold, full of burning smoke, was terrible. It was confusion, to put it mildly, with water pouring in and no way out.
>
> Someone, must have been many service men, ripped covers off the hold five decks up and passed ropes down for us to get hold; but there were too few ropes and too many men; by now some in panic. As the ship settled, water covered in oil filled our part and gradually took us nearer the top. As many as possible held onto the ropes as the intake of water was pulling the men into the ship and gangways. In time I was pulling myself up the oily sloping deck and managed to hold on until the ship settled and I reached sea level.
>
> When I looked around I could not see any part of the *Lancastria*, only men black with oil. Some distance away I saw an upturned lifeboat with men on top, I swam to the party of chaps and saw that most of them were

injured. The rest of us, who were fit and well, kept a lookout for others who were in trouble; there were many. Myself and someone else managed to get a few more bad cases onto the upturned boat, while we used the ropes for support. Many men just could not hold out and just slipped below the oily surface, we were powerless to give them any further help.

————

Lieutenant R. Haynes, AMPC, narrowly avoided death. He had been standing two yards from the hatch when the explosion occurred and was thrown to the deck. He relates his story:

> As I lay there waiting for the debris to fall I began to pray. It must have been only seconds, but it seemed like ages and I prayed like hell. Then I felt a blow against my back. A rifle had hit me. I was relieved it was not a Bren gun!

————

Private Sidney H. Dunmall, RAPC, had joined a long queue outside the purser's office to receive a bar of chocolate. He had been waiting patiently for some time and had just reached the head of the queue. As he was about to be served he had a premonition that something awful was about to happen and rushed aloft. As he reached the upper deck there was a terrific explosion. He peered upwards through the dust and smoke in time to see a twin-engined aircraft climbing back into the clouds.

As the smoke cleared he was faced with an incredible sight. Most of the deck rails had been blown away and the port Sampson post was sheared off about three feet from the deck. The only other person visible was an injured man holding a shattered arm and crying. He too experienced the change of list from port to starboard and back to port. He ran to the port, lower, side and descended a convenient rope and entered the sea. Several non-swimmers were shouting for help, which was a glaring reminder that he could not swim either. Sidney clung to the rope for support and considered his options. Just then, someone on the upper deck started throwing heavy planks of wood into the water. Seizing the opportunity he thrust himself from the side of the ship and reached the nearest plank, straddled it and hung on for dear life. Despite desperate efforts to distance himself from the sinking ship he remained where he was. A swimmer offered to pull him clear of the expected suction, an action that no doubt saved his life. The swimmer then left him to his own devices and Sidney paddled towards a distant ship. More bombs were dropped and machine-gun fire continued, causing the ship

51. Private Sidney Dunmall, No. 7662664, Royal Army Pay Corps, in July 1940.

he was paddling towards to steam off. He distinctly remembers being showered with dead fish as each bomb exploded.

Sidney continued paddling aimlessly until he heard voices; he looked up and saw a Carley float full of men, barely afloat. He was invited aboard and given a piece of wood and told to paddle with the rest.

———

A company sergeant of the Auxiliary Military Pioneer Corps, who had been allocated to one of the holds, related his story:

> I gave the order to man the hosepipes, for smoke was coming in the hatch. It was impossible to obey, because the troops were jammed so tight in the alleyways. Just then the ship gave a sudden lurch to port until she was listing at an angle of 45 degrees. We were thrown off our feet.
>
> From the bridge came the order: "Every man for himself," and I chucked hatchboards over the side to act as rafts when we got into the water. By this time the ship was beginning to sink and her propellers were right out of the sea...
>
> ... As two of the lifeboats were dropping down the towering side of the *Lancastria*, they capsized. One had about 120 people on board including

two French women and two children, aged about five. They were flung into the water. One woman flung her baby into the water and dived in after it; she was a strong swimmer, and after picking up the child she made off to one of the lifeboats...

... Forward was a soldier with a Bren gun rattling away with all he'd got. He stuck it out even when the water was up to his waist. His gun was silenced only when he was washed away from it. A grand lad. I hope he was saved.

Just before the ship capsized and went down, some of our men ... [laughed in the face of death] (we called ourselves *The Thin Red Line*) and scrambled on to her uppermost side. There they stood, ... [with an immaculately dressed British officer coolly smoking a cigarette] knowing that they had no chance. They went down like brave men, singing 'Roll out the Barrel ... [let's have a barrel of fun]!'

———

A sergeant of the AMPC had been in the stokehold during the attack. Tracing his way into the accommodation area he rushed to the side of a French woman and her eight-year-old child. He assisted them up a companionway, which was hampered by escaping steam from fractured pipes. To avoid getting burnt they held handkerchiefs over their faces. He eventually got them aboard a lifeboat and was then told to join them.

———

Royal Engineer P. K. Barker was sitting in one of *Lancastria*'s lounges when the first bomb struck the ship. He heard two more explosions in close succession. Within two or three minutes the troopship began to develop a heavy list. He describes what happened next:

I spotted a lifeboat and with two others I tried to lower it. I was once in the merchant service. While we were working on this, some man, who seemed quite mad, rushed up with an axe and chopped at the ropes shouting "Here's the way to lower a boat." The result was that one end went down and one of the men (Sergeant Chipchase) lost the fingers of one hand. His hand had been accidentally caught in the chock of the davits.

By this time the raiders were spraying the decks with machine-gun bullets. We could hear them spluttering all around. I found myself on the boat deck – slanting at a very acute angle – and, feeling very much on my own, I slid down into the water. Long afterwards I realised I was swimming with my steel helmet and glasses still on! Apart from that all I had on was my battledress trousers.

I managed to get clear of the sinking ship. There were one or two lifeboats nearby, but they were absolutely packed. Nothing for it but 'keep on swimming'. The water was covered in oil and in some places that was on fire ...

[There are several accounts accusing the German pilots of dropping incendiary bombs deliberately in order to set fire to the oil. This is entirely unfounded. The few fires that did appear were almost certainly caused by calcium flares attached to the circular lifebelts, which ignited automatically as soon as they came into contact with the sea. Designed to save lives by displaying the whereabouts of a swimmer in the dark, this feature was, nevertheless, a serious design fault when large amounts of fuel oil were present. Nevertheless, the strafing of survivors by bullets was certainly a heartless act of contempt by the Luftwaffe pilots.]

Captain C. Brooke, RAPC, remembered a muffled explosion which indicated damage below the water line. The explosion rocked the ship. He describes the scene:

> After trying to steady her by crowding from port to starboard and vice versa – a hopeless task – it then became a question of how many lifeboats could be got away in time. I don't remember how many had been released from our deck, but I was surprised at the presence of females and small children who were being helped into boats. It soon became impossible to release any more boats because of the dangerous list.
>
> I do remember clearly how members of the crew and others were working furiously to release the rafts and anything else which would float...

It was then that he decided to entrust his life to Providence and enter the water. Until this time he had been a non-swimmer. But the desire to live meant that he had at least to try. To his own astonishment he discovered that he could swim and eventually reached a crowded raft which he was able to hang onto with the aid of the rope surrounds. He continues:

> By that time [the *Lancastria*] had disappeared below the surface – the sea then became a mass of dead and dying bodies, the latter being slowly suffocated by the filthy oil in which most of us were unrecognisable. It was about that time that 'Jerry' decided to let fly again and some of his bullets were seen to strike on the oil and, if my memory serves me correct, there were small patches of fire in consequence...

A member of *Lancastria*'s crew, who had tried to launch one of the lifeboats, describes what he saw:

> As soon as we were struck I pushed my way through the mass of soldiers towards one of the lifeboats. Already it was full right up with men, and

when I moved them, others surged forward towards the boat hoping to get a place aboard.

Just then the *Lancastria* gave a terrific lurch to port and all the men were thrown from one side of her to the other. I slid on my back down the deck, which was at an enormous slant, and flung into the sea. The scene can only be described as being one of an almost solid mass of men, clinging together like flies and covered with thick black oil. Some of them were horribly burnt by the explosion. There were women and children struggling for their lives, other soldiers were swimming until they finally sank; it was every man for himself.

All this time the [aircraft] were still above us and continually swooped and bombed the oily waters [while] their machine-gunners fired on the men struggling for their lives in the water.

Acting Lieutenant Colonel Norman de Coudray Tronson was probably the oldest soldier on board; he was certainly the oldest of the army survivors. After experiencing warfare in the Boer War and the Indian frontier he had seen action in the Great War, with the North Staffordshire Regiment. He was gassed in 1917 and injured the following year. In January 1940 he celebrated his sixty-fourth birthday as town major of Dieppe with the North Staffordshire Regiment (The Prince of Wales'). Now, in the face of the enemy, his heroism, along with another officer, stood out as he coolly assisted in any way he could. He was Mentioned in Despatches (see Appendix 2) for great gallantry during the evacuation at Saint-Nazaire.

Sisters Margaret Chamley and Gladys Trott, both Church Army workers, had been put aboard the *Lancastria* after being bombed during a lorry dash to the French coast. Once on board and settled they peered through an open porthole from their allotted cabin. Their attention was drawn to what first appeared to be a fast-moving black cloud. However, on closer inspection, they soon realised that it was five or six enemy aircraft. They circled and then passed directly above the troopship, releasing their bombs as they flew over.

After the bombs exploded they rushed up onto the boat deck where they heard the order 'women and children first'. They then got into a lifeboat while men slid down ropes into the sea; others leapt overboard into a mass of oil-covered men. The German bombers continued their attack sweeping down towards the sea. The nurses saw the spurts as the bullets struck the water where men swam for their lives.

As their lifeboat was lowered falteringly, snagging the starboard side of the ship during its descent, soldiers, watching through a porthole, noticed that they were wearing life jackets and shouted "Give us a chance. Those are our only hope" The two nurses instantly removed their life jackets and managed to throw them successfully to the men. With the assistance of men above, the boat eventually reached the water safely.

The sisters remembered seeing another lifeboat, full of civilians, which was not so fortunate. One end had been lowered far too fast, spilling all the passengers into the sea, and one fat old lady was plunged into the water with an emphatic splash. Buoyed up by her life jacket she surfaced, gave out a dreadful scream, and then immersed her head under the surface and drowned herself. Such is the power of panic.

Miss Fernande Tips, whose father was the managing director of the Belgium aeroplane company Avion Fairey, tells her story:

> I was with my mother, two brothers and a maid in the dining room when the ship was bombed. We all wore lifebelts as we ate.
>
> As each bomb fell all we could see was a sort of shadow, followed by thousands of splinters. Something hit me very hard in the eye and there was a terrific bang.
>
> We tried to stick together. We went up the slanting [companionway] to the boat deck. After that I lost trace of my mother and brothers. My mother swam about for three hours before she was picked up.

Harry Pack, of 1 HRS, RASC, had just slid down the listing deck and entered the water when he heard a female voice. It was the voice of Julie Delfosse, wife of an Avions Fairey worker and mother of a son called Freddie. She was entangled in ropes from an upturned lifeboat close under the rail of the *Lancastria*. In broken English, Harry learned that she had lost her son. He urgently encouraged her to free herself from the ropes and get away from the sinking ship. By now the funnel was almost in the water, hissing with escaping steam. Freed from the ropes, they both headed towards a distant ring of ships amidst strafing and bombing. After almost four hours they were picked up by a small rowing boat and transferred to the destroyer *Havelock*, where they parted company.

E. J. Mansfield, RAF, made for the companionway as soon as he realised that the *Lancastria* had been hit. He was just about to ascend with four or five others when he heard a shout from the centre of one of the holds. One man was stranded, unable to climb the listing deck to reach the companionway. They all linked hands and managed to pull him to safety. From what he could see there was nobody else left in that part of the ship. By the time he got to the upper deck the starboard handrails were almost vertically above him. Mansfield jumped from the bulkhead of the accommodation area, on which he was now stood, and grabbed hold of the rails and pulled himself over them and onto the starboard side of the ship. He continues:

> ... I just sat there for some minutes, when in came German twin-engined bombers, machine-gunning men already in the water, and one dropped a bomb right behind the *Oronsay* (which was another liner sent to get us out). I saw the plume of water from the explosion of the bomb. Thank goodness the bomb missed. *Oronsay* was partly loaded with troops before the air raids [had] started.
>
> By this time the *Lancastria* was laying on [her] port side and the [for'd section] of the ship was well underwater. I then decided it was time I got off. I had been sitting there on my own, but men had been going into the water on each side of me. I took off my boots, tied them together by the laces, and hung them neatly over the rail. I then walked along the side of the ship. Passing the portholes, I could see men trapped in the ship, and no way was I able to help these poor chaps who would soon perish.
>
> Once in the water I started to swim away; luckily I was a strong swimmer. I had no lifebelt and the ship, I know, was very overcrowded and there were not nearly enough lifebelts to go round. As I was swimming away, four or five older men, all [wearing] lifebelts, just floating together, called out to me to help them. I towed them some distance to a capsized lifeboat which they clung to; I climbed on top. Out to sea, some two hundred yards or more, was a motor launch [belonging to] the *Lancastria*; nobody in it, just floating. I decided I could swim to it, and managed to get [aboard].

———

Civilian C. Green was standing on the promenade deck when the order to abandon ship was given and jumped from there with his daughter Claudine. After about 1½ hours they were picked up by a lifeboat full of soldiers. He relates an amusing story:

> As we came alongside the lifeboat my daughter was taken [on] board and I was quite happy holding on to the side whilst awaiting rescue from either of the destroyers present or the French tugs. However, it would appear that, despite the fact that the lifeboat was very heavily loaded they

insisted that I went aboard, and the efforts of the soldiers to row the boat in a given direction was screamingly funny. Some were pulling one way and some the other, and consequently the boat was just going around in circles. After a while an Irishman, of all people, decided to get up and control operations, and having tried for several minutes without success, in a truly Irish manner he said "Shure and begorra you (this I leave to your imagination) will you pull now," and I must say it had the desired effect.

————

Sapper Norman Driver of 159 Railway Construction Company, RE, had been directed to the upper deck of the ship with three members of his company. Norman and two friends left their kit under the watchful eye of Bert Cunliffe while they searched for food. Despite finding the ship's galley, they were disappointed to discover that they had missed lunch and decided on the next best thing: find a cabin and have a wash and brush up:

... We found a vacant cabin which contained two toilets and a washbowl. We tossed coins to see who washed first. I had a wash and shave 'ready for Blighty'. While I was in the toilet the ship was attacked. As I was adjusting my dress burning timber fell on my hand and leg. With blood on my leg I realised what had happened. [Sheffielder] Cal [Beal] shouted from the other toilet, "I've been hit. There's blood on my leg." Managing to open the door I could see a hole in the [deck] where [cockney] George Watling had been having a wash and shave. We did not see him again. He'd always carried a piece of his girlfriend's dress. His family never knew what happened to him.

With Cal Beal holding on I managed to go up the [companionway] to the loading bay, which was the full width of the ship. When we arrived at the end of the [alleyway] the ship keeled over, with men and kit bags falling to one side. As I could see some light coming from the [gunport] doors, I scrambled up. A sailor did the same, and we were able to open the top and bottom of one of the side doors. As the ship started to right itself the sailor jumped out with the bottom door closing behind him. Keeping hold of the top half, and with Cal Beal following me, I went overboard.

I was hit on the head when I surfaced. I realised afterwards that I had swum from underneath a liferaft which had broken loose from one end. For a while I swam around in search of my friend, unfortunately there was no sign of him. As I swam from the ship I recognised a lad from our company, James Reock. He was trying to pull a raft, I went to help him. We pulled men, who could not swim, up to the raft. We heard a man crying out "Save me, save me. I've a wife and three children." Swimming away from the raft in order to remove my boots, I was just in time to pull him back. James Reock and myself managed to keep the six men afloat until we were picked up by a French trawler.

––––––

Twenty-four-year-old Sergeant Harry Pettit, RASC, had boarded the *Lancastria* from a trawler. It was early afternoon and the troopship was so overcrowded that the only space left was on the upper deck. From a convenient corner Harry saw four German bombers climb into the sun and swoop down to begin their attack. He saw one aircraft cross right above him; it dropped four bombs on and around the *Oronsay*. The aircraft then sped eastwards, no doubt telling others of their fruitful attack. It was a reasonable assumption, for it was not long before a fresh offensive began. Harry relates his story:

> ... When the next attack came, all troops on deck were ordered below. The ship shuddered as a terrific explosion occurred. She listed sharply, throwing us all into a mass on one side. There was a silence for a short time, as the full significance of what had happened dawned upon us, then another lurch. Someone shouted, "She's hit, she's going down!" and there was a mad rush for the [companionway]. Many, I believe, were trapped when the [companionway] broke.
>
> My memories of the ensuing period are rather muddled, but I remember assisting, unsuccessfully, to lower a boat. The list was already very acute. I was convinced, in my own mind, that it couldn't really be happening to me. I saw a group of padres, Church Army and YMCA workers kneeling in prayer.
>
> As the *Lancastria* turned over, I climbed the rail with many others and, removing my boots, walked on her [hull] plates. I would not leave the ship if I could possibly remain on her, but, in readiness, I removed most of my clothing. The plates were now getting rather hot, and I feared the ship might blow up any minute. I was, I must say, quite calm, but had a terribly dry throat. As the *Lancastria* turned [onto her port side], revealing [one of] her vast propellers quite close to me, and sinking lower every minute, I walked towards her keel. A friend, Corporal Evans, strolled up from somewhere, shook hands and said: "Cheerio Harold, this looks like the end for us." He then said: "I'm going in," and slid down the plates into the black, oily water. I followed him, neither of us had a life jacket. I sank below the water, and – this is my most vivid recollection of all – kept going down and down until my lungs seemed on the point of bursting. I was quite convinced at that moment that I was dying, and, with a clear, calm picture in my mind of home and a widowed mother, I wished that death by drowning did not take so long. A hundred things from the past flitted through my mind in those few

seconds that seemed like hours. Almost unconscious, I must have shot up to the surface quickly, because the next thing I knew was that I was choking and gasping amidst the dreadful scene on the surface...

... The oil which covered the water in a thick layer, was keeping me warm, but was terrible to the eyes, nose and stomach.

Looking around me, I saw many men swimming and floating close by. About six of these, with myself, collected together to form a group. I did not recognise anyone, but with a thick layer of oil over us, this was not surprising. Three of the group had life jackets, the others had not, and I suggested that we made a circle, joining hands across the backs of neighbours shoulders, to make a kind of human lifebelt. This, to the everlasting credit of those fortunate enough to be wearing life jackets, we did. Occasionally, hands lost their grip because of the slimy oil and loss of strength, but we soon reformed and held on for what could have been one or three hours, I do not know...

... A screaming, panic-stricken man joined us, throwing his arms around the neck of one of our group, trying to tear the life jacket from his shoulders. Had this fellow been calm, we might possibly have accepted him, though it is doubtful if we could have supported the extra burden. He was, in this condition, a menace to our own hopes of survival, so we fought him off, thus wasting some of our precious reserves of energy. He left us, and, swimming reasonably well, reached a floating 'body', wearing a life jacket, some distance away. As he approached, the 'body' came to life and there followed an awful struggle, the sight and sounds of which still disturbs me, and which ended only in the disappearance below the surface of the poor, crazy fellow. If his opponent in this grim struggle survives, I hope he suffers no remorse. What he did, he had to do...

———

Major P. H. Fairfax, RASC, managed to get clear of the ship and came across a large black dog which was completely bemused by the situation. It swam away from him never to be seen again. His story is also very poignant for its account of unnecessary behaviour from some of the more fortunate:

... The oil now began to get very thick; this was very dangerous to the eyes, mouth, nose and ears; but on the whole [was] our salvation as the water then became warmer and we floated better and the water became calm. Just then 'Jerry' started to tracer bullet us, also dropping flares and set light to the oil, when this started I saw two pals together and heard one say "Well Charlie when you are ready I am." We looked in the direction to see a chap take from his neck a revolver and string, one then shouted "fire away" and out rang two shots; he shot his pal then himself...

... We then saw a small rowing boat coming alongside with two ... [Frenchmen] standing up moving the kit bags about with [their] oars, we cried out to them, but they were only looking for loot and pushed everyone away from them. Another boat came along full up and we saw one man reach up to catch the front part of the boat and from the distance from us it appeared to be an officer in the front with [a] revolver in [his] hand keeping others away from the boat, the man in the water made several attempts to grab the boat when we saw the revolver pointed, a shot rang out and down went the man. At the same time, I should say a second later, another shot rang out, and the officer who sent the first shot [probably] shot himself and he rolled into the sea...

———

Staff Sergeant Major A. Picken, RASC, and Corporal Frederick Purchase, of the same regiment, had both stripped off and leaped for ropes which were attached to the falls. Picken descended rather quicker than he had anticipated, burning his left hand and right leg in the process. He landed in a water-logged lifeboat which had sped uncontrollably from its davits full of soldiers and airmen beforehand, stoving in its hull and rendering the boat useless. Being a non-swimmer, Picken stayed with the boat until a kit bag dropped into the water beside him. Noticing that it floated, he tucked it under his left arm and paddled with his other arm. Gaining confidence by the minute and knowing that he had to distance himself from the sinking ship, he soon discovered that he made better progress when he used his feet. However, slowly but surely, the kit bag began to sink, and with it Picken's hope of survival. With no other option but to release the bag, he thrashed around in the water, sure that he would drown. Blessed with good fortune, however, his arm suddenly struck something solid, it was a wooden oar from a lifeboat, and this amply supported his weight.

He was becoming increasingly aware of the thick black oil which was rising and spreading outwards from the wreck. He kicked out in an effort to distance himself from it and delay the inevitable. He then came across another survivor who was on his last legs, exhausted from the efforts of swimming. Picken gladly shared the oar, suggesting that the other man held the blade whilst he held the handle. By now the oil had spread all around them as more German planes swooped down to machine-gun the survivors. The bullets zipped into the water in two neat lines. Picken was between their paths. Unfortunately his companion was in the line of one of them and was struck in the forehead, which killed him instantly.

RAF sergeant H. Strudwick saw a Hurricane pilot, who had previously been in action against the enemy, fly low over the survivors and drop his Mae West; it no doubt assisted someone.

———

Sergeant J. L. Langley, RA, had managed to swim alongside a partially submerged lifeboat. Some men were seated while about thirty, including himself, clustered around the boat hanging on to the side ropes. However, an older man, who was beside Langley, was very distressed because he did not have a life jacket, a reality that effected many more survivors. A young lad of about 17 years of age, who was sitting in the boat, moved over to the side of the lifeboat and gave him his. It was a forlorn gesture; neither of them survived the ordeal.

———

Stanley Flowers, 1 HRS, RASC, had boarded the *Lancastria* with the rest of his company. He escaped from the ship with his friend Walter Smith who also lived in Faversham. They shook hands, wished each other good luck and descended down the starboard side of the ship using two convenient ropes. Unfortunately they fell short of the water and they had to fall the rest of the way. In the confusion in the water they became separated. It was the last time that Stan saw his friend (see Chapter X for the conclusion to this story).

———

Neal Howard, RAOC, could hardly swim; he was one of the many men who were the last to leave the *Lancastria*. Here is the relevant part of his story:

> ... Afraid that I might be sucked under when the *Lancastria* finally went down, I decided that I must dive in and get away from the suction effect, but it never happened as I was standing on the side of the *Lancastria* as she went down. There were many others like myself who stayed until the end. I was told by someone who was not on the *Lancastria* but on another ship and so was able to watch, that at the end it looked like a long line of humans walking on water.
>
> There were all sorts of things being released from the *Lancastria* as she sank. To my amazement I found floating beside me a kitbag. This must have been so well packed that it floated and supported me for about five hours before I was picked up...

Three bombs, which had struck in the vicinity of Nos. 2, 3 and 4 holds, not only killed many of the occupants, but undoubtedly broached

52. Stanley Flowers pictured in 1939 when he was with 1 HRS, RASC.

53. Walter 'Wally' Smith stood in the same yard in 1939. He joined 1 HRS, RASC, as a replacement driver the following year.

the port side of the ship's hull, causing massive flooding in the for'd section of the troopship. The earlier near-misses had possibly also fractured rivets and sprung plates along the port side only minutes earlier, compounding the inrush of water, the pressure of which was substantial. Inadvertently, because the two large ships had steamed in as close as they could to the port of Saint-Nazaire, the shallowness of the anchorage meant that the forefoot actually touched the seabed before the ship had finished sinking, providing survivors with a few further minutes in which to escape, and minimising the effect of suction which normally accompanies the loss of a large ship. The area where the *Lancastria* sank was just over 62 feet deep at the lowest astronomical tide (ref. Chart No. 3216, Approaches to La Loire, August 1994).

Several aeroplanes attacked the *Lancastria* and at least six bombs were dropped, but the loss of ship was caused by four 250-kg bombs hitting their target, and these from a single aeroplane. The attack began at 15.45, the four bombs hit the ship at 15.48 and by 16.02 the bow of the *Lancastria* had sunk and she had rolled over onto her port side. At 16.12 she disappeared into the shallow waters of the Loire estuary, leaving thousands of people struggling in the water awaiting rescue. The *Lancastria* had taken just twenty-four minutes to sink (times recorded by Captain H. Fuller, OBE, master of the *John Holt*).

54. Map of the Loire Estuary showing the coastline in relation to where the *Lancastria* sank.

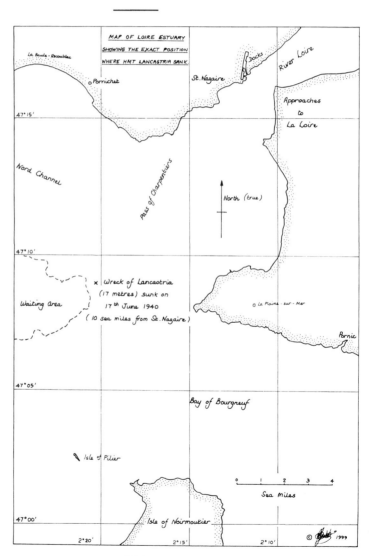

124

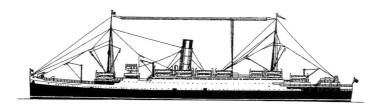

CHAPTER IX

RESCUE

As the *Lancastria* sank by the head, rolled onto her port side and disappeared beneath the surface of the Loire estuary, ships in the vicinity were compelled to postpone the rescue operation in order to first take evasive action. Groups of German aircraft were dropping bombs, strafing ships and killing survivors. Every captain was faced with the same dilemma: that of the safety of his own men and ship weighed against the natural impulse to rush to the aid of the survivors. At 16.30, as the Luftwaffe's forty-five-minute attack subsided, tugs, destroyers and smaller craft, both French and British, closed the area to begin the recovery. In the heat of the battle Captain Wilson, the master of the *Ulster Prince*, had signalled *Highlander*, offering assistance as he closed the sinking *Lancastria*. Instead, the destroyer had ordered him to leave the scene and proceed to Saint-Nazaire, where he moored his ship alongside the harbour wall.

Highlander, however, had closed the scene before *Lancastria* had even finished sinking, lowering one of her boats to begin the rescue. The destroyer *Havelock*, the trawlers *Agate* and *Cambridgeshire*, French tugs, pilot boats, trawlers and small fishing boats (which had sailed from Saint-Nazaire shortly after the *Lancastria* had been bombed) also approached the disaster area to assist. The captain of the French trawler *Paul Leferme* had just finished switching off all the lights on the buoys in the Loire estuary in preparation for the forthcoming night's evacuation when he received orders to help with the rescue. The captain describes what he saw:

> When we arrived near the indicated area we were horrified at the sight. Hundreds of men were struggling in the sea. We went down in our boats to recover the wounded and those who had escaped the sinking. It was dreadful to see. We could only take 10 to 12 men at the most, and even then our small boat was nearly awash. We made three consecutive journeys, transporting 65 men to the *Paul Leferme* after rescuing them with difficulty, for their clothes were gooey with black fuel oil. Space

55. One of the *Highlander*'s lifeboats is being prepared for rescue work,
as the *Lancastria* lists over to her port side.

being limited, we had to push back those who were dying to make room
for men with a better chance of survival.

While they were transferred on board the *Paul Leferme* the injured
survivors received medical treatment. The French sailors cleaned their
blackened faces and made them drink water to force them to vomit.
These men no longer had a human appearance; they were covered in
sores and burns, or intoxicated by the fuel oil they had swallowed. The
black oil covered them from head to foot as if they had been dipped into
a barrel of tar. Some had stripped down to their underwear to enable
them to swim better.

The three large French tugs, the *Minotaure, Titan* and *Ursus*, succeeded in
saving five hundred people between them while a ferry boat, carrying
traffic from Saint-Nazaire to Saint-Brévin, did the same. Even the pilot
schooner *La Lambarde* took part in the rescue, ferrying her charges to a
British tanker that had recently arrived in the area.

At Le Pouliguen, the fishing port of La Baule, the small French
fishing boat *Saint Michel* put to sea soon after the sinking. Michel Luciani,
the master of the vessel, had been approached by Englishman Henry
Boyd, a former engineering manager of Les Chautiers de Dunkirk, and
Monsieur Pierre Huni, a delegate of the International Red Cross. He had

immediately agreed to assist with the rescue and readily offered his services free of charge. Sailor Yves Goanvic also joined the boat to complete the crew. As they left port *Saint Michel* traversed a known minefield but, as it was the quickest way to reach the scene, he felt that he had no alternative. The *Saint Michel* was certified to carry twenty passengers, but by moving unwanted gear they made room for at least another hundred. As the little ship chugged towards the disaster area she was joined by two more ships from Le Pouliguen.

————

Fifteen-year-old Gaston Noblanc was part of a 25-man crew on the large British-built tug *Hoedic*, along with his father. When the *Lancastria* was bombed Pierre Huni contacted various fishing ports in the Loire basin. Although twenty or so small French ships had been used to ferry troops out to the transports throughout the day, Pierre's efforts ensured that at least twenty more joined in the rescue efforts. This piece of co-ordination was instrumental in saving many more lives. Gaston remembers making repeated journeys out to the struggling men, women and children in the water. He went on to become an active member of the French resistance, in the Vendée area, and was arrested and interrogated by the Gestapo. His face still bears the marks of torture.

————

J. Mansfield had slid down the convenient rope, which was secured from the deck above, only to discover that it was too short to reach the water. He dropped the remaining distance, remembering to hold his newly-acquired life jacket down as he did so. He tried in vain to distance himself from the sinking ship and noticed a lifeboat, within reach, turning away from the grey hull of the stricken liner. He grabbed hold of an oar, which was being used to propel the lifeboat away from the ship, and pulled himself along it until he was able to hook his right arm over the gunwale and grab hold of the rope safety loop with the other. He remained in this position until he, and the occupants of the lifeboat, were picked up by a small ship (probably the *Cambridgeshire*) and transferred to the *John Holt*. His friend Frank Spooner never survived the disaster and his body was never found (see Appendix 1, ref. Dunkirk Memorial).

————

Meanwhile, Staff Sergeant Major A. Picken had moved back to the centre of the oar after his unknown companion had been shot in the head by the Luftwaffe. He noticed two men paddling along, supporting an

56 (this page). Closer view showing hundreds of men clambering down her starboard side, while others huddle on the stern tube. Hundreds more are already in the water. The 'Welin' davits protrude above the ship's side; oil is just visible on the port side of the wreck. This and other photographs were taken from the *Highlander*.

57 (opposite). Oil painting of the scene, painted from memory, by survivor Corporal Robert W. May, 1 HRS, RASC whilst he was recovering in hospital. The *Lancastria* is shown here sinking on her starboard side, an understandable mistake to make.

unconscious man between them. One of them called out, asking Picken if he was okay and suggesting that he hang on to the third man's legs. Picken decided to stay where he was. Shortly after, a life-raft drifted near. It was covered with soldiers and airmen, while clusters of men clung to the ropes that trailed from it. An RAF officer encouraged the men to sing popular songs. Picken continues his story:

> ... Up ahead on the horizon I could make out a fishing trawler, perhaps half a mile away. I paddled towards it with new energy. Out of sight I could hear the struggling of other survivors, but I couldn't risk letting go of the oar that prevented me from drowning. I couldn't help anybody else.
>
> Bit by bit I neared the fishing trawler. Other survivors were already being helped aboard and I only hoped the little fishing boat would wait for me. My head and face were covered with the murky oil and I doubted if I could be seen from the boat.
>
> On and on I paddled for nearly an hour until I was under the lee. The boat was covered with other survivors, nearly all wearing as little as I, some quite naked.
>
> Two oil-blackened survivors on the trawler leaned over the side toward me. "Here, mate," one of them yelled, "Catch hold!" He threw me the end of a two-inch hawser.
>
> Still clenching the oar with one hand, I took the slippery hawser with the other. When I held the rope tightly enough I let go of the oar and it drifted away from me. All around the boat men were being fished out of the water. Some lost their grip on the ropes and fell. Many of them were more weak than I, and some drowned before they could be pulled aboard the ship.
>
> I clung to the rope as tightly as I could while the two men began pulling me up. I was almost completely out when I lost my grip on the thick, coarse rope and felt it slip. I splashed back into the water, expecting to drown.
>
> Wildly paddling, using strength I didn't know I had, I found that I had stayed afloat. Yes, I was swimming!
>
> Speedily [thrashing] my hands and kicking [my] feet, I made little circles in the water while the men above shouted encouragement. "We'll throw you a loop!" I used my new talent and kept on sculling. The rope dropped to me again and I wriggled into the loop. The two men pulled me up as quickly as they could, slipped the rope off me and I collapsed on the deck like a jellyfish...

The captain of the French fishing trawler wanted to land the survivors at Brest, as his family and livelihood remained in France. Although there were over five-hundred survivors on board, none were in a fit state to commandeer the vessel. A signalman rectified the situation when he semaphored the *Oronsay*, which was about a mile away, using two torn shirts. The large troopship eventually closed the trawler, lowering a Jacob's ladder. It was a laboriously slow operation with many falling off the wriggling rope ladder into the sea; luckily none were drowned. The problem was quickly solved by using the gunport doors for easier access into the ship.

————

When Morris Lashbrook, 1 HRS, RASC, got into the sea, he and another soldier spotted a badly burnt comrade close by. With the aid of flotsam they managed to keep the injured man afloat for some fifteen minutes. To this day Morris cannot forget the look in that young man's face, uncomplaining but with a look of despair. He eventually died and they had to let him go.

————

Tom Payne, RAF, was beginning to feel the cold and was suffering from cramp. He was almost at the point of giving up when he grabbed a folded wooden chair. Encouraged by his good fortune he kicked his stiffening legs, surprised that they were moving at all. He then tucked the chair under his chest and rested for a while. Tom continues:

> ... All was now quiet. As I floated there I heard something, or was it my imagination? Over the sea came a whisper, wafted, it seemed, from a thousand miles away. It was another song, a hymn. Very faintly I followed the tune, but clearly I heard the last line "... to our eternal home."
>
> I wanted to look back again at that tragic scene but was unable to do so. I found myself incapable of even moving, but just floated there, staring ahead. Then into my vision bobbed a head, a man's head, and his eyes were fixed on mine.
>
> He did not speak but he seemed to get nearer to me. I'd thought that he must be after my chair and if that should be then I did not have the strength to stop him from taking it. The 'head' must have sensed my thoughts for it then spoke "You got a plank or something there, pal?"
>
> I didn't reply but just stared, so the 'head' continued and said "Take it easy old man, I am alright and can swim but I am so tired I want a rest. Let me hold on for a minute." His voice was so calm that I found mine and invited him to join me and we both hung on to that precious chair. After a short rest my new-found friend said "Come on, together we can make it" and with both of us treading water, slowly we moved towards a mirage which really turned out to be a lifeboat, into which I was hoisted and promptly passed into oblivion. I never saw my good friend again.

I was taken aboard the destroyer HMS *Highlander* where I regained my senses and was given a good rubbing down, hot tea, and a good noggin of rum, which warmed me in spite of my feet being swollen up like balloons...

58–9. Some of the survivors picked up by the *Highlander*. Opposite, hot tea is poured into Sapper Percy Brown's cup, who is seated beside the *Highlander*'s torpedo tubes, and a naval rating attends others. Most of them are covered in oil.

Lieutenant Colonel F. E. Griggs saw a French fishing boat some distance away and decided to swim towards her. He eventually reached the boat's side, but was too breathless and tired to help himself. He was helped aboard, where he witnessed a sorry sight. Men were lying naked, some injured, some hysterical and some motionless. He reached into his jacket pocket and produced an unopened packet of Players cigarettes, still wrapped in cellophane. Miraculously they were nearly all bone dry. He took one out and offered the rest around. While he was waiting on board he noticed a naked man, black with oil, diving in to save men in the water. This he repeated no fewer than five times. It was later discovered that it was Major Armitage of the 159 Railway Construction Company, RE.

Armourer E. J. Mansfield, who had managed to board one of *Lancastria*'s motor launches, continues his story:

> ... Before I could attempt to start the engine, a lifeboat rowed by two army lads and a sailor shouted for me to "Hold on." They tied the lifeboat behind the launch and we set off, picking people from the sea.

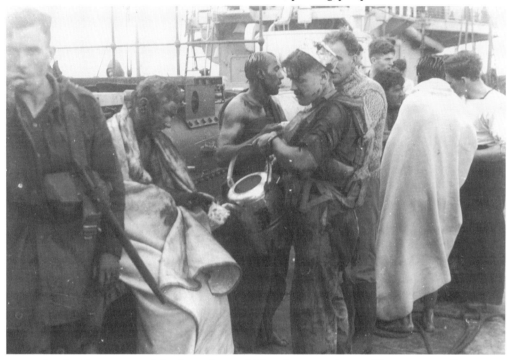

> In the front part of the launch would be about twelve to fifteen men, all strangers to one another. With the launch full, and two-thirds of the lifeboat, we were taken to the destroyer *Highlander* and put aboard...

This little contingent of survivors was one of the first groups to be picked up by the destroyer; in fact the *Lancastria* was still barely afloat:

> ... Although it was a lovely summer's day and the sea was calm, by this time I was beginning to feel very cold. No enemy aircraft had been around for some time, and rescue work was [under way] when next minute in came the German aircraft again, very low and machine-gunning men in the water.
>
> From HMS *Highlander* I could see hundreds of men round the [stern] of *Lancastria* and with this machine-gunning they never stood a chance. *Lancastria* was well down in the water by this time, only the stern above the water, and then the next minute it seemed to rise up and plunge to the bottom. French boats of every size put out and picked up many men from the sea.

Later, on [board] HMS *Highlander* the call went out. All that were not wounded were to be transferred aboard SS *Oronsay* (*Highlander* was very overloaded). They put a plank between the two ships (from the deck of the *Highlander* to a [gunport] door on the *Oronsay*) and then as the two ships rolled together we ran across, which was very frightening, even then some dropped in the water between the two ships ...

———

Squadron Leader E. M. C. Shipp, MBE, had managed to reach the upper deck with fellow officer Bob Doig, by which time the list to port had increased considerably. He continues the story:

... we came face to face with those army boys, many suffering from terrible wounds, others showing on their faces mental havoc which had been wrought in so short a time. The cries of suffering from those badly wounded and needing help was the worst problem, others obviously suffering from shock and those whom we can only assume had become demented, leaping over the starboard (higher) side of the ship to drop maybe 80-100 feet into the sea and perhaps death, or drowning due to concussion, we could do little.

The Hun intent on securing evidence of his kill, came over again, no doubt to gloat over his kill, so I clutched the Bren gun and gave him a burst before he vanished. Then Doig and me did what we could to help those about us.

Time was running out fast, though, to do much for any of them. The list of the ship was increasing at an alarming speed, so I said to Doig 'Directly the deck touches the 'drink' we'll push off and hope for the best.' It was at this point I heard an army lad shout out "I can't swim" – I was lucky, I could – so I whipped off my shoes, life jacket and tunic, fixed him up with my jacket, shouted to Doig to dive in – gave the army boy a ruthless push and I followed him into the water...

Shipp was picked up by a French tug. After a massage and a warm drink he was put in the wheelhouse and wrapped in a blanket to thaw out. He soon revived and, smoking a cigarette stub, walked around the small deck looking for anyone he knew. More and more survivors were being pulled out of the sea. He asked the time; it was 18.05. Shipp continues:

... On the other side of me, rigid as a robot, was an army lad; his head looked stiff as though it was in a vice. I learned as a result of one of the bomb explosions in the Lancastria a thin fillet of wood was driven into his neck, possibly six or eight inches just behind his ear and any movement might cause sudden death – his calm patience and fortitude was beyond my conception.

I began to wonder what our next move would be. Within a few minutes however, one of the crew said something to the skipper in

French and departed. The Captain lost no time in taking action on what I assumed were orders received by wireless, indicated by the man who had spoken to him, as the engine room was given the signal for full steam ahead by the mate. The tug turned completely round. In the distance could be seen a number of large ships spread out and I felt pretty certain we were making for them.

Just after 19.00 we [secured] alongside the *Oronsay*. A gangway was lowered, the wounded were taken aboard first and the rest of us followed. I was directed to a saloon on the main deck, it was packed with survivors, sitting, standing and others lying down, so I followed the general pattern and having been given a cigarette by the fellow next to me, sat, taking stock of the surroundings. Confirmation of the result of her having been bombed earlier in the day was hardly necessary, as fittings, furniture and structure bore conclusive evidence, in addition there was the usual smell, consistent with fire...

———

Second Lieutenant 'Peter' Petit was eventually picked up by the *Highlander* and transferred to the *Oronsay*. He was to learn, later, that the three of his men he had found on the starboard side of the sinking ship had also survived the ordeal.

———

Acting Lieutenant Colonel Norman de Coudray Tronson was picked up by a French lightship and transferred to *Havelock* after being in the water for over three hours.

———

Jesse Fenton was eventually sighted by a small two-man rowing boat and pulled out of the water by a young French soldier. His father, the other crew member, fished out another friend of Jesse's, Peter Moore. Both were then taken to the *Havelock* where they were given mugs of hot tea and some clothing.

———

Chief Officer Grattidge tells how he and Captain Sharp left the ship. This narrative has been extracted from Harry Grattidge's book, entitled *Captain of the Queens*:

... "It's time now, Harry," Sharp said. "I'm going to swim for the after end." I looked at my watch: 16.08. Somehow we had only one lifebelt on the bridge, so, knowing he was a poor swimmer, I made him take it. "Good luck, sir," I said. The water was so close to the bridge now it lapped and chuckled like bathwater. The *Lancastria* quaked once under my feet, a last gesture of farewell. Then she was gone, and I walked from the bridge into the sea off Saint-Nazaire.

The oil crept up my body like cold black syrup. Just beside me, as I swam for clear water, was a man, staring and exhausted. I grasped at him spitting out oil, swimming at right angles to the ship. When I struck clean water I wriggled to help him further, and my stomach turned over. There was only his head.

I grasped a spar to keep me afloat, and kept swimming. High overhead the planes were still buzz-sawing across the horizon; each burst of machine-gun fire and the recoil of the *Oronsay*'s pom-poms seemed to jump like a nerve in my stomach. Suddenly above the shattering explosions and the cries of the wounded, I heard one single superb tenor's [voice] float across the water:

> There'll always be an England
> Where there's a country lane
> As there's a cottage small
> Beside a field of grain...

For all this time, more than half an hour, I had been swimming on my breast, but as the noise of the planes grew louder I strained upwards to see them. A terrible fear shot through me. Why couldn't I see them? Why could I see nothing but darkness? My head, I thought, the top of my head has been blown away and my eyesight has gone. Then a foolish and blessed relief flooded through me, for I had overlooked the fact that I had entered the water wearing my tin hat and that it had jammed forward over my eyes.

I was so light-headed, despite the black oil that emptied from my mouth and burned my lips and nostrils, that I moved over to a little Cockney who was swimming stark naked not far away and asked how he was getting on. He gave me a look of superb disgust. Then he said, "What's the good of hanging on under conditions like this, eh? What's the good? I tell you I'm so fed up I've got a perishing good mind to sink."

I was half inclined to agree with him, but I said, in my best Chief Officer's voice, "Now, don't talk like that. Here, hang on to this bit of wood and I'll swim alongside you, and there's no reason why we shouldn't both be saved." I saw him glance at the gold braid on my sleeve, for I was still wearing my uniform, but eventually he did what he was told. Though I could almost have sworn he shrugged there beneath the surface of the water, as he said with true Cockney philosophy, "Well, guv'nor, I'll tell yer this. If my old mother had known before I was born that I was due to suffer like this, she'd 'ave drunk more gin."

Grattidge was eventually picked up by a small French rowing boat, taken to a tug and transferred to the *Oronsay*. Meanwhile, small boats had come to within twenty yards of Captain Sharp, but it was not until he spotted and hailed his quartermaster Murphy, in boat No. 10a, that he was picked up. Here he learned that ten lifeboats had been successfully launched. Murphy steered alongside the destroyer *Havelock* where Captain Sharp and the other survivors were taken aboard. He was also taken to the *Oronsay*.

––––––

Neal Howard was picked up by a lifeboat belonging to the destroyer *Havelock*. It was manned by two sailors, one controlling the boat while the other, a giant of a man, was naked and knelt in the bows of the boat fishing out survivors. Once full the helmsman steered back towards the *Havelock*, offloaded and continued the search for more survivors. Men were sprawled out along the deck resting and trying to keep warm. Neal describes the scene:

> ... There was one man lying on a bench with his arm stretched upwards with a lot of skin hanging down from various parts of it and someone said that he had been [burnt]. In spite of his injuries however he was laughing and joking with others around him, but next morning, when I went to look for him, I was told that he had died during the night and had been removed.
>
> After drinking my tea I decided that the safest place to be was up on deck, just in case, and I made my way to the [after end] of the destroyer and made myself comfortable, sitting down and leaning against something. I must have fallen asleep. I was awakened by some shouting and a lot of activity, to find the destroyer was listing over at quite a serious angle, and that some of the sailors were undressing and going over the side. I thought it must be serious if the sailors were jumping off the side but was informed that the destroyer had fouled a buoy which was pushing upwards and causing it to [list]; the sailors were going over the side to try to release the buoy from the propeller. To attempt this the destroyer had to stop and the decision was taken that this would make a very good target for any U-boat that might be prowling around, the other destroyer and all other ships should go ahead. Our *Havelock* sailors tried and tried but were unable to [disentangle] the buoy and so it was decided to take it with us back to England. We still had our [list] and the buoy slowed us down quite a bit, but at least we were going in the right direction...

––––––

Likewise, Private J. H. Drummond was picked up by a small French vessel and later transferred to the *Havelock*. As he boarded the destroyer he was directed to the galley and given a hot mug of tea. As he took a sip he noticed a very large man, who was propped up on a bench and shaking badly from shock, a distressing sight. The next thing he just keeled over and died. Drummond walked outboard to witness the rescue. As each survivor was brought aboard a naval officer examined them, ordering some to be thrown back. Drummond questioned the action, only to be told "We only have room for the living." It was a sad but true fact.

––––––

Sapper Leslie Bailey had clung to the wooden ladder with three others for three hours when they were picked up by a French trawler and transhipped to the *Havelock*. However, Leslie was nearly left behind when a sailor was ordered to withdraw the gangplank. He shouted across to the sailor, asking him where they were bound. "Plymouth," he replied.

Leslie said, "but that's where I live!" Luck was with him; the sailor quickly allowed him to board. Now he would make that date at the altar and marry Marie Horrill.

––––––

Captain Williams, master of the *Dundrum Castle*, who was carrying about five-hundred troops, embarked at Saint-Nazaire, had been slow to clear the South Channel. It was fortunate for the survivors of the *Lancastria* that his ship was still in the vicinity, for two of the *Dundrum Castle*'s lifeboats, under Chief Officer D. P. Klasen and Second Officer W. G. Shannon, played a major role in the rescue, recovering over 120 men in oily and difficult conditions. They made repeated journeys to French ferry boats which were standing by. After this gallant and successful effort, the *Dundrum Castle*'s boats were recovered, being some of the last to leave the scene (see Appendix 2).

––––––

Sergeant Strudwick eventually closed the small ship he had been swimming towards. It was the *Cambridgeshire* and he thought how strange it was that he could spell his girlfriend's name, Madge, from letters in the ship's name. He was hauled aboard the ship on the second attempt, still fully clothed in his airman's uniform. He continues his story:

> ... I was immediately relieved of my life jacket and it was put into the ship's small rowing boat together with the life jackets from the others rescued. ... [The boat] was [then] rowed out among the still struggling thousands and thrown to them. Men were now being hauled over the sides of this small ship at quite a fast rate and it was quickly filling up with men in all stages of dress, varying from naked to fully dressed...

... By this time the *Cambridgeshire* was packed with survivors and the skipper spoke to us assembled in the well deck to the effect that it was impossible for him to cram any more onto his ship and consequently he was going to put us back into Saint-Nazaire so that he could return empty and pick up more survivors.

On our way into Saint-Nazaire we were passing quite near another ship and the skippers spoke to each other by loud hailers. As a result of their conversation the *Cambridgeshire* drew alongside the other ship, which turned out to be an empty cargo ship [named] *John Holt...*

60. Leading supply rating, Dennis Maloney; without his fortitude many more people would have died.

Leading supply rating, Dennis Maloney, RN, had witnessed the attack on board the *Highlander*. As his ship closed the mass of survivors one of the *Lancastria*'s lifeboats came alongside the destroyer and the survivors were helped aboard. On the spur of the moment Dennis saw the empty lifeboat, jumped in and hailed two more shipmates to join him. Once aboard, Dennis manned the tiller while the other two rowed, making slow progress towards a small group of survivors. They hauled several aboard and two of the fittest were given two spare oars, to speed up progress. They then proceeded towards larger groups of survivors, taking all on board. When they had forty or so survivors aboard, they decided to turn about and make back towards the *Highlander*. To their utter dismay they saw their ship heading out into the open sea, presumably bound for England. Now the three ratings, instead of becoming rescuers, had become survivors themselves! As the light began to fade they realised that four or five men had died since being rescued; they were gently lowered over the side of the boat, leaving room for more men to be picked up. In the growing darkness they were eventually spotted by a French pinnace which towed them back into Saint-Nazaire. After all the survivors had disembarked, Dennis noticed that one soldier remained in the boat. He went over and checked his pulse. He was dead. Dennis left him in the lifeboat with his identity disc still around his neck. However, he did remove some letters from his pocket, letters he intended to return to the soldier's next of kin at his convenience.

One of the survivors who was pulled out of the sea by Dennis was Joe Sweeney. He was a non-swimmer and was one of the last to leave the *Lancastria*. After escaping the deathly clutch of another non-swimmer, he saw a large plank of wood with four men already clinging to it. He inexpertly splashed his way towards it and clung on for dear life. By then one of the men had got on top of the plank, where he lay prostrate, refusing all pleas to return to the water. Another man, who was injured, held on with one hand while another gave him support.

During the long hours in the water they saw live men, without life jackets, struggling to stay afloat, while dead men, wearing them, bobbed along and passed them by. They all looked as if they had simply gone to sleep. It was a sad but true fact that many of them had jumped from high parts of the ship without holding the front of their life jackets firmly downwards. The resulting force of the impact had wrenched their necks upwards, causing instant death.

———

Sergeant Percy Manley had been recovering from an industrial accident, in which he had lost the tops of three of his fingers. He reached the safety of the *Highlander* only to receive another injury. An enemy aircraft had near-missed the destroyer, lifting her stern out of the water. The ship returned seawards with such a force that the hatch cover sliced though Percy's toes. Although thankfully alive, he was helped below for treatment.

———

The Tillyer family were eventually picked up by the *Highlander*, where baby Jacqueline had to be revived, for she had lapsed into unconsciousness. When the *Highlander* had her quota of survivors on board she steamed over to the *Oronsay*, where the survivors boarded the troopship, using scrambling nets, which enabled them to reach and enter the ship through the gunport doors.

———

It was around 19.00 when the *Saint Michel* and the two other fishing vessels reached the scene. By then most of the survivors had been picked up. Seemingly, all that remained were the inert oil-blackened shapes of dead men. Grim faced they set about their task. As Luciani slowly steered his vessel through the bodies the other three checked them for any signs of life. Amazingly they found some still alive and eventually transferred twenty-three of them to a nearby transport. Others, who were severely wounded, were taken back to La Pouliguen for treatment, along with nineteen more that they picked up from a tanker, after instructions from the captain of a British destroyer who had taken them there. Held up by the tide, it was almost midnight before Luciani could berth his vessel and despatch the injured men to hospital.

———

C. W. Cornish's lifeboat was approached by a French fishing trawler to which they all transferred. Once on board he was given a pair of long johns and a night shirt to restore his dignity. The *Oronsay* was listing ten degrees to port, but was still seaworthy. Some, like Tom Hutchison, were still in the water as dusk fell. He was lucky enough to be picked up by a small French fishing trawler. The crew worked tirelessly, picking up motionless bodies from the water. If it was discovered that they were dead they were returned to the sea, reserving precious space for the living. Like the *Highlander*, once fully loaded the trawler captain despatched his human cargo to the *Oronsay* before repeating the process in another area.

The trawlers *Cambridgeshire* and *Agate* had also steamed into the disaster area and began picking up survivors, as did the Ellerman Lines' steamship *Fabian*. Her master, Captain M. Hocking, picked up many survivors before proceeding into Saint-Nazaire to embark another eight hundred troops. Although his small cargo ship had no passenger accommodation he still managed to carry many hundreds of troops, and reached Plymouth safely. As the crew of the *John Holt* finished their evening meal Captain W. G. Easton (*Cambridgeshire*) hailed Captain Fuller for information about the navigable depth near the entrance of Saint-Nazaire. He was told it was eighteen feet. Easton's ship was drawing twenty-three feet, due to the near one-thousand survivors he now had aboard; which, for a 443-ton ship, was quite incredible. Captain Fuller signalled him to come alongside. She was made fast by 18.15 and began off-loading her cargo of men via six rope ladders, three alongside No. 2 hatch and three further aft.

The men clambered aboard; some were partially clothed, some naked and most were smothered in black oil. Those that were injured or

61. HM trawler *Cambridgeshire* comes alongside the Commodore's ship *John Holt* and disembarks her human cargo. Her captain and crew had seemingly performed a miracle.

62. Another dramatic view showing the last of the *Lancastria*'s survivors boarding the *John Holt*.

burnt were tended by Chief Officer Hind in the smoke room, which served as a hospital. Later he was ably assisted by a sergeant and sappers Norman Jones and Freddie Friswell. By 19.15 the embarkation was complete: all but three severely wounded survivors had been taken aboard. The three wounded men had been left aboard the *Cambridgeshire* because the *John Holt* did not carry a doctor. The *Cambridgeshire* then proceeded to Saint-Nazaire to await further orders. Shortly after, the

63. A couple of survivors pose for a photograph on board the *Cambridgeshire* before joining the *John Holt*. The injured man was taken back to Saint-Nazaire.

signal station at Saint-Nazaire sent a message to Captain Fuller, instructing him to bring the survivors ashore; to him this seemed a ludicrous demand, especially with the evacuation in full swing. He reasoned that these destitute men had already gone through enough trauma for one day. So, Fuller spoke to the naval commodore, Admiral J. Burgess-Watson, persuading him to let him sail immediately, despite the consequences, should there be any. A signal was then sent to the *Robert L. Holt* (Vice Commodore) instructing Captain Kendall to take over the responsibilities of the convoy. Shortly before 19.30 the French pilot was landed and the *John Holt* sailed for England. Fearing an aerial attack Captain Fuller purposely avoided Quiberon Bay, trusting his luck through a minefield without the usual guidance of a French minesweeper.

The Blue Funnel Line's 7,405-ton steamship *Teiresias* was seen near the entrance with a 10-degree list to port. This ship had originally been requisitioned to carry Admiral Burgess-Watson, but this arrangement had been changed, hence him being aboard the *John Holt*. At around the same time that the *Lancastria* had been attacked and bombed the *Teiresias* was hit on her port side between Nos 2 and 4 lifeboats. A second bomb had missed by about 40 feet while a third exploded 10 feet from her port

64. The *Cambridgeshire* steams away towards Saint-Nazaire. The French coast is visible in the distance.

side, amidships. The bo'sun was killed and a crew member injured. The ship gradually listed to starboard and at around 16.20 all the starboard lifeboats were cleared, leaving only Captain J. R. Davies and six crew on board. The ship was attacked by nine planes. Bombs exploded all around the ship between twenty and thirty feet away, but none hit her. At around 18.00 the SS *Holmside*, which had been about a mile away during the action, went alongside the three lifeboats to offer assistance. At that point they were still assuming that they would be able to return to their own ship, so they politely declined the offer of help, but Captain Davies then ordered the third officer's lifeboat alongside and he and the six remaining crew members also abandoned ship. All were then taken aboard the 3,433-ton *Holmside*, including the body of the ship's bo'sun. The injured crewman, who was Chinese, received medical attention and later made a full recovery. Attempts to reach the other two lifeboats, which had drifted south-east, were hampered, however, by the shallow water. They were making for Ile de Pilier lighthouse and eventually reached England safely by another ship. At 21.00 the *Teiresias* was reboarded and the starboard anchor was dropped to prevent the ship drifting into the fairway. She eventually broke in half and sank later the same day.

65. Blue Funnel Line's steamship *Teiresias*. She too was sunk off Saint-Nazaire on 17 June 1940.

Meanwhile, as the *John Holt* steamed into the open sea they were instructed, by a destroyer, to make for Falmouth. Captain Fuller now had another concern: how to feed so many men. He discussed the matter with Chief Steward Lange and it was decided to make buckets of tea, laced with a bottle of rum and served with biscuits. As the ship normally carried a crew of forty-five, there was a distinct shortage of crockery and cutlery. This problem was partially overcome by the crew, some of whom carried their own sets. Every space in the ship was packed with men, even the lower holds and 'tween decks. Clothes were given out and curtains, tablecloths and bedding were also improvised for use as clothing.

The following day, 18 June, the crew's boiler was put to good use, making hot stew, which was served in soup plates. With no escort, Captain Fuller prudently steered a course well west of Ushant, instructing everyone to keep under cover in case of a chance sighting by enemy aircraft. Responding to Admiralty instructions the *John Holt* entered Plymouth Sound that evening and was cheered in as she passed the fort. After anchoring for an hour she proceeded to Smith Bay Pier and made fast in darkness. People lined the shore and threw biscuits, tins of milk and corned beef. Girls came along with trays of cigarettes. Naval and military doctors and nurses soon followed. Ambulances collected about 170 casualties and thirty or so stretcher cases. Some were lucky enough to receive a bag of fish and chips, purchased from a nearby shop and handed out by local ladies. Postcards were also provided to enable the survivors to inform relatives that they were home and safe; all were posted free of charge.

––––––

Young Roger Legroux had survived the fall from the lifeboat and had got clear of the *Lancastria* with his mother and Mrs Tips. In the confusion Emilie had been lost. The other three had spent 3½ hours in the water, supported by their life jackets. They were picked up by a small French fishing boat and transferred to the destroyer *Havelock* (Captain E. B. K. Stevens). By this time Roger was unconscious, cold and apparently lifeless, and it was only because Mdm. Legroux insisted that artificial respiration be continued for twenty minutes that her son survived; he had swallowed a great amount of sea water and fuel oil during his struggle in the water. The *Havelock* had rescued several hundred survivors, including a dozen civilians who were part of the Avions Fairey group. Unfortunately there was no news of Roger's father or sister. The previous evening, the *Havelock* had sustained damage to her bows when she was near-missed by a bomb; a little later she snagged a loose buoy around her port propeller shaft, rendering her useless for convoy duties. Captain Stevens, commander of the 9th Destroyer Flotilla, transferred his flag to another destroyer. The first lieutenant, who was left in charge, was then ordered to pick up as many survivors as he could and proceed to Plymouth, using his starboard propeller; some of the badly-injured army survivors died during the voyage and were buried at sea. As day broke on the 18 June the English coast was visible to all on deck. Without doubt the temporary 'captain' of the destroyer had forwarded a message explaining the circumstances aboard ship, for as the warship berthed, with the help of another naval ship, the crew could see doctors, nurses and ambulances lining the quayside, waiting to tend the wounded and traumatised survivors. The first to be disembarked were the stretcher cases.

––––––

Julie Delfosse was thankful to be reunited with her son Freddie, reaching England in the destroyer *Havelock*. Whilst on board she searched, with the help of two Church Army sisters, for one Harry Pack. She could only recognise him by his eyes but, when she found him, using one of the sisters to translate, she thanked Harry for helping her get away from the sinking ship. In England, she was reunited with her husband and the Belgian family lived in Earlstown, Lancashire until the end of the War. In September 1940 Julie wrote a letter to Harry; part of which reads: ... 'I am the person whose hand you held until I was safely aboard the rescue ship ... Please, I should like to tell you once more how grateful I am to you for saving my life for, had it not been for your courage and bravery I should never have seen England...'

———

When Jesse Fenton landed at Plymouth he was temporarily taken to Devonport Barracks, where a petty officer saw his state of undress and asked him "Where's your shoes, soldier?" Jesse replied "I haven't got any, sir." Just then a naval rating appeared and the petty officer asked him "What size shoes do you take, sailor?" "Seven, sir," he replied. "Then give this soldier a pair of yours. I'll make sure they are replaced."

———

The *Oronsay* eventually got under way in darkness at around 21.30. Captain A. E. Nicholls had to navigate using a compass from one of the lifeboats, and he was without the luxury of proper charts, instead he used a school atlas supplied by the purser. The steering gear had been temporarily rigged up using chain blocks. All this damage had been caused by the bomb which had wrecked the bridge after it had landed in the captain's toilet. Fortunately he was not sitting on it at the time!

The next morning, news spread around the ship about the army lad who had the piece of wood lodged in his neck. He had sadly died during the night and had been buried at sea; to quote Shipp's words – "a sad ending to his heroic and magnificent courage, and the skill of those who tried to save him." Approaching her destination, *Oronsay* was escorted the last few miles by the cruiser *Shropshire* and a Sunderland flying boat. She arrived in Plymouth just after 21.00 on 18 June. It was not until the following day that Shipp learned that his friend, Bob Doig, had also survived. He had been brought back to England in a different ship.

Captain Nicholls, despite the deafness he suffered after the bomb had exploded on his bridge, continued his service with Orient Line in the *Orontes*, from 3 March 1941 to 17 December 1945, when he retired.

———

66. Captain A. E. Nicholls, master of the *Oronsay*. This photograph was taken on 5 September 1945, shortly before he retired.

Sergeant G. Miller belonged to the 159 Railway Construction Company, RE. As the ship deepened he and his Irish friend, Michael Coffey, had stripped ready to jump, but neither men could swim at all well. The Irishman jumped first, but failed to surface. Still hesitating, Miller was approached by Bill Collier, another friend from his company. They jumped together and Collier, being a strong swimmer, stayed with Miller until they were fortunate enough to reach a submerged lifeboat, which was already overcrowded with survivors. Here they hung on for hours, somehow escaping the machine-gun bullets and tracer. During that time many dropped off the side of the boat, probably suffering from exhaustion or hypothermia. There was nothing else that they could do, except hold on and hope for rescue.

After four hours both men were rescued by a French fishing boat and taken ashore. They were then taken to a convent where nuns tried to clean them up with hot water. However, the relief of rescue was short-lived when an English-speaking nun informed them that the Germans were already entering the outskirts of Saint-Nazaire. Dressed in blankets they reached the dockside and found some abandoned officers' uniforms. Miller was standing in a lieutenant colonel's jacket and trousers – very rapid promotion indeed! Alongside him a medical orderly stooped, tending a number of stretcher cases.

They eventually boarded the 2,918-ton *Robert L. Holt* at Saint-Nazaire docks and were taken to Plymouth. Four men died during the 57-hour voyage and were buried at sea. The crew had given up their cabins for the wounded and shared their rations with the survivors. On arrival, all the survivors were taken to the Prince of Wales' Hospital. After 48 hours Miller and Collier, who had been suffering from shock, were detailed to take a party of men to Derby, despite Miller's insistence that they should report to Longmoor. When they reached their destination no one knew anything about them, so they were redirected to Longmoor where they were given a generous 48 hours leave!

———

At around 20.00/17 June a message was sent from shore by Aldis lamp instructing all ships to proceed into the River Loire. Several ships moved to a position off Saint-Nazaire. Throughout the night troops were ferried out to the ships at anchor. In darkness the *Glenaffric* set sail from Saint-Nazaire during a heavy air raid. Once clear of the harbour she set course for England and disappeared in the darkness. By 09.00 the next morning the *Robert L. Holt* still remained at anchor empty. Soon after, a pilot boat appeared and the pilot steered the ship into a large lock where troops swarmed aboard, filling the holds and decks to capacity. Once full she sailed alone, catching up with and joining a slow-moving 21-ship convoy, codenamed 'Stable 2', that had sailed at 11.00/18 June. The convoy included the *Baharistan, Clan Ferguson, City of Mobile, City of Lancaster, Royal Ulsterman, Beltoy, Maurice Rose, Glenlea, Floristan, Harpathian, Glendinning, Pollux* (Estonian) and *Lechistan* (Polish), all carrying troops from Saint-Nazaire, including some who were survivors from the *Lancastria*. Also in company were the oiler *Caspia*, the Polish ship *Lewant* and the British ship *Orama* with the trawlers *Cloughton Wyke, St Melante* and *Armana*, escorted by the *Highlander* and the sloop *Wren*. All twenty-two ships reached Plymouth safely around midday on 20 June.

———

The 8,082-ton oil tanker *Cymbula* had finished discharging her cargo of benzene at Donges, just after noon on 17 June. Without the aid of tugs or pilot, Captain Clatworthy steered his ship out into the Loire estuary, where he anchored and continued to wash tanks, a necessary procedure to reduce fire risk. Survivors from the *Lancastria*, who had been taken back into Saint-Nazaire were taken out to her by tugs and small fishing vessels before she sailed. However, as with any tanker that is carrying (or has carried) flammable cargo, Captain Clatworthy insisted on the retention of his ship's 'No Smoking' rule, despite the craving of numerous passengers.

The destroyer *Beagle* was also used to bring back some 600 *Lancastria* survivors (see Appendix 8).

––––––

Throughout the evening of the disaster the *Ulster Prince* embarked some of the survivors that had been landed at Saint-Nazaire. Most were in a pitiful state. Plenty of paraffin and water were made readily available for cleaning purposes, while spare clothing was issued to the lucky few. By 21.00 the ship had run out of fresh water. Lieutenant (E) Gerald Hughes, RNR, who was one of the ship's engineering officers continues:

> ... as more survivors piled on board they were forced to clean themselves as best they could with engine room cotton waste and any other material lying around. It was a completely hopeless task. By [22.00] every inch of space on board was closely packed with survivors from the *Lancastria* and other troops who had been ashore. I had ten in my cabin (all covered in oil). They had used my towels and sheets which had to be destroyed afterwards.
>
> Captain Wilson made a careful tour of inspection and decided it was high time to sail. The supply of lifebelts had long since been exhausted and there was no way of checking the exact numbers on board save by a long and painstaking count which the circumstances neither permitted or warranted. It was enough to know that the ship could not take any more aboard.
>
> A request to move off was refused by the Naval Control Officer on the grounds that despite a fortuitous full moon and flood tide the buoys in the river were all extinguished. So we were forced to stay in harbour until 05.30 the next morning, 18 June.
>
> That night another heavy air attack was made on Saint-Nazaire and we all waited anxiously, crew and troops alike, knowing that it needed only another unlucky bomb or two to cause a repetition of the *Lancastria* tragedy, but fortune was either more merciful or the gods of war were glutted to satiety with their recent feast, for the *Ulster Prince* lay alongside the harbour wall untouched, and at 05.30, just after dawn, we were able

to join an assembling convoy. Slowly out into the gathering day moved ships of all sizes and the *Ulster Prince* was forced to dawdle along, the 18 knots speed reduced to the [8-knot] saunter of [the slowest ship]; and so it was that we made our way safely to Falmouth.

After disembarkation had been completed Captain Wilson was amazed to find that the *Ulster Prince* had brought back more than 2,850 men, all squeezed aboard a cross-channel ship which in peace time did not carry more than 500 passengers.

––––––

If Joe Sweeney thought that his adventure was over he was mistaken. After hours in one of *Lancastria*'s lifeboats, the one which had been manned by three of the *Highlander*'s crew, he was eventually landed in Saint-Nazaire, black with fuel oil and wearing only his underwear. After adventures in a French *estaminet* he dressed in some tight-fitting clothes supplied by a local French girl, which she had obtained from her younger brother. Joe eventually gained passage back to England in a collier.

––––––

After five hours in the water Frank Brogden was picked up by a French tug. On board the survivors were given a mug of hot wine; this was purposely served to induce regurgitation and remove the fuel oil that many had involuntarily swallowed during their struggle to survive. The tug then took them back to Saint-Nazaire where Red Cross workers tended the sick and wounded. From midnight to around 02.00 ambulances transported them to a nearby convent hospital. Here nuns led them to a special room where they cleaned the oil from the survivors as best they could. It was a difficult task which was not helped by a scarcity of both soap and hot water. Bed sheets were ripped up and handed round, allowing the fitter survivors to clean themselves as best they could. They were then wrapped in blankets and taken to various wards and told to lay down on palliasses which had been placed on the floor between patients beds. The patients must have had a shock when they woke next morning to see so many black faces!

Many soldiers and airmen died during the night at the convent and just after midday various local people came to the hospital with an assortment of clothing. Those fit enough, dressed as best they could. They were then advised to make for the port, as it was known that a small number of Germans were entering Saint-Nazaire. Brogden continues the story:

> ... We walked down to the quayside to see if there was any chance of picking [a ship] up, but [the dock area] was in a complete state of disarray. Various people, crews from ships and troops, were just lying

there; some were injured, some were in a state of shock, some were clothed, some weren't clothed at all – all were black from head to toe with oil fuel. They had just been put on the quayside and covered in blankets. People were coming around with drinks from time to time and tried to wipe you down. There were no lights on at all because there were intermittent air attacks.

One yacht came in which turned out to be the [745-ton *Osprey*], in peacetime ... [she had been owned by W. D. & H. O. Wills, the tobacco company, as a pleasure yacht and handed over to the Royal Navy for use as an anti-submarine vessel and renamed HMS *Oracle*]. She was in the area and had heard about this terrific episode and came in to see if she could pick anyone up. We were very fortunate, they picked up [44 survivors from the *Lancastria*] and brought us back to Plymouth.

We left around midnight on the 18 June and we had a near miss with a submarine as we were leaving Saint-Nazaire. One of the junior lieutenants, who had let us use his [cabin] to get cleaned up, told us about it. He came back to see if we were alright and, when asked what was up, told us that they had picked up the sound of a submarine and then had let the depth charges go...

———

Sergeant S. Clarke, RAOC, substantiates the above story; he too had been rescued after spending three-and-a-half hours in the water. He, like many others, was taken to a Saint-Nazaire hospital suffering from exposure. After remaining in the hospital for a day they heard on the radio that the Germans were just a couple of miles away from Saint-Nazaire. He and Sergeant Adams, RAOC, asked the matron if they could be discharged; she refused. So a number of survivors, who considered that they were fit enough to travel, discharged themselves. Sergeant Clarke continues:

... We made our way to Saint-Nazaire docks in army vehicles that had been abandoned by troops that had evacuated from France. On arrival at the docks we tried to get aboard an American ship without success as the captain informed us that at that time America was neutral. He said that when his ship reached outside the three-mile limit, he would have a message sent out, hoping that a British ship would receive it. This apparently had the desired [effect], as at 21.30 [18 June] HM yacht [*Oracle*] entered the docks, and after the captain satisfied himself that we were British, allowed us to board his ship and we were brought back to Plymouth...

During the voyage to Plymouth a German [U-boat] was encountered and the ship discharged several depth charges.

———

General Sir Alan F. Brooke proceeded to Saint-Nazaire where he boarded the armed trawler *Cambridgeshire* at 21.30. The destroyer, sent for his use by the Commander-in-Chief, was being used to ship *Lancastria* survivors back to England. The *Cambridgeshire* remained in the harbour throughout the night despite three German air raids, which were concentrated on land targets.

At 03.00/18 June the *Cambridgeshire* sailed as escort to the slow convoy to Plymouth mentioned earlier. The trawler reached Plymouth safely at 18.00/19 June, allowing General Brooke and his staff to catch the midnight train to London, where he reported to General Sir John Dill, Chief of the Imperial General Staff, the next morning.

67. General Sir Alan F. Brooke on board the *Cambridgeshire* with other senior officers who were to take passage back to Plymouth.

Corporal G. Youngs, RASC, had survived the sinking, minus his new bicycle, and was picked up by a French trawler. The vessel then returned to Saint-Nazaire, where the survivors were landed. Youngs ended up in a convent hospital with ten others from the *Lancastria*. Here they received attention and were cleaned up by the nuns who ran it. Two days later a German officer and two soldiers entered the hospital and, in perfect

English, they were warned not to attempt to escape. The Germans then disappeared, seemingly returning to their front line.

On 19 June the Tribal class destroyer *Punjabi*, which had just completed repairs at Devonport after shell damage in the second Battle of Narvik, was ordered to proceed to Saint-Nazaire to pick up about two hundred French and Polish soldiers, who had dispersed into hiding. What made the operation even more hazardous, was that some Germans were known to be already in the area. Closing the coast near Saint-Nazaire, the captain put a group of crew members ashore. Here they rounded up the soldiers, who were taken on board. Corporals Youngs, Cyril Woolston and another soldier, noticed the destroyer steaming close to the shore and piled into a Red Cross ambulance. They drove to where the crew had landed and informed them of other survivors left at the hospital. Acting upon this information Surgeon Lieutenant John Thomas jumped into the ambulance and returned to the hospital. Of the eight *Lancastria* patients, two were unfit for transportation and had to remain, while the other six were taken back along the coast and embarked in the destroyer. The *Punjabi* returned to Millbay Dock, Plymouth, where the injured soldiers and airmen were taken to hospital. Surgeon Lieutenant John Thomas was awarded the Distinguished Service Cross for his efforts.

When Corporal Youngs did get ashore he and five other soldiers were escorted by an army sergeant and taken to the Ballard Institute, which was a large building commandeered by the Army. Here he met two other *Lancastria* survivors from his own unit. They had got back to England a few days earlier. As no new uniforms were readily available, they were given ten shillings and allowed to walk around Plymouth in their shabby civilian clothes. Youngs and a few others went in search of Woolworth's to purchase some shaving gear. When they found it, the manager was locking the store up for the night. They explained who they were and what they wanted to purchase. The manager eyed the dishevelled party carefully and, believing their story, reopened the store and told them to take any necessary items they required. He then listed the items but refused payment – such was the spirit of Britain in those days.

———

G. Skelton, who had survived straddled across a sizeable piece of wood, eventually drifted towards an upturned lifeboat, which had a few survivors clinging to its keel, to which he transferred. At first he enjoyed the company of his new found friends, but as time went by more people joined them, testing the displacement of the buoyancy tanks and the stability of the boat. Sensing another imminent disaster he abandoned the lifeboat for another piece of wreckage. He was eventually picked up by a French trawler and taken back to Saint-Nazaire, where he was transported by ambulance to a nearby hospital. There he washed and had his injury cleaned and stitched. The following day he decided to try his luck at getting home, a decision sharpened by the knowledge that the Germans were near at hand. Thanking the nurses and doctors he made his way outside the hospital where a number of survivors had gathered discussing the same issue. Three men were standing together, deep in discussion. He approached them and asked if he could join their company. After a quick analysis of the situation they decided to head south to try their luck in another port. It resulted in a 350-mile journey along the coast of France.

They hitched a ride in a truck driven by a young French boy who had lost his family through enemy action. Other passengers included a Salvation Army officer and some nurses. Their journey brought no success at the ports of La Rochelle or Rochefort. At Bordeaux the four soldiers parted company with their friends, who continued their journey south, and reported to the British Consul. Here they learned that there were still no ships heading for England, although an RAF officer did provide shoes and clothing for Skelton who, at that point in time, was very poorly dressed.

Travelling further south they finally arrived at the port of Bayonne where their luck changed. A Dutch liner named *Queen Emma* was preparing to leave for England. After gaining permission to board her they were reunited with their former travellers, including the French driver who had also been granted passage after a lengthy debate between the Salvation Army officer and the ship's captain. The uneventful voyage terminated at Weymouth, where Skelton was reprimanded for wearing an RAF uniform, when it was discovered that he was a soldier! Such was officialdom even in those days. Skelton was taken away for questioning before being allowed to continue his journey back to his headquarters in Durham.

———

Dennis Maloney, and his two companions from *Highlander*, eventually made it home by ship and reported back to Devonport Barracks. During two days leave, Dennis took time to visit the dead soldier's family, explaining what had happened and returning the letters he had rescued at the same time. He felt that it was the least he could do and hoped that it gave them some sort of comfort. It was some time before the 'three delinquents' rejoined their ship. When they did, the ship's officers lined the deck in front of the gangway. The three rescuers did not know what to expect. Perhaps they would be court martialled for desertion or, at the very least, receive a serious reprimand. Instead, as they boarded, each officer shook their hands and congratulated them. Promises of recognition never did materialise, but the knowledge of what they had done was reward in itself.

––––––

One final, poignant story comes to light in a Second World War recollection written by Sister Ann Reeves, QAIMNS(R) and held at the Imperial War Museum Archives Department, listed under 'Unpublished recollections of Second World War nurses'. When she was a student nurse at a London hospital, she treated a *Lancastria* survivor. Let her own words describe the story:

> ... We found the burns casualties from the *Lancastria* even more awesome. They made my flesh creep. Few of them could walk. Most of them had been covered in flaming oil and were indescribably, horrifically, burnt. These were the days of tannic acid treatment for burns. Sometimes even cold tea leaves were used for agonising burns. We also used saline.
>
> Sister said to me, "Nurse you will apply Bunyan bags to Corporal Campbell's arms and legs and treat the rest of his body with tannic acid. Call me if you want any help."
>
> Bunyan bags were enormous cellophane bags filled with saline solution into which the whole of a charred arm or leg could be inserted so that it was surrounded by salt water.
>
> Corporal 'Jock' Campbell was an unrecognisable bulk of burnt flesh with a human soul. He had been enveloped in burning oil and had jumped from the *Lancastria* as a living torch. Perhaps the salt water had at first saved him but the flaming oil, thick and cohesive, had burnt right through his tissues. He was never free of pain except when mercifully drugged with morphine.
>
> All severe burns cases suffer from dehydration which can be remedied by giving the patient a saline solution. But if, as in Corporal Campbell's case, the lips are too corroded and swollen, and the tongue too painful for fluid, then a saline solution can be given through a vein. But they could not find a vein in Jock's charred body. So Corporal Campbell died...

Twenty-one-year-old Corporal Gordon Grant Campbell, 7517192, RAMC, had worked in 24 General Hospital, France; he died on 11 January 1941 after a long and painful struggle. He is buried in a joint grave, No. 69, at

St Pancras Cemetery, Finchley. His parents lived in Hendon, and his father, William Campbell, was a highly qualified bacteriologist, gaining experience in Cape Town, Edinburgh and London Universities. He joined the RAMC as captain during the Great War and was mentioned in despatches.

Although Corporal Gordon Grant Campbell had been counted, initially, as a survivor (although not named) his name has been included in the Roll of Honour listed in Appendix 1. There are, no doubt, many other cases like his, whereby a man was listed as a survivor but subsequently died as a result of his injuries, counted separately from those who died during the immediate circumstances of the sinking of His Majesty's Troopship *Lancastria*.

68. The memorial window at St Katharine Cree Church by Mr M. C. Farrar Bell.

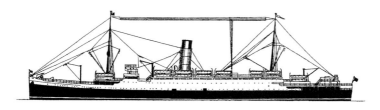

CHAPTER X

AFTERMATH AND THE FINAL PILGRIMAGE

The bodies of seamen, airmen and soldiers drowned or killed as a result of the sinking of the *Lancastria* were washed up on various beaches from Piriac to the Vendée. The currents of the Loire estuary eventually washed many bodies into the sandy reaches of Bourgneuf Bay. In the district of Moutiers-en-Retz, the first body did not reach the coast until 28 June, eleven days after the disaster. It was not until 11 July that sixteen more bodies were found, a result, no doubt, of a storm that had pounded the French coast the day before. The last bodies were washed ashore on 19 July. Local people were anxious to dispose of them quickly.

On the whole it was impossible to make coffins for the bodies being washed ashore. Instead council workers at Moutiers-en-Retz dug one long trench where the bodies were laid to rest between two layers of straw. The date and number of bodies washed ashore at the district of Moutiers-en-Retz were as follows: 28 June – 1; 11 July – 16; 12 July – 34; 13 July – 9; 16 July – 33; 17 July – 6; 19 July – 30. A total of 129, of which 45 were 'known only unto God', were found in that district. When the trench at Moutiers was full, additional bodies were buried behind the sea wall at Minselles, in the sand dunes between Les Moutiers and Le Collet. They were exhumed after the war and reburied at Pornic, but the place where they were temporarily buried still carries the name 'The English Cemetery' and the lane that leads there is called '*Lancastria* Way'. After a municipal council meeting on 4 December 1949 the village gave some land, in their communal cemetery, to the Imperial Commission of British Military Graves.

Certain districts were able to put the bodies in coffins. At Clion-sur-Mer, for example, the mayor had all the large trees chopped down in Millassière to make them, although this was an exceptional gesture.

At La Baule the council employees were faced with the problem of rocky soil, making the task of digging a trench extremely difficult. The land had been given as early as 1939 to be a military cemetery. Once it was dug the bodies were wrapped in cotton sheets and covered in lime before the grave was closed. During the war, and while still under the German occupation, flowers were placed occasionally on the graves. At La Baule one French woman, Mademoiselle Louise Jaouen, regularly looked after the war graves and, despite the risk to her own safety, placed a white cross above every seaman, airman and soldier who had been lost in the *Lancastria*. Without her courageous and compassionate action many of the graves in this area would have remained anonymous. It was a similar story in other areas of the Vendée, however, where the bodies of so many were eventually washed ashore.

At Prefailles, near Saint-Nazaire, a resident named Madame Ruth Audra revealed her story:

> The *Lancastria* sank before our eyes; for nearly a month, both before and after the Germans entered our village, my gardener helped rescue the bodies that came ashore along the coast. The sea was calm and lovely all that summer, the fuel oil with which they were covered was apparently protective; none of the bodies was injured or disfigured, and my gardener came in again and again dead tired and heart sick, as we all were, to say to me "Madame, indeed I'm telling you the truth, he looked like a child asleep." There are 72 of these Englishmen in our cemetery. The last time I was allowed to go there, in 1942, when there were some 2,000 Germans in the village of 450, there lay on a long grave a wreath of China roses with on it one word, "Reconnaissance" [a French word for "Gratitude" or "Recognition"].

On 1 November 1941, the day of the *Toussaint* (All Saints' day) the vicar from Escoublac blessed the war dead with a small number of German officers present. The same sort of ceremonies took place all over the surrounding areas.

At Moutiers a similar ceremony took place on the same day, throughout the war, at the cross in the middle of the cemetery. A mass was sung for all the dead, including the British who had flowers placed on their graves. The Lamp of the Dead in the centre of Moutiers is still lit for those who dissappeared in Britain's biggest sea disaster.

This letter was written to Gaston Noblanc, near the end of the 1980s by Brian Reynolds, the President of The HMT *Lancastria* Association:

> The history of the people of Saint-Nazaire is tied irrevocably to our story – we are linked together by our suffering which is as strong as our unity which comes from subsequent glorious and joyful events. The painful memory of those who died in the *Lancastria* belongs not only to us but also to the city of Saint-Nazaire. We are happy that The HMT

Lancastria Association is represented so faithfully by you. I thank you in the name of all the members for your devotion to us.

Sincerely Brian.

———

The first *Lancastria* reunion was organised by survivor Major Cyril V. 'Peter' Petit on 18 June 1946 at the Marlborough Club, London. Major Petit, who was the district supervisor of HQ NAAFI for the Berlin district, requested an insertion in 'routine orders', inviting all serving survivors at HQ BTB (British Troops Berlin) to attend. Shortly after, the *Lancastria* Survivors Association was formed by 'Peter' Petit; it was the start of an annual parade, reunion and service of remembrance.

69. Major Cyril V. 'Peter' Petit, survivor and founder member of the *Lancastria* Survivors Association.

On Sunday 19 June 1955, two days after the fifteenth anniversary of the sinking, a two-part remembrance schedule was organised; one in London and the other at Saint-Nazaire. The original *Lancastria* tie and badge was designed and woven by Major Petit (some of which still exist to this day). The Service of Remembrance was held at the Cenotaph and, after a two-hour cruise on the Thames, the survivors were landed at Tower Pier. Here they entered the Tower of London for the Association's tenth annual reunion in the Yeoman Warders Club, which was chaired by Major J. A. Cousins, RAOC. It was at this gathering that Robert May's famous oil painting was unveiled and presented to the Association (see picture No. 57).

Meanwhile, the flying pilgrimage to Saint-Nazaire, the first of its kind, began (on Sunday 19 June 1955) at Victoria Coach Station where a coach took a small number of survivors, including the leader of the party, Lieutenant Colonel C. Booth, to the Aguila flying station at Southampton. From there they took off at 12.45, arriving at Saint-Nazaire around 14.00. They then circled the spot where the *Lancastria* had foundered before landing in the Loire estuary; here they were taken ashore by launch. They were met by HM Consul, Lieutenant Commander F. C. Bishop, RN (Rtd.), the sub-prefect, mayor, senior officers of the French services and members of the French parliament. The service was held near the Commando Memorial, to coincide with the service at the Cenotaph in London, where other members of the Association also paid their respects. The French government organised the presence of an army unit while the experimental asdic trials ship, the frigate HMS *Brocklesby*, brought the C-in-C, Portsmouth, supported by the commanding officer and members of the ship's company. After the service they were taken to Escoublac-La-Baule war cemetery, near Saint-Nazaire, where seventy-seven of *Lancastria*'s victims are buried, before flying back to Southampton later the same day.

Sunday 16 June 1963, the day before the *Lancastria* survivors' twenty-third anniversary, marked the eighteenth annual parade and march which took place in the City of London. It was attended by the Lord Mayor of London, Sir Ralph Perring, Kt, and representatives of all sections of the Royal Navy, Royal Air Force, Army, Merchant Navy and delegates from France, including M. Pierre F. Huni and his wife. At St Katharine Cree Church a memorial window, the work of Mr M. C. Farrar Bell, was unveiled by the Admiral of the Fleet, Lord Fraser of North Cape. The main part of the three panels depict Christ walking on water as he assists Peter, who is sinking and calling for help. In the bottom of the left panel is a version of the famous picture by survivor Robert May. A wooden plaque, below, commemorates many of the names of the ships involved in the rescue, or the transportation of *Lancastria*'s survivors from France to England.

After the death of Major Petit in 1969 the *Lancastria* Survivors' Association ceased to exist and Major Petit's effects were deposited in a local authorities' repository. In 1978 these effects were bought at auction by Mr Browne, who lived near Clapham Common. On 17 June 1979 Brian

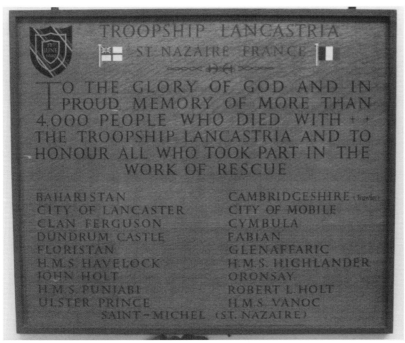

70. The wooden plaque which commemorates many of the ships involved in the rescue.

Reynolds went to St Katharine Cree Church to say a prayer on behalf of his late father, WO II Tom Reynolds, RASC, who had survived the sinking of the *Lancastria* and had always paid tribute at the church on the anniversary (he died on 11 November 1978, aged 73). Whilst there Brian met three survivors, Gordon Sullivan, Wally Forney and Don Fullerton, and it was decided there and then to meet again the following year.

On 15 June 1980, Brian and the three survivors were joined by the church's vicar, the Reverend Hereward Cooke, and the church archivist, Miss K. E. Campbell (who agreed to assist Wally Forney, who was a regional manager for a petroleum company in Wellingborough, in the search for more survivors). That evening evensong was said for the *Lancastria*'s victims.

In the *Daily Telegraph* Brian had noticed an article about the 40th Anniversary of the evacuation of Dunkirk and decided to write to the paper about the forgotten story of the *Lancastria*. Headed 'The Worst Day', a brief four-paragraph précis appeared in the Tuesday 17 June 1980 edition of the *Daily Telegraph* in the 'London Day by Day' column. The article, which had been read by Mr Browne, spurred him into contacting Brian Reynolds and he gave him some of Major Petit's archives and memorabilia concerning the *Lancastria*, including a list of the members of the disbanded *Lancastria* Survivors Association.

In 1981, on the 41st anniversary, it was decided to form a new association, which was named The HMT *Lancastria* Association. Its first committee comprised Brian Reynolds (President), Wally Forney (Secretary) and Jack Lumsden (Treasurer). Membership, it was decided, was to include survivors' relatives.

The second pilgrimage did not take place until 1985, when one coach, organised by the new HMT *Lancastria* Association (greatly assisted by John Duggan) travelled down to Saint-Nazaire to perform similar ceremonies. It was repeated the following year, when the design of a proposed memorial, to commemorate those lost in the *Lancastria* on 17 June 1940, was presented to the mayor of Saint-Nazaire. (The third, fourth and fifth pilgrimages were organised by Major and Mrs Holt's Battlefield Tours of Sandwich in conjunction with The HMT *Lancastria* Association).

In 1988 two coaches were used to transport survivors and relatives on the fourth pilgrimage, when the new memorial, designed by Brian Reynolds, was unveiled by Chief Royal Engineer, General Sir George Cooper, GCB, MC. It was placed, temporarily, on the esplanade wall. The polished grey granite memorial carries the gold inscription:

> Opposite this place lies the wreck of the troopship *Lancastria* sunk by enemy action on 17 June 1940 whilst embarking British troops and civilians during the evacuation of France. To the glory of God, in proud memory of more than 4,000 who died and in commemoration of the people of Saint-Nazaire and surrounding districts who saved many lives, tended wounded and gave a Christian burial to victims. We have not forgotten. HMT *Lancastria* Association, 17 June, 1988.

Two years later, during the fifth pilgrimage, the memorial was repositioned on a stone plinth where it exists to this day. The sixth pilgrimage was organised by the Royal British Legion's Pilgrimage Department (Remembrance Travel) and The HMT *Lancastria* Association in 1998.

In June 2000 the present author was privileged to attend the 60th Anniversary gathering, and to meet and interview many of the twenty-four survivors present. The nine-day pilgrimage, the seventh and possibly the last of its kind (certainly to consist of such relatively large numbers), comprised two coaches and was again organised by the Royal British Legion's Pilgrimage Department and The HMT *Lancastria* Association. Pick-up points were at the Union Jack Club, London and Portsmouth ferry terminal. After a five-hour passage to Cherbourg and an overnight stay at nearby hotels the journey continued south to St Jean de Monts, where all were accommodated in two hotels.

The following morning the cemeteries at Noirmoutiers-en-l'Ile, L'Herbaudiere, L'Epine and Olonne-sur-Mer were visited before the group continued south to a small village called Triaize, about fifteen miles north of La Rochelle and approximately 100 miles, by sea, from Saint-Nazaire.

Two years before Triaize had attracted London historian Stanley Smith, who had been holidaying with friends living in the area. He was told about one of Triaize's proudest possessions, the grave of 'our English soldier', as local people described it. His friends took him to the level spot within the stone walls of the sloping graveyard. There, marked by a simple cross, lay the grave of an army driver named Walter James Smith. Carved in the cross was the following epitaph: *Ici Repose Dalher James Smith, Soldat Anglais, deceden Aout 1940* (Here lies Walter James Smith, English soldier, died August 1940).

In August 1940, the body of Walter James Smith, identified by his army identity disc, had been washed up on the Vendée coast. Fearing an unpleasant attitude from their German occupiers, the people of Triaize buried his body in marshland, near where he was found, but marked it regularly with fresh flowers. After the Allied victory in Europe, his body had been exhumed in September 1944 and reburied in Triaize's communal cemetery, with a service attended by the residents of the village. Although unknown, he had come to be accepted by the people of Triaize as one of their own. Stanley Smith (no relation of Walter, who had been known to his army friends as Wally) sent photographs of the grave to the Commonwealth War Graves Commission at Maidenhead. The HMT *Lancastria* Association became involved when a relation of Stanley Smith visited St Katharine Cree Church. By pure chance an Association committee meeting was taking place during his visit. Colonel Terry Sharman conversed with the visitor; Terry Sharman had been a corporal in Walter Smith's unit, No. 1 HRS, RASC, and survived the sinking. As a result of this, the efforts of survivor Stanley Flowers and the support of the Royal Logistic Corps, in collaboration with the Commonwealth War Graves Commission, moves were made to update existing records and, more importantly, mark the grave officially.

In April 1999, more than half a century after his burial, the simple wooden cross was replaced by a Commonwealth War Graves Commission's headstone, bearing his name, corps and number, and confirming his death as 17 June 1940. The grave was dedicated by ex-Army chaplain, the Reverend John Salter, TD, AKC, in the presence of members of The HMT *Lancastria* Association, civic heads, villagers, French ex-servicemen and a local band. Stanley Smith, Stanley Flowers

(Wally's friend) and standard-bearer Fred Coe also attended the ceremony. Stan Flowers had known Wally from his school days at Faversham, where they both lived and had been educated. Ironically, they were to meet again in France, when Wally was transferred to Stan's section of 1 Heavy Repair Shop, RASC, at St Étienne de Montluc, as a replacement driver in April 1940. They soon renewed their friendship.

During the open air service the local mayor, Monsieur Francoise Cart, marked the sadness of the occasion with the following oration, which was translated by John Duggan:

> Here lies the body of a 21-year-old soldier who was probably full of hope and purpose; who wanted nothing more than to live ... He was one link in the huge chain which drove out the invasion forces so that we may now live in peace.

71 (left). Stan Flowers lays a wreath on Walter James Smith's grave at Triaize communal cemetery on 12 June 2000; and 72 (right). Survivors of 1 HRS (MT) RASC at Triaize. From the left: Fred Coe, Morris Lashbrook, Tom Hutchison and Stan Flowers.

Walter's sister, Flossie Giles (née Smith) and her family, who were traced through the *Faversham News*, also attended the service. Local people were a little anxious that she might have wanted to have his body exhumed and reburied in a CWGC cemetery, but she reassured them that she felt that he belonged in Triaize, where he had been cared for since his discovery, months after the tragedy.

The reception at Triaize was no less hospitable in 2000. A sizeable number of villagers, dignitaries and flag bearers were waiting patiently for the sixtieth-anniversary visit of *Lancastria* survivors when they arrived an hour later than expected.

The following days saw similar services at Bouin, Les Moutiers-en-Retz, La Bernerie-en-Retz, Le Clion-ser-Mer, St Marie, Prefailles, La Plaine-sur-Mer and Escoublac-La-Baule cemeteries. Two epitaphs, carved into separate headstones in different cemeteries, stated *To the world you were just a soldier, but to me you were all the world* and *Only to feel the clasp of his hand and to hear his voice again.*

On Saturday 17 June two coaches took the pilgrims to the Saint-Nazaire Memorial where the Act of Remembrance began with a piper's lament. Speeches followed before wreaths were laid by two survivors, Arthur Snow and Harry Pettit, the deputy mayor of Saint-Nazaire, civic dignitaries, and representatives of the Army, Royal Air Force and Royal

73. Memorial to those lost in the *Lancastria*. It was designed by Brian Reynolds and stands, facing in the direction of the wreck, at Saint-Nazaire.

Navy. Survivor Henry Harding then recited Lawrence Binyon's poem: *They shall grow not old, as we that are left grow old; Age shall not weary them, nor the years condemn. At the going down of the sun and in the morning, We will remember them.* Everyone present repeated *We will remember them.* A bugler then sounded the last post to begin two minutes' silence. Reveille marked the end. Survivor Bill Rose, who had later been a Japanese prisoner of war, then said the Burma Star Association's dedication: *When you go home tell them of us, and do not fail to say For your tomorrow we gave our today.* A rendition of 'God Save the Queen' and 'The Marseillaise' followed.

74 (above). Survivor Harry Pettit, on the 60th Anniversary of the sinking.

75 (opposite page). The splendid model of the *Lancastria*, on display at Saint-Nazaire. Fred Coe (left) and Denis Holland (right) describe their experiences to the author while Henry Harding points to the position where he was standing when the ship was bombed (he still has his watch – it stopped at 16.05).

76 (right). Gaston Noblanc and his charming wife Jacqueline. Gaston had helped in the rescue when he was 16 years old and went on to join the resistance. His face still bears scars after interrogation by the Gestapo.

Everyone was then transported to the Hotel de Ville for *vin d'honneur*. Here a large and splendid model of the *Lancastria* was on display; it had been built by Raoul Sébilo and completed shortly before

his death. Survivors, whom the author interviewed throughout the week, were keen to show me exactly where they had been standing at the crucial time.

The climax of the pilgrimage was yet to come, however. We were transported to the dockside where the survivors boarded the Hunt class MCMV (Mine Counter Measure Vessel) HMS *Chiddingfold*, under the command of Lieutenant Commander C. Davis, RN. Others, like myself, boarded the French MCMV FS *Verseau*, while the remainder boarded RLCV (Royal Logistic Corps Vessel) *Aachen*, commanded by Staff Sergeant A. Smith, RLC. All three vessels then proceeded slowly to the site of the wreck, which was clearly marked by two buoys. Strangely, dolphins had encircled the *Chiddingfold*, some way out, and followed her to the scene. The weather conditions were almost identical to 17 June 1940 – cloudless, hot and calm. The little flotilla was soon joined by three French lifeboats, one carrying six French flag bearers, another carrying French dignitaries and the third, Pornic's lifeboat, boasting a very large Union Jack. On board this vessel was Madame Rosie Guorio, the most decorated coxswain in France and former skipper of the lifeboat for over twenty years.

As the time of the actual sinking approached the three larger vessels closed over the wreck, forming a triangle with the three lifeboats in the middle. The commemorative service was supposed to have been relayed ship to ship, but technical problems intervened. However, the

169

piper's lament drifted across the olive-green water before the wreath-laying ceremony began. A French priest, who was standing for'd on Pornic's lifeboat, said inaudible prayers and sanctified the grave. Fifty or so wreaths drifted in the six-knot current while a lone bugler played the last post and reveille, marking the beginning and the end of two minutes' silence. All the ships then sounded their sirens for at least a minute – and there was not a dry eye to be seen. It was a sobering and sombre occasion, reminding everyone of the horror that had taken place sixty years before, tragically taking the lives of so many people, both young and old.

77. HMS *Chiddingfold* moves in over the wreck carrying the survivors of the *Lancastria*, who are stood on the starboard side behind the bridge. A French priest, who is standing on the prow of the Pornic lifeboat, blesses the grave at the exact time of the sinking, sixty years before.

The other vessels left the scene and the *Verseau* waited a respectful time before traversing slowly over the wreck to show its image on two sonar screens. The record clearly showed that the wreck was virtually upright and intact; at one point the curvature of the *Lancastria*'s forward profile, from the port and starboard sides of the ship to the point of the bow, was clearly visible (see photograph No. 80). Later, I spoke to Lieutenant Commander Guillaume de Roquefeuil (the captain of the ship) and Lieutenant Bertrand de Lorgeril (second in command and the ship's diver). Bertrand had dived on the ship earlier that morning and, when I spoke to him, he told me that the hull of the *Lancastria* was intact and 180 metres long (in other words, still her original length). When the *Verseau* was over the wreck that afternoon the keel lay 27 metres down and the highest point, which was not visible, was just eight metres from· the surface. When I asked him about the dive, he said that the distance of visibility was barely an inch; he could not see a thing, although he could feel the side of the great ship and judged that it was nearly upright. He revealed that about one third of the hull is immersed in soft mud, no

78. Dennis Maloney throws a wreath from HMS *Chiddingfold* while the mayor of Saint-Nazaire and survivors, Stan Flowers and Michael Sheehan, look on.

doubt a result of the flow of the River Loire into the Bay of Biscay. The wreck, which is still facing west-north-west, has long been recognised as a war grave and, perhaps, it is fitting that nobody will ever be able to cast their eyes in or around it.

After corresponding with Pierre L. Guillou, a retired pilot of the Loire estuary, certain aspects concerning the wreck of the *Lancastria*, became much clearer. Pierre had worked in the vicinity of the wreck for a great many years, as did his father, who was a co-owner of the pilot schooner *La Lambarde*, which had assisted in the rescue. When the

Lancastria disappeared beneath the surface she lay on her port side. In a recent letter he told me that during the winter of 1941 the wreck was brought back almost upright for a few hours, before falling back onto her port side during the following ebb tide. The ghostly scene, a result of storm-force westerly winds and a spring tide, was witnessed by a few pilots who almost doubted the evidence of their own eyes. His father thought that the bizarre incident was suitable for a role in Edgar Allan Poe's *Tales of Mystery and Imagination*.

Later, in March 1942, the *Lancastria* was again witnessed in an upright position. This time it was during one of the most daring raids of the Second World War, codenamed 'Operation Chariot'. In the late hours of 27 March 1942 the two masts and the funnel of the wreck were clearly visible in the hazy and sporadic moonlight. The flotilla, led by Commander R. E. D. Ryder, comprised one MGB (motor gun boat), the destroyer *Campbeltown*, two MTBs (motor torpedo boats) and fifteen MLs (motor launches), carrying 611 commandos and Royal Navy personnel. They were beginning a clandestine attack on the docks of Saint-Nazaire, scheduled for the very early hours of 28 March. However, the first part of the attack, the bombing of the *Normandie* Dock and the northern end of the Penhouet Basin by the RAF (a diversionary ploy), had been foiled by cloudy weather. The element of surprise had been unavoidably lost, but despite this disappointment Lieutenant Colonel A. C. Newman, who was in command of the military force and empowered to call off the assault at any time, decided to continue.

The main objective was to destroy the vital equipment serving the dual-purpose *Normandie* Dock, the largest structure of its kind in the world, measuring 1,148 feet long by 164 feet wide. Two large moveable caissons, north and south of the dock, allowed it to be used as a lock when full of water, or a dry dock when empty. Being in enemy-held territory, it became Germany's only dock in western France capable of holding the new and large battleship *Tirpitz* (sister ship to the *Bismarck*, which had been sunk by the Royal Navy on 27 May 1941). If serviceable, the *Normandie* Dock would allow Germany the comfort of repair facilities and instant access into the Atlantic.

The raid, which was against very difficult odds, achieved considerable success. The *Campbeltown*, under the command of Lieutenant Commander S. H. Beattie, was successfully rammed onto the south caisson where she was scuttled to impede removal. Within a short space of time the pump room/switchboard and electric motors, the north and south winding huts and equipment, several gun emplacements and two tugs were destroyed and sunk. The north caisson was only partly damaged, because of lethal crossfire and the failure to gain access into the caisson itself, despite several determined attempts.

The *Campbeltown*'s fuses and explosives, which were planned to explode no later than 09.30, remained undetected despite a thorough search by the enemy. Satisfied that the ship was 'safe', many inquisitive German officials swarmed aboard the destroyer to collect trophies and look around the ship; some brought their wives or girlfriends. With over two hundred personnel either on board or stood nearby, the *Campbeltown* inflicted the biggest death toll of the raid, when twenty-four 400-lb Mk VII depth charges, weighing four and a quarter tons, exploded at 10.35 with devastating effect, killing the majority of the visitors. More importantly, the force of the huge explosion breached the one-hundred-and-sixty-ton caisson. Like a gigantic tidal wave the sea poured into the empty dock and crashed into the weakened caisson at the north end, but the structure held. Two tankers, the *Passat* and the *Schledstadt*, which were undergoing repairs at the time, were flung against the dock walls and damaged, while the mutilated *Campbeltown* was washed into the centre of the dock. (Although British Intelligence did not discover the exact details of the raid until much later, the *Normandie* Dock remained out of commission until 1952).

Further damage materialised days later when two delayed-action torpedoes exploded, destroying the outer lock gates at the Old Entrance to the port. During the attack and the withdrawal, and under the cover of darkness, many motor launches were illuminated by searchlights, hit by enemy gunfire and caught fire, fuelled by the extra petrol that was being carried in tanks on deck to extend their range. One motor launch, *ML 177*, commanded by Lieutenant Mark F. Rodier, had successfully landed Troop Sergeant Major Haines' assault party in the Old Entrance and embarked Lieutenant Commander S. H. Beattie and some thirty or more of the *Campbeltown*'s crew before beginning its withdrawal minutes before 02.00. As *ML 177* emerged from the cover of the quay wall it was once more exposed to the blinding glare of the probing searchlights and the staccato accompaniment of enemy gunfire. At first Rodier avoided being hit and, under the cover of smoke, managed to reach the safety of the broadening estuary.

His luck was not to last, however. Searchlights further down the river illuminated his retreat. Three miles from Saint-Nazaire the small vessel was hit twice by 75-mm shells, killing Rodier and several others and setting the launch on fire. The crew fought the blaze for nearly three hours before abandoning ship. A few wounded ratings managed to get away in the only serviceable carley float, while other men entered the cold

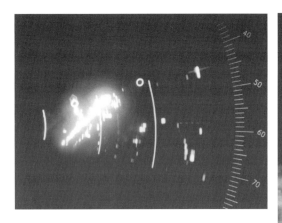

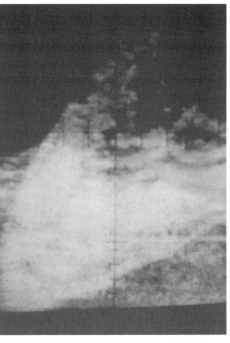

79 (above). General sonar image of the
Lancastria, taken by the FS *Verseau*, showing
that the ship's hull is still intact.

80 (right). Sonar image revealed by the FS *Verseau* on 17 June 2000 from the port
quarter, showing the bow section of the *Lancastria*. The curvature of the starboard
side is clear to see, while the profile of the port side of the ship is not so well
defined, because the side of the hull is partially buried in soft undulating mud.
This picture verifies that the *Lancastria* is now virtually upright.

water, where they were to remain for well over four hours; many
succumbing to the ordeal. *Campbeltown*'s chief boatswain's mate, Petty
Officer Stocker, was carried out to sea with several others. By some
strange and somewhat ironic twist of fate, however, they found refuge on
the protruding masts and davits of the wreck of the *Lancastria*, where they
were picked up by a German patrol trawler at 09.30 and became prisoners
of war. (For awards and casualty numbers see end of Appendix 2).

The last entry made on the *Lancastria*'s final voyage record card
stated the following in April 1951: 'Attempt being made to refloat'.
According to Pierre Guillou the wreck was considered a major
obstruction to shipping. However, a survey soon demonstrated that
salvage was impossible, and the operation was abandoned in September
1951. It seems reasonable to assume that the *Lancastria* was demasted,
either by German gunfire (as they apparently used the wreck for gunnery
practice during the war) or by the later use of demolition charges.
Initially, at very low tides, the uppermost parts of the wreck were visible
(davits and the edges of main decks). Slowly, over the course of twenty

174

years, the wreck has progressively disappeared beneath the surface, never to be seen again by the naked eye.

During the course of the last sixty years the wreck has settled deeper and deeper into the sea bed. In the words of ex-pilot Pierre Guillou 'Over the years the wreck of the *Lancastria* has proved to be a little additional trouble, but has also provided a good opportunity for pilots to prove their efficiency!'

Before the Pilgrimage left France there were two more ceremonies to perform; both took place in Pornic on 18 June 2000. The first, which was held in the French communal cemetery, marked the anniversary of General de Gaulle's call to the French people to fight on. The second, just across the road, took place at the CWGC's cemetery, where an Act of Remembrance was performed by the Reverend John Salter. It is in this beautifully kept cemetery that a great many of *Lancastria*'s dead are buried, along with others who stormed Saint-Nazaire docks nearly two years later.

81. Jacqueline Tanner (*née* Tillyer) and Arthur Snow at Pornic's *vin d'honneur*. The youngest and the oldest survivors to attend the ceremonies marking the 60th anniversary of the loss of HMT *Lancastria*.

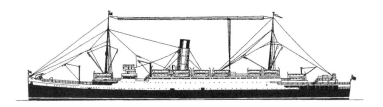

CHAPTER XI

CONCLUSION

As with any major disaster many questions arise, concerning what actually happened and whether any blame should be attached to any individual or any procedure. This chapter is an attempt to reach some conclusions.

According to Captain Sharp the *Lancastria* was carrying 1,407 tons of surplus fuel oil, in deep tanks situated in No. 3 hold, and just over 5,200 troops, women and children, plus 330 crew, when the ship was attacked.

Fred Coe, who saw the first attack develop out of the sun, was sure that the first two bombs, although they did not hit the ship, exploded close enough to the port side to cause structural damage to the hull, although this cannot be substantiated without an archaeological investigation.

It is almost certain that at least four bombs subsequently hit the ship. Many eyewitnesses saw one bomb enter No. 2 hold through the hatch cover on the deck. Undoubtedly this bomb was still moving towards the stern of the ship after entry (due to the speed of the bomber that dropped it). It is believed that it penetrated the bulkhead between Nos. 2 and 3 holds, as witnessed by Private J. H. Drummond who was in the latter. This is a plausible explanation for why so many tons of fuel oil were released into the river estuary. The force of the explosion must have fractured or weakened the bulkhead between Nos. 3 and 4 holds.

Another bomb almost certainly landed in the vicinity of No. 4 hold as oil and water was seen by Bill Slater and Sid Chenery in that hold and the starboard baggage space.

A third bomb probably landed near the after port side of No. 4 hatch cover, for Lieutenant Colonel F. E. Griggs, who had just entered the first-class dining room, saw it crash through the deckhead and deck

A fourth bomb (all of which must have been dropped more-or-less simultaneously by the same aircraft) landed to the port side of the funnel, crashing through the deckhead of the waiting room, which had been set

176

up as a hospital. The explosion also disrupted the accommodation areas on B and C decks, including the cabin on C deck just occupied by Sapper Norman Driver and his two friends, killing George Watling who was having a wash and shave alongside Cal Beal.

These explosions certainly also damaged the ship's hull in the area of the holds and may have penetrated or fractured the double bottom tanks which formed the deck of the hold, as witnessed by Chief Officer Grattidge, who saw a furious core of water rising in No. 4 hold. The second bomb had miraculously missed the boiler room, for had it done so 3rd Engineer Frank Brogden, and others on duty in the engine and boiler rooms, would surely have been killed, scalded or injured.

Although most survivors state that they heard two explosions, a split second apart, it is more than probable that the aircraft dropped its full bomb load – four bombs, two at a time to increase the chances of hitting the ship. This must have been the case because damage was reported by survivors in more than three locations.

This theory is substantiated by Captain Sharp's report (see Appendix 12) which states that four bombs hit the ship, three entering Nos. 2, 3 and 4 holds and the fourth going down the funnel. Nevertheless, photograph No. 51 clearly shows that the funnel was still intact at the time of the sinking, suggesting that this bomb, known to have caused considerable damage below deck, must have entered the ship near the funnel, not through it. If it had entered through the funnel, substantial damage would have been caused to the engine room instead.

With the bulkheads between Nos. 2, 3 and 4 holds broached, the ship's port side holed or fractured and, without doubt, No. 4 hold taking in water at a tremendous rate, there could only be one outcome; the *Lancastria* was going to sink. However, because of the shallow depth of the sea bed (12 fathoms or 72 feet, according to Captain Sharp) the forefoot came to rest upon it, giving survivors more time to escape. Had the *Lancastria* been in deeper water she would have sunk in half the time, and the suction, too, would have been prolonged and greater. Several survivors reported the surprising lack of suction. The ship, however, certainly turned on her side as she sank. Had the *Lancastria* sank upright some parts of the ship would have remained above the surface – masts, funnel etc. – and escape through conventional means, such as companionways, would have been easier and more lives would have been spared.

Causes of death were more varied than one might suppose; many were killed instantly as a result of the explosions, of course (by sudden suffocation as well as blast damage), and others by falling debris, and many must have drowned inside the ship, unable to escape in time; but also many could not swim and had no life jackets. There were not enough jackets for everyone on board and those fortunate enough to acquire one were not given proper instructions on how to use them, especially, tragically, many of those jumping into the water from a height. Many survivors therefore must have been lost to drowning unnecessarily.

Those that initially entered the water from the port side of the ship were immediately enveloped in fuel oil, which spilled freely from the ruptured tanks in No. 3 hold. The thick toxic morass made breathing and swimming difficult; eyes and mouths stung, and hands became so slippery that survivors found it almost impossible to grip anything that could keep them afloat. Added to this was the heartless machine-gunning of survivors by the Luftwaffe pilots.

The accusations that the pilots dropped incendiary bombs to ignite the fuel oil are almost certainly mistaken. An incendiary bomb has to hit something solid before it will ignite; if they were dropped into water they would simply sink, with no visible effect. The source of combustion undoubtedly came from calcium flares which, according to Captain Sharp, had become detached from the ship's rafts and lifeboats, drifting on the sea of oil and designed to ignite when they were immersed in water. Had the fuel oil caught fire the death toll would have been much higher.

We know also that some died after their rescue, as a result of their injuries. Finally, a number of lives were also lost unnecessarily through suicide or murder, in the immediate circumstances of panic following the sinking.

Undoubtedly the key factor in the saving of so many lives was the ability of the Royal Navy and the local French to respond quickly. That, coupled with the fine, warm weather and the closeness of the near-empty, but bomb damaged, *Oronsay*, allowed survivors to be transferred immediately to her, where they could receive immediate help.

The *Dundrum Castle*, which had just left Saint-Nazaire dock full of troops, launched two of her lifeboats to assist in the rescue and went on to save over 120 men. The naval trawlers *Agate* and *Cambridgeshire* also took part in the rescue, the latter saving nearly 1,000 men. Dennis Maloney's quick thinking enabled one of the *Lancastria*'s lifeboat's to be immediately recycled, with the assistance of the two crew members from *Highlander*, saving another forty or more. The resourcefulness of naval architect Pierre Huni, who later became the mayor of Saint-Nazaire, and Henry Boyd undoubtedly helped to save the lives of many more. It was because of their efforts that more French ships, which were alerted by them in nearby ports, took part in the rescue.

What happened on the sunny afternoon of 17 June 1940 has been largely forgotten by the media and by naval historians, almost as if Churchill's directive not to release the news was still in force. Those who visit the shores of Brittany and Loire Atlantique near Saint-Nazaire today, however, and see the cemeteries listed in Appendix 7, will begin to understand the enormity of this disaster – by far Britain's worst.

82. Dunkirk Memorial at Nord, Dunkirk, France. Here, over 750 names of *Lancastria*'s missing are recorded. The chapel, boasting a beautiful stained glass window, can be seen at the end of the lawn. The inscription at the entrance reads: 'Dunkirk. Here beside the graves of their comrades are commemorated the soldiers of the British Expeditionary Force who fell in the campaign of 1939–1940 and have no known grave'.

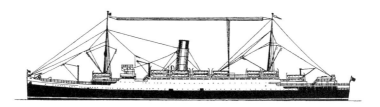

APPENDIX 1

ROLL OF HONOUR
KNOWN LIST OF CASUALTIES LOST IN THE SINKING
OF HMT *LANCASTRIA* ON 17 JUNE 1940

The sheer size of the *Lancastria* disaster, the fact that no manifest could be recorded as the ship was boarded, and the fact that many passengers must have died trapped inside the hull, means that it is a difficult task to compile an accurate list of the casualties.

The first step in any attempt to list the *Lancastria* casualties is to consult either the relevant registers of the Commonwealth War Graves Commission or use their database which, unfortunately, is only accessible by name, service, rank and number, and then only one at a time. All the names which follow which are marked by an asterisk (*) are recorded by the Commission as having been lost in the *Lancastria* disaster and have been supplied by them from their database; 1,189 names were produced by them using this method. However, although the Commission reassures the author that they have a complete list of all the Commonwealth service personnel lost during the war, not all the names of those relevant to this enquiry are necessarily recorded as having been *Lancastria* casualties. This is due to a variety of reasons, such as the variant recording methods of clerks from different army regiments and RAF squadrons, the fact that men may be initially recorded as missing, but with no subsequent clarity as to their fate, the fact that bodies washed ashore may not always be identifiable, or because personnel sometimes died later, in different locations and circumstances, but as a result of injuries received in the disaster. As an example the CWGC's *Lancastria* list, supplied to me by them, only records two victims of the disaster buried in Pornic and two in Escoublac-La-Baule cemeteries; there are, in fact, 181 named servicemen buried in Pornic and another 77 named servicemen buried in Escoublac-La-Baule; clearly illustrating, that if the name *Lancastria* does not appear in their details, the computer will not locate them, and they are, accordingly, missing from their list.

The absence of an asterisk does not necessarily, therefore, mean that the man was not on board the ship, and the list can be supplemented from other sources of information. The CWGC registers are the starting point for supplementary enquiries because they can also be searched for the names of men who died on a particular day, in a particular locality. A second search for the names of those lost in the vicinity of Saint-Nazaire within two days of the *Lancastria* sinking, but excluding those names already recorded, produces an extra 443 names. These can then be cross-checked against other sources. The other sources include the records of The HMT *Lancastria* Association, the lists of those found and buried ashore (where the bodies could be identified), the records of individual RAF squadrons and army regiments and the general lists of those recorded missing at the time.

The following list can therefore be presented with some confidence in its accuracy, whether the name is marked with an asterisk or not. The details of each serviceman is presented as recorded in the CWGC registers or database, against which all uncertainties have been systematically checked.

The CWGC assure the author that every Commonwealth serviceman or woman lost during the Second World War is recorded somewhere in the world, either on a headstone or on a memorial, and that all such lists are duplicated in their respective registers; they have also assured me that there were no Royal Navy casualties connected with the loss of the *Lancastria* (a fact substantiated by the MOD).

It is not impossible that the CWGC registers and database includes the names of other casualties from the *Lancastria* but which the systematic search has not identified as such. The Dunkirk memorial, for instance, includes some names which may well be of *Lancastria* casualties, because the date and regimental details make that likely, but with no absolute certainty involved. There are 177 of these 'also possible' names and they are nevertheless included here, but at the end of the list. The five known civilian casualties are also listed.

If any names are actually missing from the following list, the author would like to apologise; but if an incorrect date for a person's death is recorded, or if a survivor died after having been rescued, it will always be difficult to associate all the known casualties of the time with this particular tragedy. The compilation of this list took an inestimable number of hours of research, but it was not compiled to prove or disprove any previous estimations. It is purely to record all the known and likely names, together, as a memorial to those who died on 17 June 1940.

Their Name Liveth for Evermore

<u>Army and RAF abbreviations used in the following list of names:</u>

AASF:	Air Advance Striking Force.
AMPC:	Auxiliary Military Pioneer Corps.
A&S Highlanders:	The Argyll and Sutherland Highlanders.
attd:	attached to.
BAFF:	British Air Forces in France.
B&H Regt:	The Bedfordshire and Hertfordshire Regiment.
Bn:	Battalion.
Bty:	Battery.
Buffs:	The Buffs (Royal East Kent Regiment).
BW:	The Black Watch (Royal Highland Regiment).
C*:	Communal Cemetery.
Coy:	Company.
C Regt:	The Cheshire Regiment.
dra:	death recorded as (i.e., the date of death recorded by the CWGC in the appropriate register).
D Regt:	The Devonshire Regiment.
E Regt:	The Essex Regiment.
EL Regt:	The East Lancashire Regiment.
ES Regt:	The East Surrey Regiment.
EY Regt:	The East Yorkshire Regiment (The Duke of York's Own).
GH:	The Green Howards (Alexandra, Princess of Wales Own Yorkshire Regiment).
H Regt:	The Royal Hampshire Regiment.
KORR:	The King's Own Royal Regiment.
KOSB:	The King's Own Scottish Borderers.
KSLI:	The King's Shropshire Light Infantry.
KRH:	The King's Royal Hussars.
L Fus:	The Lancashire Fusiliers.
MP:	Corps of Royal Military Police.
MT:	Motor Transport.
N&D Regt:	Nottinghamshire and Derbyshire Regiments (The Sherwood Foresters).
NS Regt:	The North Staffordshire Regiment (The Prince of Wales's).
QOCH:	Queen's Own Cameron Highlanders.
QORWK:	The Queen's Own Royal West Kent Regiment.
QR Regt:	The Queen's Royal Regiment (West Surrey).
R Fusiliers:	The Royal Fusiliers (City of London Regiment).
R Sigs:	Royal Corps of Signals.
RA:	Royal Regiment of Artillery.
RAC:	The Royal Armoured Corps.
RAMC:	Royal Army Medical Corps.

APPENDIX 1: ROLL OF HONOUR

RAOC:	Royal Army Ordnance Corps.
RAPC:	Royal Army Pay Corps.
RASC:	Royal Army Service Corps.
RB Regt:	The Royal Berkshire Regiment (Princess Charlotte of Wales's).
RE:	Corps of Royal Engineers.
RF:	The Royal Fusiliers (City of London Regiment).
RNF:	The Royal Northumberland Fusiliers.
RUR:	The Royal Ulster Rifles.
RW Fusiliers:	The Royal Welch Fusiliers.
SS Regt:	The South Staffordshire Regiment.
SL Regt:	South Lancashire Regiment.
SQMS:	Squadron Quartermaster Sergeant.
SWB:	The South Wales Borderers.
WO I and WO II:	Warrant Officer, Class 1 or 2.
Y&L Regt:	The York and Lancaster Regiment.

ARMY PERSONNEL
COMMEMORATED AT THE DUNKIRK MEMORIAL (NORD)

Abbott Robert Norman	(22)	Pte	1 Base Supply Depot RASC	S/63242*
Able Leonrard Walter	(38)	Gnr	5 Bty 2 HAA Regt RA	1426292*
Ainsworth William Rhodes	(21)	L/Cpl	2 Field Bakery RASC	S/98848*
Airey John Alan	(35)	Pte	York & Lancaster Regt attd AMPC	4742642
Akeroyd John	(22)	Spr	159 Railway Construction Coy RE	1892866*
Alcock Harold	(26)	Spr	663 Artisan Works Coy RE	1910047*
Aldom Colin Henry James	(30)	Spr	663 Artisan Works Coy RE	1913266*
Aldred Ernest Emanuel S.	(22)	Pte	2 Ordnance Workshop Coy RAOC	7622115*
Alexander Arthur Gordon	(26)	Pte	1 Base Ordnance Depot RAOC	7593143*
Allen Horace	(36)	L/Cpl	South Staffordshire Regt attd AMPC	4910570
Allen Robert	(26)	L/Cpl	1 Supply Base Depot RE	1867988
Allinson Albert Edward	(38)	Pte	73 Coy AMPC	13005223*
Anderson Albert Charles	(?)	Pte	2 Bn B & H Regt	5945648
Andrews Joseph (MM)	(42)	Sgt	75 Coy AMPC	4737269*
Aplin Harold Frederick	(28)	Spr	663 Artisan Works Coy RE	1914278*
Arends Richard	(28)	Sgt	1 Base Supply Depot RASC	S/3767249*
Arey Clifford William	(39)	Pte	73 Coy AMPC	13002461*
Armstrong David	(40)	L/Sgt	1 Base Supply Depot RASC	T/33910*
Armstrong Thomas Spencer	(22)	Dvr	7 Res MT Coy RASC	T/121391*
Ash Frank Stanley	(47)	Sgt	RASC	S/147853*
Ashcroft John	(31)	Pte	2 Base Ordnance Depot RAOC	7603156*
Astle Norman Ernest	(31)	Pte	115 Coy AMPC	2185475
Attwood William Henry	(34)	Pte	4 Motor Ambulance Coy RAMC	7536057*
Avis Arthur George	(42)	Pte	53 Coy AMPC	13001811*
Ayears Horace Ernest	(37)	Cpl	579 Field Coy RE	2030311*
Baines Edmund Charles	(35)	Gnr	3 Bty 1 Searchlight Regt RA dra 18.6.40	
				3707167
Baldwin Charles	(37)	Pte	50 Coy AMPC	13001467*
Ball Arthur	(35)	Pte	46 Coy AMPC	2188568

Ballam Harold Collins	(39)	Pte	46 Coy AMPC	2022442*
Ballard James	(25)	Dvr	1 Base Supply Depot RASC	S/88502*
Balls Kenneth Arthur	(21)	Spr	6 Movement Control Group RE	1505919
Barnard Kennth Lawrence	(24)	Spr	663 Artisan Works Coy RE	1911259*
Barnes Francis Meredith	(38)	Dvr	'C' Park MT Veh Rec Depot RASC	110617*
Barnes Peter	(37)	Pte	108 Coy AMPC	7607102*
Barnsley George	(47)	Pte	50 Coy AMPC	13002420*
Barr Ernest	(36)	Pte	53 Coy AMPC	13006023*
Barrie David Kerr	(24)	L/Cpl	159 Railway Construction Coy RE	1899079*
Barry John	(37)	Pte	73 Coy AMPC	13006077*
Bateman Harry James	(24)	S/Sgt	Royal Engineers	1868848*
Batt Raymond Harold	(21)	Pte	4 Bn Buffs (Royal East Kent Regt)	6288403*
Batten Frederick John	(25)	Pte	46 Coy AMPC	13002841*
Baty Richard Stanley	(34)	Pte	King's Own Scottish Borderers	3183638*
Baugh Albert	(38)	Pte	46 Coy AMPC	2188534*
Bayliss Richard	(24)	Pte	RASC	105711*
Beames Frederick William	(32)	L/Cpl	159 Railway Construction Coy RE	777043*
Beaumont Alfred	(31)	Pte	73 Coy AMPC	2188368*
Beck Frank	(21)	Pte	Sherwood Foresters (N&D Regt)	4976666*
Beckwith John George	(24)	Gnr	3 Bty 1 Searchlight Regt RA dra 18.6.40	
				831673
Bedell Arthur Joseph	(41)	Pte	73 Coy AMPC	3902029*
Bell John Edward Scott	(29)	Spr	1 Supply Base Depot RE	1914607
Belshaw James	(33)	Gnr	204 Bty 51 Anti-Tank Regt RA	1073264*
Bendall Frank William	(43)	Pte	46 Coy AMPC	2188369*
Bennett Albert Sephton	(21)	Pte	1/5 Bn Sherwood Foresters (N&D Regt)	
				4978040*
Bennett David William	(26)	Pte	62 Coy AMPC	2191159*
Bennett Harry	(30)	Sigmn	Air Form Signals R Sigs	2587164*
Bennett James Ivor	(36)	Pte	73 Coy AMPC	13005272*
Bennion Frank	(44)	Pte	50 Coy AMPC	13002340*
Benson Arthur	(45)	Pte	50 Coy AMPC	13002444*
Bentley Ralph	(38)	Cpl	46 Coy AMPC	2188379*
Beresford George Charles	(20)	Pte	115 Coy AMPC	2185835
Betteridge Arthur George	(44)	Spr	156 Transportation Stores Coy RE	1926501*
Bevington Philip Redmond	(40)	Pte	75 Coy AMPC	13005493*
Bignall Arthur Percival	(24)	Pte	1 Base Ordnance Depot RAOC	7607554*
Biles William Edward	(38)	L/Cpl	2 Field Bakery RASC	S/74275*
Billings George Henry	(42)	Pte	50 Coy AMPC	13003803*
Black Bernard Richard	(35)	Spr	116 Railway Construction Coy RE	2187336*
Black Charles	(20)	Spr	6 Movement Control Group RE	1891863
Black Hamish Addis	(24)	L/Cpl	1 Armd Div Provost Unit MP	7687025*
Blackburn George Henry	(32)	Pte	115 Coy AMPC	2183203*
Blackman Horace Walter	(21)	Spr	579 Army Field Coy RE	2079626*
Blake Lionel Bruce	(39)	Pte	50 Coy AMPC	13001450*
Blyth Alexander	(22)	Dvr	2 Field Bakery RASC	S/98429*
Bodimeade George Alfred	(31)	Dvr	RASC attd 50 Coy AMPC	T/118174*
Bowdidge Charles Edward	(?)	Lt	1 Base Supply Depot RE	S/126096*
Bowen George	(26)	Pte	RASC	S/105301*
Bower Ernest	(32)	Pte	York & Lancaster Regt attd AMPC	4742538

APPENDIX 1: ROLL OF HONOUR

Bown Sidney	(21) Pte	Sherwood Foresters (N&D Regt)	4978811*
Boyle Joseph	(37) Pte	46 Coy AMPC	2188943*
Braddock Albert	(41) Tpr	2 Gen Base Depot RAC	3644831*
Brady Edward	(40) Pte	73 Coy AMPC	13005273*
Brady John	(38) Pte	50 Coy AMPC	13003391*
Braidwood George	(?) Cpl	75 Coy AMPC	13005638*
Bramley Alan Devenport	(21) Cpl	RASC	S/73417*
Brand Robert	(20) Pte	7 Bn A&S Highlanders	2982611*
Bridle Frederick William	(34) Pte	46 Coy AMPC	2188500*
Brind Lorraine Ernest Walter	(23) Spr	663 Artisan Works Coy RE	1914330*
Britton Reginald Charles	(25) Pte	RASC	S/147440*
Brookhouse Francis Joseph	(29) Cpl	RASC	S/147757*
Brown Eric George	(20) L/Cpl	579 Army Field Coy RE	2067340*
Brown George William	(22) Pte	2 Bn Buffs (Royal East Kent Regt)	6466737*
Brown Herbert	(38) L/Cpl	663 Artisan Works Coy RE	1917041*
Brown James Buchan	(20) Spr	159 Railway Operating Coy RE	1887700*
Brown Thomas Henry	(37) L/Cpl	50 Coy AMPC	6909735*
Brown William	(37) Pte	50 Coy AMPC	13000452*
Brown William Ernest	(20) Gnr	5 Bty 2 AA Regt Royal Artillery	1518173*
Bryans Joseph William	(22) Pte	46 Coy AMPC	2188374*
Bryant Robert Edward John	(39) Pte	68 Coy AMPC	13001139*
Buckley Eric	(22) Spr	11 Movement Control Group RE	1905283*
Budby Samuel	(45) Pte	73 Coy AMPC	13004946*
Bull Frank Desmond	(22) Pte	2 Bn Buffs (Royal East Kent Regt)	6466508*
Burke Brian Lonsdale	(32) Pte	RASC	S/105077*
Burke James William	(37) Sgt	Royal Artillery attd HQ 12 AA Bde	1417330*
Burke Thomas	(38) Pte	50 Coy AMPC	13002050*
Burleigh Harold	(?) Capt	Royal Engineers	107035*
Burns Owen	(44) Pte	26 Coy AMPC	13004622*
Burns William	(39) Cpl	115 Coy AMPC	529164
Busby Ernest Alfred	(44) Pte	53 Coy AMPC	13000535*
Butterworth Thomas Taylor	(27) Pte	115 Coy AMPC	2182540
Butterworth Walter	(39) Pte	75 Coy AMPC	13005513*
Byne William Horace	(33) L/Sgt	RAPC	7658670*
Bytheway Harold	(38) Cpl	73 Coy AMPC	13005058*
Caborn Davis	(38) Pte	73 Coy AMPC	7253152*
Caddy Cyril Herbert	(26) Pte	1 Base Ordnance Depot RAOC	7594680*
Cail Arthur James	(25) Pte	RASC	105985*
Cairns John	(22) Pte	1 Base Ordnance Depot RAOC	7619679*
Campbell Reginald Mumford St Clair	(41) Pte RASC		147499
Candlin Walter John	(20) Pte	1 Base Supply Depot RASC	S/57251*
Carbury George	(22) Cpl	46 Coy AMPC	2188410*
Carless Francis Henry	(29) Pte	115 Coy AMPC	5104872
Carr William Robson	(44) L/Cpl	73 Coy AMPC	13005016*
Carroll Donald	(21) Dvr	7 Res MT Coy RASC	T/121336*
Carroll Thomas	(50) Pte	75 Coy AMPC	13005496*
Casey James Patrick	(24) Pte	108 Coy AMPC	7615198*
Casson Daniel	(34) Spr	Royal Engineers	3518207*
Caulfield John	(30) Pte	6 Bn A & S Highlanders	4341767
Chamberlain Robert	(26) Pte	RASC	T/2654738

Champley Albert Norman Winston (31)	Gnr	157 Bty 53 AA Regt RA	881931*
Chandler Percy William (24)	Cpl	RASC	105576*
Channing Reuben Holly (39)	Pte	108 Coy AMPC	1032425*
Charlotte John Edward (38)	Pte	75 Coy AMPC	13005382
Cheetham Reuben (29)	L/Cpl	2 Bn SS Regt attd 113 Coy AMPC	4911894
Chilton James (36)	Cpl	RASC	94132*
Chowns John James (41)	Pte	50 Coy AMPC	3590558*
Clacher Alexander Johnston (20)	Pte	RAPC	7663275*
Clark George John (36)	Pte	46 Coy AMPC	13001209*
Clark Roy (21)	Tpr	1 General Base Depot RAC	7901391*
Clarkson Edward (48)	Pte	50 Coy AMPC	13002477*
Clay Albert (24)	Sgt	1 Supply Base Depot RE	1872270
Clay Donald (21)	L/Cpl	1 Supply Base Depot RE	2193464
Clay John Frederick (21)	Pte	2 Field Bakery RASC	S/98553*
Clements Lionel William (28)	Pte	SS Regt attd 15 Coy AMPC	4912693*
Cliffe Harry (42)	Pte	50 Coy AMPC	13002053*
Cloake John William George (27)	Pte	46 Coy AMPC	6284318*
Clyne John (21)	Pte	32 Coy AMPC	2183857*
Cobb Allan Roland John (26)	Pte	2 Bn Hampshire Regt	2694234*
Cocklin George (36)	Pte	50 Coy AMPC	13004219*
Coffey Michael (36)	Sgt	159 Railway Construction Coy RE	2717668*
Colbridge Frank (29)	Pte	1 Base Ordnance Depot RAOC	7593720*
Collins Alfred Eric (24)	Tpr	Royal Armoured Corps	409508*
Collins George (36)	Pte	50 Coy AMPC	13001404*
Connor Peter (22)	Gnr	5 Bty 2 HAA Regt RA	1528702*
Cook Jeffrey (31)	Pte	NS Regt attd AMPC	5045351*
Coomber Henry (21)	Pte	2 Bn Buffs (Royal East Kent Regt)	6289218*
Cooper Daniel (22)	Pte	46 Coy AMPC	2188397*
Cooper Walter Alan (23)	Pte	115 Coy AMPC	2184102
Copley Leonard (37)	Pte	73 Coy AMPC	13004995*
Cornish John (25)	Pte	RASC	S/94927*
Cort William (34)	Dvr	RASC attd 73 Coy AMPC	T/91432*
Cour Arthur (24)	Spr	663 Artisan Works Coy RE	1914323*
Coward Cyril George (21)	Dvr	1 Base Supply Depot RASC	T/97760*
Cowlishaw Sydney (21)	Pte	Sherwood Foresters (N&D Regt)	4978980*
Cox Cecil (36)	Cpl	RAPC	7658735*
Cox Cecil Charles (24)	L/Cpl	1 Base Ordnance Depot RAOC	7594509*
Cox Charles (49)	Pte	75 Coy AMPC	13005433*
Cracknell Harold (30)	Spr	159 Railway Construction Coy RE	1887420*
Craggs Godfrey (34)	Spr	116 Road Construction Coy RE	2186735*
Crips Reginald Edward (24)	Pte	1 Base Ordnance Depot RAOC	7611778*
Croft Walter (36)	Pte	46 Coy AMPC	13001821*
Crow Guy Allen (36)	Gnr	159 Bty 53 HAA Regt RA	2037797*
Cruickshank Alexander (38)	Pte	2 Field Bakery RASC	S/2812343*
Cummings James Joseph (34)	Cpl	115 Coy AMPC	2185400
Cummings Stanley Victor (20)	Pte	5 Bn KOSB dra 18.6.40	3193730
Cunliffe Herbert (20)	Spr	159 Railway Construction Coy RE	1891840*
Cunliffe William Edward (38)	Sgt	50 Coy AMPC	4850010*
Currey Reginald Francis R. (33)	Capt	1 Base Supply Depot RASC	S/52451
Curry Robert Frank (38)	Pte	RASC	S/94749*

Cusick Thomas	(50)	Pte	50 Coy AMPC	13002300*
Dale George William	(41)	Pte	50 Coy AMPC	13001451*
Dalgarno William James	(24)	Pte	1 Base Supply Depot RASC	S/2034530*
Daniel Thomas Edward	(35)	Pte	46 Coy AMPC	2188548*
Darby Ray	(22)	Spr	116 Road Construction Coy RE	1883072*
Davies Bert	(50)	Pte	73 Coy AMPC	13005230*
Davies Charles Rees	(25)	Pte	RASC	147923*
Davies Ernest Edward	(36)	Pte	62 Coy AMPC	2191495*
Davies Richard	(45)	L/Cpl	RASC	T/7576367*
Davis Edwin Stanley	(26)	Gnr	157 Bty 53 HAA Regt RA	835333*
Davis Walter George	(27)	Gnr	210 Bty 73 HAA Regt RA	5568314*
Day Eric	(28)	Sgt	159 Railway Construction Coy RE	1870057*
Day William Arthur	(22)	Pte	RASC	T/109261*
Deards Frederick	(34)	Pte	46 Coy AMPC	2188360*
Delaney John Frederick	(37)	L/Cpl	2 Bn Y&L Regt attd AMPC	4741171*
Dennison James	(34)	Pte	73 Coy AMPC	102344*
Dewis William Henry	(40)	Cpl	50 Coy AMPC	2186767*
Dickens Stephen	(22)	Pte	4 Base Ammn Depot RAOC	7605198*
Dicks Thomas John	(37)	Pte	50 Coy AMPC	13001478*
Diviani Joseph William P.	(22)	Pte	1 Base Ordnance Depot RAOC	7589067*
Doherty Andrew	(41)	Pte	50 Coy AMPC	13001945*
Donald David Forbes	(22)	Pte	46 Coy AMPC	2188394*
Donald David Theodore	(34)	Pte	RASC	S/119050*
Donovan Ernest Charles	(22)	Spr	159 Railway Construction Coy RE	1908941*
Dorkins Reginald Leonard	(46)	Sgt	RAPC	7658221*
Douglas Herbert Kitchener	(24)	Pte	2 Field Bakery RASC	S/132854*
Dowling Frank	(29)	Sgt	1 Supply Base Depot RE	1867367
Downey Albert Ernest	(30)	Pte	50 Coy AMPC	2181356*
Downs Edward Arthur	(26)	Pte	50 Coy AMPC	2188975*
Drabble James Alfred	(26)	Sigmn	2 Air Forn Sigs R Sigs	2587538*
Draper William Frederick	(22)	Pte	Ordnance Workshop Coy RAOC	7621647*
Driscoll Daniel	(42)	L/Cpl	73 Coy AMPC	5875691*
Dubery Samuel William	(30)	Cpl	QR Regt (West Surrey) attd AMPC	772805*
Duncan Walter	(44)	Pte	50 Coy AMPC	13001409*
Dunphie Samuel	(21)	Pte	RAPC	7663192*
Durrant Donald Phillips	(24)	Cpl	RASC	105133*
Dutson Donald Walter	(30)	Pte	1 Base Ordnance Depot RAOC	7593501*
Dwyer Edward George	(24)	Pte	RASC	S/119036*
Dwyer Richard	(35)	Pte	RAOC	7625084*
Dyke Albert Edward	(23)	Cpl	2 Field Bakery RASC	S/54849*
Earlie Thomas	(33)	Pte	115 Coy AMPC	2184038*
Eden Harry	(22)	Pte	108 Coy AMPC	7613264*
Edge John	(22)	Pte	50 Coy AMPC	5249871*
Elliott Alfred Andrew	(36)	Pte	46 Coy AMPC	5878067*
Ellis James Charles	(21)	Pte	1 Heavy Repair Shop (MT) RASC	T/99502*
Elvin Leonard	(40)	Pte	73 Coy AMPC	13003422*
Elvin Reginald John	(31)	Pte	1 General Hospital RAMC	5769299*
Elward William John	(21)	Spr	154 Railway Operating Coy RE	1927417
Embury Edward	(40)	Pte	63 Coy AMPC	13003804*
Emsell Cyril	(37)	L/Cpl	1 Base Ordnance Depot RAOC	7593660*

England Lionel	(39)	Cpl	50 Coy AMPC	5718466*
Etherington Thomas	(42)	Pte	1 Base Supply Depot RASC	T/43579*
Evans Albert Edward	(44)	Pte	RASC	132843*
Evans George Percy	(35)	Bdr	158 Bty 53 HAA Regt RA	875805*
Evans John Raymond	(27)	Pte	RASC	S/73506*
Evans Percy Llewellyn L.	(26)	Spr	159 Railway Construction Coy RE	4194872*
Evans Walter Cyril	(?)	Pte	115 Coy AMPC	2184039
Eyles Harry	(35)	Pte	115 Coy AMPC	5104434*
Fahie Charles Thomas (MM)	(46)	Pte	Base Supply Depot RASC	T/47931*
Fairhurst John	(39)	Pte	50 Coy AMPC	13002427*
Falconbridge Arnold Lawrence	(23)	Pte	RASC	S/108399*
Faragher William	(22)	Spr	159 Railway Construction Coy RE	1892864*
Farline Francis Robert	(31)	Spr	663 Artisan Works Coy RE	1912306*
Farrer Albert	(22)	Pte	46 Coy AMPC	2188411*
Ferrie James	(37)	Pte	115 Coy AMPC	15957
Fetigan Thomas	(44)	Pte	50 Coy AMPC	13002474*
Finlay William	(41)	Pte	75 Coy AMPC	4380141*
Finnie Kenneth Douglas	(22)	Gnr	158 Bty 53 HAA Regt RA dra 4.7.40	1428756
Finnigan Peter Paul	(28)	L/Bdr	RA attd HQ 12 AA Bde	819180*
Fishwick Edward Terry	(23)	Pte	Durham Light Infantry	4459151*
Fitch Stanley Lashwood	(32)	Spr	663 Artisan Works Coy RE	4384911*
Fitzmaurice Walter James	(33)	Pte	115 Coy AMPC dra 18.6.40	2183322
Flaherty John	(25)	Pte	46 Coy AMPC	2188449*
Fleisher Soloman	(20)	Pte	2 Field Bakery RASC	S/98215*
Fletcher Albert	(33)	Cpl	NS Regt attd 15 Coy AMPC	5044351
Flowers Gerald	(26)	Pte	4 Bn Buffs (Royal East Kent Regt)	6286543*
Fone Albert	(25)	Pte	73 Coy AMPC	4691095*
Forrester James	(42)	Pte	75 Coy AMPC	13005497*
Forshaw Dennis Erktwald	(?)	L/Cpl	7 Army Field Workshop RAOC	7593606*
Forsyth John	(35)	Pte	115 Coy AMPC	2189224*
Fowler Richard	(36)	Sgt	115 Coy AMPC	2186362
Fox Michael Gerard (*served as* Switzer Gerald Wiseman)	(26)	Pte	RASC	105844*
Franks Charles William	(40)	Sgt	RAPC	7811580*
Freeman Leslie	(22)	Pte	2 Bn Buffs (Royal East Kent Regt)	6466563*
Frostick Walter Sydney	(37)	L/Cpl	159 Railway Construction Coy RE	2313455*
Fryer Fred	(19)	L/Cpl	29 Railway Survey Coy RE	1872703*
Fuller Francis Victor	(27)	Pte	1 Base Ordnance Depot RAOC	7593913*
Gallagher John	(36)	Pte	75 Coy AMPC	13005546*
Galloway William	(26)	Pte	2/6 Bn Duke of Wellington's Regt	4612249*
Galvin Jeremiah	(32)	Pte	QORWK Regt attd AMPC	6198942*
Gardiner Alfred Arthur	(22)	Pte	2 Bn Buffs (Royal East Kent Regt)	6466566*
Garside William	(27)	Pte	73 Coy AMPC	102127*
Gaskell Joseph	(22)	Pte	RAOC	7616967*
Gawith Thomas	(34)	Pte	46 Coy AMPC	2188462*
Geekie Douglas Laing	(42)	Pte	53 Coy AMPC	13003554*
Gibbs Ernest George	(38)	Pte	E Regt attd AMPC	5822542*
Gibson Charles	(25)	Pte	46 Coy AMPC	2188590*
Gibson Norman	(36)	Pte	RASC	T/63177*
Glendinning William John	(33)	Pte	5 Bn KOSB dra 18.6.40	3188162
Gordon John	(21)	Pte	51 Div Ammunition Coy RASC	T/109069*

Gordon John Lessels	(21)	Pte	RAPC	7661757*
Gorringe Joseph Francis	(35)	Cpl	73 Coy AMPC	399387*
Graham Daniel	(32)	Tpr	1st Lothians & Border Horse RAC	420063*
Graham Thomas George	(41)	Pte	46 Coy AMPC	4440783*
Grant Alphonso Kinmont	(25)	Pte	115 Coy AMPC	2184064
Grant Forbes	(43)	Pte	RASC	S/147451*
Grant Roy	(29)	WO II (SQMS)	1 Base Supply Depot RASC	S/52977*
Gray George Henry	(46)	L/Sgt	663 Artisan Works Coy RE	1904582*
Green Eric	(22)	Pte	1 Base Ordnance Depot RAOC	7617144*
Green Frederick William	(22)	Spr	159 Railway Construction Coy RE	1892877*
Green William Albert	(36)	Pte	73 Coy AMPC	13006032*
Greenhill Albert	(40)	L/Cpl	663 Artisan Works Coy RE	1904568*
Greenwood Fred	(43)	Pte	50 Coy AMPC	3847072*
Gregg George Oswald	(40)	Pte	75 Coy AMPC	13005465*
Greig Walter	(46)	Pte	46 Coy AMPC	13002783*
Griffin Montague Raymond	(20)	Spr	663 Artisan Works Coy RE	1911237*
Griffiths Alfred Rees	(39)	Cpl	50 Coy AMPC	392162*
Griffiths Edwin	(38)	Pte	RASC	S/52034*
Griffiths James	(31)	Cpl	KSLI attd AMPC	4029688
Griffiths John Edward	(38)	Pte	67 Coy AMPC	4026258*
Griffiths Stanley	(28)	Pte	SS Regt attd AMPC	4913025
Grimshaw George Frederick	(25)	Dvr	116 Road Construction Coy RE	2189393*
Grinnall Francis Henry	(20)	WO II (SQMS)	RASC	S/54779*
Hale Peter John	(20)	Pte	4 Base Ammunition Depot RAOC	7612364
Hall Cecil Pinnington	(24)	Spr	Stores Base Depot RE	1880671
Hall Horace	(39)	Pte	73 Coy AMPC	13002274*
Hall John William	(34)	Cpl	115 Coy AMPC	4445255
Hall Samuel	(43)	Pte	50 Coy AMPC	13003373*
Halliday Cyril Robert	(21)	Spr	116 Road Construction Coy RE	1882253*
Hancock Hugh Stanley	(26)	Pte	Base Ammunition Depot RAOC	7594020*
Hancock Lewis William	(24)	Pte	115 Coy AMPC	2182526
Harris Frederick John	(32)	Pte	RASC	S/147280*
Harris Harold	(21)	Pte	2 Field Bakery RASC	S/98870*
Harris Trevor Haig	(21)	Spr	159 Railway Construction Coy RE	1898654*
Harris William James	(42)	Spr	154 Railway Operating Coy RE	1980425
Harrison Edward	(37)	Pte	46 Coy AMPC	4535726*
Harrison Ronald James	(25)	Pte	46 Coy AMPC	2188423*
Harrison Thomas	(26)	Pte	46 Coy AMPC	2188455*
Harrison William	(22)	Dvr	RASC	T/120291*
Harrison William John	(32)	WO I	1 Base Ordnance Depot RAOC	7582340*
Hart Albert	(31)	Spr	663 Artisan Works Coy RE	1917091*
Hartigan Edwin Albert	(20)	Spr	159 Railway Construction Coy RE	1889958*
Hartley Walter	(22)	Pte	40 Coy AMPC	101096*
Harvey Richard Harry	(26)	Dvr	1 Base MT SD RASC	T/5724429*
Haselton John H.	(32)	Pte	1 General Hospital RAMC	315951*
Hassell Thomas Henry	(41)	Spr	156 Transportation Stores Coy RE	5565591*
Hatton Thomas Henry	(28)	Pte	2 Bn Buffs (Royal East Kent Regt)	6284468*
Hay George Edward	(27)	Spr	663 Artisan Works Coy RE	1912487*
Hayward William Edward	(?)	2/Lt	663 Artisan Works Coy RE	120577*
Healey James Naylor	(26)	Pte	1 Base Ordnance Depot RAOC	7589208*

Heath Frederick William	(37)	Pte	73 Coy AMPC	13005001*
Hellyer Alfred CharlesWm.	(25)	Pte	1 Base Ordnance Depot RAOC	7593299*
Henson Harry James	(21)	Pte	1 Base Ordnance Depot RAOC	7594369*
Hepworth Samuel	(42)	Pte	SS Regt attd AMPC	4910583*
Herbert David M.	(20)	Dvr	RASC	T/81722*
Herring Douglas Edward	(21)	Tpr	1st Lothians & Border Horse RAC	7899967*
Heselden Eric Philip	(20)	Pte	2 Bn Buffs (Royal East Kent Regt)	6289138*
Heywood Clifford Gordon	(22)	Pte	115 Coy AMPC	3856961
Hibbins Harry Lawrence	(32)	Sgt	Cheshire Regt attd AMPC	4119665*
Hickerton Hubert Thomas	(25)	Pte	73 Coy AMPC	2188669*
Hicks Horace	(38)	Pte	46 Coy AMPC	6908838*
Hiscock Norman Harry	(25)	Spr	663 Artisan Works Coy RE	1912462*
Hoban James Patrick	(37)	Pte	73 Coy AMPC	13005931*
Hodgekinson Walter Bertram	(22)	Dvr	2 Field Bakery RASC	S/3132126*
Holmes Leslie Nelson	(23)	Dvr	2 Bulk Petrol Coy RASC dra 18.6.40	T/100731
Holsworth Henry John	(26)	Pte	NS Regt attd AMPC	4800138
Holt Harold Atkin	(38)	Pte	RASC	T/74668
Hope Gideon	(27)	Pte	46 Coy AMPC	101368*
Hopgood Edwin Walter	(43)	Pte	46 Coy AMPC	1028969*
Horan Stephen Anthony	(20)	Pte	115 Coy AMPC	2185416
Horne Percy Cecil	(20)	L/Cpl	4 Bn Buffs (Royal East Kent Regt)	6286979*
Horsfield Arnold	(24)	Pte	1 Base Ordnance Depot RAOC	7624255*
Horton John Eden	(28)	Spr	663 Artisan Works RE	1914279*
How Arthur George	(33)	Cpl	RASC	S/94761*
Howard Frederick	(35)	L/Cpl	115 Coy AMPC	4906284*
Hughes John Oliver	(24)	Pte	RASC	105540*
Hullah Ernest	(32)	Spr	116 Road Construction Coy RE	2186736*
Hulme Fred	(29)	Tpr	Royal Armoured Corps	558044*
Hulme John	(23)	Cpl	46 Coy AMPC	2188456*
Hunt Cyril	(21)	Gnr	158 Bty 53 HAA Regt RA	1512207*
Hunter Neil Grant	(31)	Pte	1 General Hospital RAMC	7260657*
Hutchinson Thomas Allen	(30)	L/Cpl	SS Regt attd AMPC	4911193
Hutchinson William	(38)	Pte	46 Coy AMPC	4793945*
Ireland John Edward	(23)	Pte	46 Coy AMPC	2188312*
Irvine John	(42)	Pte	50 Coy AMPC	13003839*
Isaac James Brewer	(33)	Pte	115 Coy AMPC	315521*
Jackson Thomas William	(28)	Pte	1 Base Ordnance Depot RAOC	7624263*
Jacobs William Frederick	(22)	Pte	2 Ordnance Workshop Coy RAOC	7616143*
James Henry Augustus	(37)	Pte	46 Coy AMPC	13002605*
James Stanley Arthur	(24)	Spr	116 Road Construction Coy RE	809775*
Jarvis David	(?)	Pte	39 Coy AMPC	3955763*
Jeffries Reginald Soloman	(39)	Cpl	RASC	T/5932*
Jenkins William Henry	(30)	Gnr	202 Bty 51 Anti-Tank Regt RA dra 18.6.40 824105	
Jenkins William Rees	(24)	WO II (SQMS) 1 Base Supply Depot RASC		S/54601*
Jessop John William	(39)	Pte	75 Coy AMPC	13005279*
John John	(26)	Spr	154 Railway Operating Coy RE	1927266
Johnson Harold Edward	(20)	Pte	8 Bn Sherwood Foresters (N&D Regt)	4976758*
Johnson Leonard William	(31)	Cpl	4 Base Ammn Depot RAOC	7583809
Johnson Robert	(44)	Dvr	663 Artisan Works Coy RE	1913414*

Johnson Robert Edward	(38)	Pte	50 Coy AMPC	102164*
Johnson Stanley	(40)	Pte	73 Coy AMPC dra 18.6.40	4736768
Johnstone John Robertson	(22)	Pte	1 Base Supply Depot RASC	S/2756655*
Jones Eric Sydney Rolston	(27)	Pte	1 Base Ordnance Depot RAOC	7593967*
Jones Evan Dilwyn Charles	(27)	Cpl	3 Supply Petrol Coy RASC	T/150007*
Jones Ieuan	(20)	Fus	RW Fusiliers attd AMPC	4194037*
Jones Kenneth Lewis	(22)	Pte	1 Base Ordnance Depot RAOC	7593679*
Jones Robert Denman	(31)	Pte	1 Base Ordnance Depot RAOC	7594116*
Jones Talieson	(28)	Cpl	159 Railway Construction Coy RE	802912*
Jordan Henry Williams	(31)	Cpl	46 Coy AMPC	1061600*
Judson Joseph	(25)	Pte	50 Coy AMPC	2190235*
Kearney Phillip	(41)	Pte	75 Coy AMPC	13003852*
Keenan Arthur	(31)	Pte	Cheshire Regt attd AMPC	4188090*
Kelly Albert Denis	(27)	Pte	NS Regt attd AMPC	5046758*
Kelly Frank Matthew	(47)	Pte	46 Coy AMPC	13000243*
Kelly Owen	(22)	Pte	52 Coy AMPC	7615077*
Kelly William	(32)	Pte	108 Coy AMPC	7613263*
Kemp Victor	(36)	Pte	46 Coy AMPC	2188951*
Kendall Frederick	(29)	Fus	2 Bn Royal Fusiliers	6457504*
Kerry Timothy	(32)	Pte	2 Bn Sherwood Foresters (N&D Regt)	4968691*
Keywood Charles James	(30)	Dvr	1 Heavy Repair Shop RASC	T/44567*
Kidd William	(35)	Tpr	1 Fife & Forfar Yeomanry RAC	7890659*
Killeen Michael	(38)	Pte	115 Coy AMPC	2186598*
King Hubert James	(23)	Spr	156 Transportation (Stores) Coy RE	1987233*
King Ronald Ernest Harold	(23)	Pte	46 Coy AMPC	2188501*
Kinsey John	(39)	Pte	1 Base Supply Depot RASC	S/52692*
Kitching Arthur Fairbrother	(21)	Pte	Sherwood Foresters (N&D Regt)	4978210*
Knibb Wilfred Henry	(21)	Spr	159 Railway Construction Coy RE	1898241*
Knight Albert	(25)	Pte	RASC	S/147907*
Lamb John Stephen	(23)	Pte	1 Base Ordnance Depot RAOC	7594035*
Lappin Jack	(?)	Pte	4 Motor Amb Coy RAMC	7264851*
Laquanello Tony Lawrance	(27)	Pte	46 Coy AMPC	2188295*
Larkin Allan	(27)	Pte	2 Field Bakery RASC	S/163195*
Latham Albert Ernest	(37)	Pte	73 Coy AMPC	13004963*
Law Joseph	(41)	Pte	50 Coy AMPC	13002453*
Lawley John Thomas	(30)	L/Cpl	115 Coy AMPC	2183077
Lawman Charles Sidney	(21)	Pte	2 Field Bakery RASC	S/5952096*
Lawrence William	(43)	Pte	46 Coy AMPC	1009693*
Lea Leonard	(34)	Pte	108 Coy AMPC	7613262*
Leahy John	(42)	Pte	73 Coy AMPC	13005027*
Lees Richard Henry	(47)	Pte	50 Coy AMPC	13002332*
Leighton William	(36)	Pte	53 Coy AMPC	13001292*
Leishman Arthur	(22)	Pte	5 Base Supply Depot RASC	S/137045*
Lester John Thomas	(36)	CQMS	15 Coy AMPC	4904890
Letch Stanley Louis	(23)	Spr	159 Railway Construction Coy RE	1887884*
Lewis Ronald	(20)	Cpl	Royal Armoured Corps	5184346*
Lightbown Frank	(21)	Pte	RASC	T/98980*
Ling John Henry	(37)	Pte	46 Coy AMPC	2188551*
Lloyd Alun Rees	(20)	Spr	159 Railway Construction Coy RE	1898023*
Lobley Harold	(36)	Dvr	116 Road Construction Coy RE	2184641*

Loff Victor Charles	(40)	Pte	46 Coy AMPC	13002604*
Logan John	(38)	Pte	73 Coy AMPC	2188640*
Long Frederick	(36)	Pte	1 Bn East Surrey Regt	6768903*
Loudon Alexander	(27)	L/Cpl	1 Base Ordnance Depot RAOC	7593810*
Love Thomas Frederick	(36)	Pte	75 Coy AMPC	13005469*
Lovett Thomas Curry	(37)	L/Cpl	116 Road Construction Coy RE	4441190*
Lowe Edmund	(30)	Pte	SS Regt attd 15 Coy AMPC	4911306*
Luff John Philip	(22)	Pte	1/5 Bn Queen's Royal Regt	6093154*
Lupton Clifford Allen	(22)	Pte	5 Bn KOSB dra 18.6.40	3192650
Luther Charles Stanley	(27)	L/Bdr	5 Bty 2 AA Regt RA	819307*
Lyrick Dennis Arthur	(20)	Pte	2 Bn Buffs (Royal East Kent Regt)	6289166*
Macleod Donald Gunn	(21)	Dvr	1 Base Supply Depot RASC	99019*
Macleod Ian Francis	(25)	Pte	1 Base Ordnance Depot RAOC	7593789*
Malam James	(23)	Pte	39 Coy AMPC	2190054*
Manning John	(33)	Pte	46 Coy AMPC	2188446*
Markey Reginald John	(46)	Lt	50 Coy AMPC	43239*
Marsden Frank	(35)	Pte	Y&L Regt attd AMPC	4741358
Marsh William	(44)	Pte	50 Coy AMPC	13002733*
Marshall Benjamin	(36)	Pte	73 Coy AMPC	13001642*
Marshall Cyril Arthur	(34)	L/Cpl	1 Base Ordnance Depot RAOC	7593681*
Marshall John	(35)	L/Cpl	1 Base Ordnance Depot RAOC	7589191*
Martin Albert Reginald	(21)	Spr	154 Railway Operating Coy RE	1889532*
Martin Daniel	(23)	Pte	46 Coy AMPC	2188308*
Massey Frank	(36)	Pte	46 Coy AMPC	2188547*
Mather Frank	(20)	Pte	AMPC	13006456*
Matthews Charles	(30)	Pte	108 Coy AMPC	7607008*
Matthews Joseph Henry	(26)	Pte	73 Coy AMPC	830282*
Matthews Philip	(24)	Pte	115 Coy AMPC	2182395
Mayer Harold Samuel	(21)	Spr	663 Artisan Works Coy RE	1913115*
Mayers Edward Frederick	(20)	Pte	108 Coy AMPC	7606821*
McCamley Thomas	(32)	Pte	115 Coy AMPC	2182015
McCormick William	(28)	Pte	46 Coy AMPC	2188553*
McCue William	(28)	Pte	115 Coy AMPC	2183234
McDonald William Henry James	(33)	Pte	46 Coy AMPC	2870263*
McDonough John Joseph	(35)	Pte	115 Coy AMPC	2183261
McDougall James	(25)	Spr	159 Railway Construction Coy RE	1899083*
McGee Francis	(23)	Pte	5 Base Supply Depot RASC	S/127363*
McGowan Ernest	(26)	Sigmn	2 Air Form Sigs R Sigs	2587688*
McKeown Gerard	(30)	Gnr	99 Bty 20 Anti-Tank Regt RA	788435*
McKigney Joseph	(39)	Pte	51 Coy AMPC	13001124*
McLuckie William Bennie	(22)	Pte	4 Base Ammunition Depot RAOC	7612303
McMillan Donald	(21)	Pte	RASC	99020*
McMillan John	(29)	Pte	46 Coy AMPC	2188934*
McNally James Francis	(21)	Pte	1 General Hospital RAMC	7263312*
McNamara Leo	(26)	Pte	46 Coy AMPC	2188472*
McVeigh Daniel	(40)	Pte	50 Coy AMPC	7006739*
Michell Douglas Herbert	(25)	Spr	663 Artisan Works Coy RE	1912461*
Middleton William James	(38)	Pte	4 Ordnance Workshop Coy RAOC	7869653*
Milburn George	(40)	Pte	53 Coy AMPC	13001931*
Miller Alfred	(30)	Pte	SS Regt attd 15 Coy AMPC	4911522

Miller David	(24)	Pte	1 Base Ordnance Depot RAOC	7603217*
Mills John Cecil	(28)	L/Cpl	RASC	T/74384*
Mills Lloyd Herbert	(21)	Spr	159 Railway Construction Coy RE	1898460*
Milton William Thomas	(27)	Pte	NS Regt attd AMPC	5046962
Mison Frederick William	(35)	Dvr	2 Res MT Coy RASC	T/49747*
Mitchell Hudson Taylor	(35)	Pte	53 Coy AMPC	2870283*
Mitchell Samuel Philip	(21)	Cpl	11 Ord Ammunition Coy RAOC	7613317
Monaghan Thomas	(37)	L/Cpl	73 Coy AMPC	101154*
Monk Philip John	(28)	Cpl	46 Coy AMPC	2188497*
Moon Anthony James	(29)	Lt	RAMC	127123*
Moore Cecil Harry	(31)	Dvr	RASC	T/53753*
Moore Joseph James	(38)	Pte	46 Coy AMPC	392826*
Moorhead Thomas	(48)	Cpl	50 Coy AMPC	13002064*
Morgan Roger	(49)	Pte	50 Coy AMPC	3513210*
Morgan Sydney	(20)	Pte	108 Coy AMPC	7607121*
Morgan Vincent	(31)	L/Cpl	1 Heavy Repair Shop Coy RASC	T/6457118*
Morgan William	(22)	Pte	46 Coy AMPC	2188586*
Morphet Stanley	(26)	Sgt	73 Coy AMPC	4535382*
Moyle Robert	(20)	Pte	4 Base Ammunition Depot RAOC	7612934
Muller Charles William	(36)	Spr	159 Railway Construction Coy RE	2064323*
Murphy John Joseph	(43)	Pte	50 Coy AMPC	13003876*
Murphy Patrick Joseph	(38)	Pte	AMPC	7615087*
Murray James Strachan	(26)	Spr	663 Artisan Works Coy RE	1913127*
Murray John Forbes	(41)		WO II (CSM) AMPC	2872401*
Murray Leonard Frederick	(21)	Pte	1 Base Ordnance Depot RAOC	6463478*
Murray Walter	(33)	L/Cpl	46 Coy AMPC	7341103*
Myers Alfred Edward	(36)	Pte	75 Coy AMPC	13005470*
Naylor John Walter	(39)	Pte	75 Coy AMPC	13005344*
Neave James	(33)	Pte	46 Coy AMPC	13002780*
Newton James	(39)	Pte	50 Coy AMPC	13001431*
Nichol George William	(22)	Spr	159 Railway Construction Coy RE	1901882*
Nicholson Horace Vincent	(22)	Gnr	RA attd 1 Salvage Unit AMPC	2183493*
Norman Brinley Charles	(36)	Pte	53 Coy AMPC	13003649*
Nunn Sidney James	(47)	Pte	53 Coy AMPC	13000801*
Oakford Arthur Robert	(40)	Sgt	RASC	148809*
Oakley William Frederick	(34)	Pte	115 Coy AMPC	2182016
O'Connell Simon	(31)	Pte	115 Coy AMPC	2182529
O'Neill Frank	(31)	Pte	115 Coy AMPC	2182011
Orr Robert	(34)	L/Cpl	1 Base Supply Depot RASC	T/63410*
Orton Frank	(23)	Spr	663 Artisan Works Coy RE	4857083*
Owen Clifford	(20)	Spr	159 Railway Construction Coy RE	1891810*
Owen Douglas Frank	(24)	L/Cpl	579 Army Field Coy RE	2075951*
Owen Edward	(33)	Pte	SWB attd 5 Rly Labour Coy RE	3907155*
Owens Thomas William	(47)	Cpl	73 Coy AMPC	13004970*
Parker Robert	(?)	Sgt	2 Field Bakery RASC	S/52283*
Parker Willis Roy	(21)	Pte	RASC	T/104178*
Parkin William	(37)	Cpl	46 Coy AMPC	2188570*
Parkinson Harry	(37)	Spr	116 Road Construction Coy RE	2183817*
Parrington John Rogerson	(?)	Spr	159 Railway Construction Coy RE	1899069*
Patchett Herbert	(40)	Pte	50 Coy AMPC	804718*

Payton Sidney Thomas	(41)	Spr	190 Railway Operating Coy RE	1898948
Peacock John Robert	(42)	Cpl	50 Coy AMPC	13000976*
Peek Leonard	(35)	Dvr	3 Motor Amb Convoy RASC	T/33960*
Peel Arthur	(33)	Pte	75 Coy AMPC	1426643*
Penfold Edward	(30)	Cpl	RASC	S/148531*
Penny George Ernest Ward	(31)	L/Cpl	RASC	T/63441*
Pepperell Charles Henry	(30)	Pte	1 Base Ordnance Depot RAOC	7593914*
Perkins Edward	(26)	WO II (SQMS) RASC		S/105535*
Perry William George	(37)	Pte	4 Bn Devonshire Regt	5612030*
Pitson Edward Harold	(29)	Dvr	9 Res MT Coy RASC	T/158079*
Place Arthur Austin	(21)	Pte	1 Bn SL Regt dra 18.6.40	3654799
Place George Forster	(35)	Pte	RASC	T/109856*
Plummer Ernest Edward	(24)	L/Cpl	579 Army Field Coy RE	2036306*
Potter John	(22)	Spr	159 Railway Construction Coy RE	1923011*
Potter Robert Frederick	(38)	Pte	RASC	T/146558*
Powell Randel	(36)	Pte	50 Coy AMPC	13001434*
Powell Thomas William	(30)	Dvr	2 L of C MT Coy RASC	T/125462*
Prager Joseph Arthur	(42)	Pte	46 Coy AMPC	13001164*
Preston Josiah	(50)	Pte	53 Coy AMPC	13000785*
Price Arthur Edward	(39)	Pte	115 Coy AMPC	3645404
Price Charles	(31)	Pte	1 Base Ordnance Depot RAOC	7594346*
Price William	(?)	Dvr	1 Div Supply Col RASC	T/125459*
Prince Douglas Harry	(21)	Spr	159 Railway Construction Coy RE	1898382*
Probert Albert Joseph	(?)	L/Cpl	4 Base Ammunition Depot RAOC	3527803
Puddicombe Frederick James R.	(30)	WO II (SQMS) RASC		148116*
Pullin Arthur Mervyn	(22)	Tpr	Royal Armoured Corps	7896959*
Raddings Joseph Edward	(?)	Spr	113 Artisan Works Coy RE	1914322*
Ramsay Albert Marshall	(38)	Spr	663 Artisan Works Coy RE	1913181*
Randall Victor Cyril	(22)	Pte	46 Coy AMPC	410467*
Raper Philip Arthur Whitham	(28)	Pte	46 Coy AMPC	803248*
Rastall Frederick Charles	(20)	Spr	Royal Engineers	1913102*
Ratcliff Arthur Ernest	(23)	Pte	RASC	T/73927*
Rayner Arthur	(36)	L/Cpl	159 Railway Construction Coy RE	1055118*
Rayner Sidney	(21)	Gnr	159 Bty 53 HAA Regt RA	1491015*
Rayner Stanley George (MM)	(43)	Spr	190 Railway Operating Coy RE	1898804
Reader Joseph	(41)	Pte	50 Coy AMPC	5242548*
Reed Michael James	(21)	Pte	RASC	T/104051*
Reekie Frederick	(22)	Pte	5 Bn KOSB dra 18.6.40	3193080
Reynolds William Joseph	(32)	Pte	115 Coy AMPC	2183168
Rhodes Arthur Cecil	(21)	Pte	4 Base Ammunition Depot RAOC	7611557
Richards Leslie John	(20)	Pte	4 Base Ammunition Depot RAOC	7612531*
Richards Robert Dennis	(22)	Pte	HQ 1 Base Ordnance Depot RAOC	7613957*
Richards Thomas Ronald	(25)	Pte	46 Coy AMPC	2188337*
Richards William John	(25)	Pte	1 Base Ordnance Depot RAOC	7604032*
Richardson Austin Easton	(20)	Tpr	Royal Armoured Corps	421137*
Richardson William Hensley	(39)	Pte	RAOC	3591571*
Ridley Alfred Hedley	(31)	Cpl	2 Field Bakery RASC	S/54511*
Rigler William John	(31)	Pte	2 Field Bakery RASC	S/74338*
Riley Thomas	(34)	Pte	75 Coy AMPC dra 18.6.40	7894815
Ritchie Adam	(36)	L/Cpl	115 Coy AMPC	2971379

Roberts Thomas	(28)	Pte	Sherwood Foresters (NS Regt)	5046778*
Robertson Adam Cail	(37)	Pte	46 Coy AMPC	2188967*
Robinson William	(20)	Spr	228 Field Coy RE	2047649
Rodgers Thomas Henry	(21)	Cpl	1 Base Supply Depot RASC	T/99956*
Rowe Frank Stanley	(23)	Spr	159 Railway Construction Coy RE	1907341*
Rozier James Charles	(33)	Pte	NS Regt attd AMPC	5044148
Ruck Sydney James	(27)	Spr	579 Field Coy RE	2067518*
Rudman John	(27)	Fus	Lancashire Fusiliers attd AMPC	3525214
Rumsby Douglas Eric	(19)	L/Cpl	1 Base Ordnance Depot RAOC	7595973*
Russell George Arthur	(26)	Pte	Y&L Regt attd AMPC	4745010*
Salloway Raymond Arnold	(21)	Pte	1 Base Supply Depot RASC	S/115221*
Sams Leslie Ernest	(47)	L/Cpl	73 Coy AMPC	13005076*
Sanders Eric Mons	(21)	Tpr	1 Arm'd Reconnaissance Bde RAC	7901263*
Sanderson Charles Frederick	(37)	Cpl	116 Road Construction Coy RE	2189404*
Sapsford John Charles	(32)	Gnr	157 Bty 53 HAA Regt RA	1491050*
Saxton Joseph Lambley	(20)	Pte	6 Bn Sherwood Foresters (N&D Regt)	4978856*
Saxton Thomas	(19)	Pte	1/5 Bn Sherwood Foresters (N&D Regt)	4976867*
Schlesinger Terence John	(20)	Spr	59 Railway Survey Coy RE	1874916*
Scholfield Arthur	(39)	Pte	75 Coy AMPC	1046579*
Scotney Charles	(43)	Pte	75 Coy AMPC	13005477*
Scott George	(35)	Spr	116 Road Construction Coy RE	2189397*
Shadwick William Robert P.	(20)	L/Cpl	1 Store Base Depot RE	1875632
Sharp Joshua William	(44)	Pte	50 Coy AMPC	7252124*
Shearing Stephen Tom	(20)	Spr	159 Railway Construction Coy RE	1898164*
Shears Frank James	(23)	L/Sgt	1 Stores Base Depot RE	1873141
Sheen William Charles T.	(29)	L/Cpl	QORWK Regt attd AMPC	6199269*
Shelbourne Walter	(36)	L/Cpl	NS Regt attd AMPC	5044759*
Shephard Arthur James	(47)	Pte	50 Coy AMPC	5097497*
Shepherd Stanley George	(22)	Spr	154 Railway Operating Coy RE	1908948
Shepherd William	(38)	Pte	50 Coy AMPC	396897*
Sherlock Joseph Heath	(44)	Pte	RASC	T/63055*
Sherratt David George	(21)	Pte	1 Bn Sherwood Foresters (N&D Regt)	4978638*
Shirley James	(31)	Pte	115 Coy AMPC	2183062
Short John	(44)	Pte	RASC	T/48038*
Short John Henry	(21)	Dvr	1 Heavy Repair Shop RASCT	/137854*
Shotter Ralph William John	(21)	L/Cpl	1 Heavy Repair Shop RASCT	/64474*
Shute Ernest Percy	(31)	L/Cpl	Cinque Ports Fortress Coy RE	1982775*
Silvester Joseph	(43)	Pte	46 Coy AMPC	2188306*
Simpson Robert Douglas	(45)	Pte	35 Coy AMPC	13004640*
Skeen George Andrew	(25)	Cpl	42 Royal Tank Regt RAC	6142199*
Slate Oswald	(38)	Pte	46 Coy AMPC	3848792*
Slater John	(39)	Pte	50 Coy AMPC	13002468*
Smallman Harry Norman	(21)	Pte	RASC	99772*
Smith Benjamin	(29)	Pte	46 Coy AMPC	2188677*
Smith Charles	(23)	Sgt	Sherwood Foresters (N&D Regt)	4974626*
Smith Charles Henry	(21)	L/Bdr	158 Bty 53 HAA Regt RA	1491072*
Smith David	(31)	L/Cpl	Cheshire Regt attd AMPC	4122024*
Smith Eric Hudson	(21)	Pte	RAPC	7662375*

Smith George Edward	(27)	Pte	1 Bn Sherwood Foresters (N&D Regt)	4971600*
Smith Harold	(19)	Pte	Sherwood Foresters (N&D Regt)	4977532*
Smith John	(?)	Pte	RAPC	7662418*
Smith Reginald Clifford Edwin	(26)	Pte	RASC	147498*
Smith Robert	(34)	Pte	A&S Highlanders attd AMPC	2974231*
Smith Robert William	(31)	Pte	75 Coy AMPC	13005428*
Smith Samuel	(47)	Pte	67 Coy AMPC	3435408*
Smith Stanley Thomas	(27)	Pte	53 Coy AMPC	13001169*
Smith Walter James *see* list of Army personnel buried in France.				
Snell Reuben	(35)	Pte	1 Bn East Surrey Regt	6136583*
Soden Henry Ernest	(27)	Pte	46 Coy AMPC	2188507*
Spencer Frederick Alan	(24)	Spr	Royal Engineers	835946*
Spencer Henry Radford	(21)	Pte	2 Base Ordnance Workshop RAOC	7620328*
Spooner Francis Percy	(21)	Pte	1 Base Supply Depot RASC	S/114034*
Stevens Robert	(29)	L/Cpl	RASC	S/11824*
Stewart Alexander Aitken	(20)	Pte	53 Coy AMPC	2878226*
Stewart Eric Harold	(20)	Gnr	5 Bty 2 AA Regt RA	1427608*
Stewart Thomas James	(34)	Pte	RASC	T/53609*
Stewart William	(43)	Pte	AMPC	13009588*
Storer Jack	(32)	Pte	Sherwood Foresters (N&D Regt)	4977731*
Storey Nicholas	(55)	Pte	46 Coy AMPC	13002766*
Sugrue James	(22)	Spr	663 Artisan Works Coy RE	1911265*
Sutton George	(31)	Pte	NS Regt attd 15 Coy AMPC	5044881
Swalwell John	(30)	Pte	46 Coy AMPC	2188473*
Switzer Gerald Wiseman (*see* Fox Michael Gerard)				
Sykes Samuel	(38)	Cpl	46 Coy AMPC	103834*
Tacey Leslie	(21)	Pte	Sherwood Foresters (N&D Regt)	4978640*
Taggart Wilson	(39)	Pte	40 Coy AMPC	101483*
Tanner Walter Henry	(31)	Pte	Royal Berkshire Regt	5333700*
Taylor Albert	(21)	Dvr	2 Field Bakery RASC	S/99997*
Taylor Arnold	(43)	Pte	50 Coy AMPC	3436576*
Taylor Harry James	(35)	Pte	73 Coy AMPC	13006099*
Taylor Isaac Joseph	(38)	Pte	73 Coy AMPC	13005257*
Taylor John Henry	(20)	Pte	Sherwood Foresters (N&D Regt)	4978266*
Teagle Arthur	(20)	Pte	Sherwood Foresters (N&D Regt)	4978944*
Theobald Donald	(28)	L/Cpl	HQ L of C MP	796474*
Thomas Benjamin	(19)	Fus	2 Bn Royal Northumberland Fusiliers	4271946*
Thomas James Harold	(32)	Pte	RAPC	106147*
Thomas John Colin	(22)	Pte	1 Base Ordnance Depot RAOC	7594156*
Thomas Leonard	(33)	Pte	York & Lancaster Regt attd AMPC	4744281
Thomas Tom Smith	(36)	Cpl	1 Base Supply Depot RASC	T/53773*
Thomas William Edward	(43)	Pte	68 Coy AMPC	13000389*
Thompson James	(30)	Gnr	9 Bty 3 Searchlight Regt RA	1465636*
Thompson William Arnold	(27)	Pte	1 Base Ordnance Depot RAOC	7624821*
Tindall Henry Edgar	(22)	Gnr	53 HAA Regt RA dra 18.6.40	1491110
Tomlinson William	(27)	L/Cpl	King's Shropshire LI attd AMPC	4031197
Townsend Percy Norman	(34)	Pte	1 Base Ordnance Depot RAOC	7593570*
Tracey Joseph	(29)	Pte	RASC	S/148889*
Treves Frederick George	(36)	Pte	RAPC	5998256*
Trevethan Richard Ernest	(27)	Pte	RAPC	7667979*

Trill Hubert Lorimer	(22)	Sgt	8 Army Field Workshop RAOC	7605139*
Tucker Cecil John Leonard	(28)	Cpl	RASC	6457199*
Tucker Reginald Robert	(29)	L/Sgt	154 Railway Operating Coy RE	1983641
Turnbull Edward Arthur	(38)	Gnr	307 Bty 37 Searchlight Regt RA	2036531*
Turner Ernest	(20)	Pte	4 Base Ammunition Depot RAOC	7601686
Turner George Frederick	(23)	Spr	663 Artisan Works Coy RE	1914201*
Turner George Henry	(30)	Sgt	1 Base Supply Depot RASC	T/36856*
Turner James Edward	(25)	Pte	2 MT Supply Depot RASC	T/119518*
Tynan James	(40)	Pte	50 Coy AMPC	13003783*
Underhill Herbert Francis	(35)	Gnr	5 Bty 2 HAA Regt RA	6538895*
Unsworth Frederick	(38)	Pte	50 Coy AMPC	13002428*
Van William Henry	(36)	Pte	1 Bn East Surrey Regt	5243496*
Vass William	(31)	Cpl	RASC	S/94401*
Verity David	(35)	Cpl	50 Coy AMPC	13001448*
Vince Harry George	(39)	Pte	73 Coy AMPC	13005175*
Voce Thomas Dennis	(22)	Pte	Sherwood Foresters (N&D Regt)	4975703*
Waine Sidney	(20)	Gnr	209 Bty 73 HAA Regt RA	871153*
Walkden Francis Oliver	(21)	Tpr	15/19 King's Royal Hussars RAC	7899228*
Walker Harry	(32)	Pte	North Staffordshire Regt attd AMPC	5044931
Walker James Maitland	(20)	Spr	159 Railway Operating Coy RE	1891912*
Wall Robert William	(22)	L/Cpl	1 Base Ordnance Depot RAOC	7593560*
Wallwin James Leslie	(34)	Pte	2 Field Bakery RASC	S/11982*
Walsh Simon Christopher	(26)	Dvr	RASC	T/127304*
Walsh William	(38)	Spr	29 Railway Survey Coy RE	3380854*
Walters Thomas	(47)	Pte	52 Coy AMPC	13001592*
Walton Sidney Cantle	(44)	Pte	73 Coy AMPC	7250994*
Ward Charles	(38)	Pte	50 Coy AMPC	13002083*
Ward George Albert	(37)	Sgt	115 Coy AMPC	2186859
Ward Harry James	(34)	Lt	RAOC	127985*
Ward Henry Aidan	(33)	Spr	154 Railway Operating Coy RE	1928050*
Ward William Henry	(38)	Pte	73 Coy AMPC	13006070*
Warren Edward Allan	(?)	Capt	Royal Engineers	104659*
Warren Joshua William Albert	(32)	Pte	North Staffordshire Regt attd AMPC	5044408
Warwick Albert Cecil	(33)	Pte	RASC	S/148726*
Watling George Moses	(22)	Spr	159 Railway Operating Coy RE	1907557*
Watson David (DCM, MM & Bar)	(44)	WO II (CSM)	1 Bn QOCH	2923773*
Watson George Edward	(37)	Pte	46 Coy AMPC	5097986*
Watson John	(48)	Pte	50 Coy AMPC	13004209*
Watson Joseph Henry	(37)	Pte	1 Bn QORWK Regt	6336894*
Watson Robert	(50)	Pte	75 Coy AMPC	13005347*
Watson Thomas	(27)	Pte	RASC	S/105697*
Watt Ernest Anthony	(25)	Pte	46 Coy AMPC	2188441*
Webb Samuel	(38)	Pte	50 Coy AMPC	4436857*
Webster Herbert John	(42)	Capt	Royal Fusiliers (City of London Regt)	46277*
Webster Joseph George James	(28)	Pte	115 Coy AMPC	2185190*
Webster William Charles	(34)	Pte	115 Coy AMPC	2185188*
Wedderburn Peter Elder	(26)	Pte	1 Bn Gordon Highlanders	811676*
Weekley George Bowmer	(21)	Pte	Sherwood Foresters (N&D Regt)	4978725*
Weir James	(38)	Cpl	115 Coy AMPC	264229
Wells Raymond Edward	(21)	Pte	1 General Hospital RAMC	7263977*

West Graham John	(21)	Gnr	158 Bty 53 Lt AA Regt RA	1452462*
West William	(41)	WO	I (Clk of W) CRE (Works) AASF RE	1861885*
White John	(21)	Pte	1 Bn York & Lancaster Regt attd RASC	4747156*
White John Francis	(40)	Spr	Royal Engineers	1894926
White Patrick Godlovton	(?)	WO II (SQMS)	RASC	94924*
White Thomas Henry	(20)	Spr	159 Railway Construction Coy RE	1922558*
Whitestone Berkeley Frederic (MBE, MC)	(44)	LtCol	RE Cdg RE, AASF	9079*
Wickham Albert Clarence	(35)	Pte	73 Coy AMPC	6394471*
Wickham George Ambrose	(27)	Pte	1 Base Ordnance Depot RAOC	7594472*
Wigley Alec Herbert	(31)	Sgt	AMPC	6895683*
Wigley Henry Raymond	(30)	Pte	RASC	148734*
Wild John Matthew	(33)	L/Cpl	1 Bn East Surrey Regt	6083113*
Wilkins Dennis	(30)	Pte	2 Bn Manchester Regt attd AMPC	3522627
Wilkinson Clifford	(30)	Gnr	HQ 73 HAA Regt RA	1446244*
Willcock Albert Edward	(41)	Pte	RASC	S/94386*
Williams George Ivor Maurice	(20)	Fus	Royal Welch Fusiliers attd AMPC	4195077*
Williams John Stanley	(28)	Pte	Sherwood Foresters (N&D Regt)	4977756*
Williams Thomas Francis	(20)	Spr	46 Coy Royal Engineers	1901134*
Williams Thomas William	(41)	Pte	50 Coy AMPC	13003443*
Williams William	(40)	Cpl	50 Coy AMPC	13001532
Wilmot Charles Morgan	(26)	Pte	1 Base Ordnance Depot RAOC	7593889*
Wilson Frederick Charles	(33)	Pte	South Staffordshire Regt attd AMPC	4910105*
Winer Jack George	(35)	Pte	RAPC	7659901*
Woodhouse Richard	(30)	Pte	York & Lancaster Regt attd AMPC	4743120
Woods Edward Gardiner	(27)	Cpl	104 Coy AMPC	65940*
Woodward Douglas	(21)	Pte	Sherwood Foresters (N&D Regt)	4978795*
Wort Albert Edward	(29)	Tpr	12 Royal Lancers RAC	551922*
Worthington James	(21)	Pte	115 Coy AMPC	2182534*
Wright Alfred	(32)	Pte	Cheshire Regt attd 13 Coy AMPC	4121385*
Wright Charles Richard	(21)	L/Cpl	2 Field Bakery RASC	S/934599*
Wright James	(34)	Pte	North Staffordshire Regt attd AMPC	2215645
Wright Sydney George	(25)	Pte	1 Base Ordnance Depot RAOC	7624595*
Wynne Frederick Thomas	(25)	Pte	4 Base Ammunition Depot RAOC	7603738
Yeaman James	(38)	Pte	46 Coy AMPC	2188953*
Young Alexander	(22)	Pte	46 Coy AMPC	2188528*
Young Henry	(47)	Pte	50 Coy AMPC	13003461*
Young Thomas	(45)	Pte	46 Coy AMPC	13002854*

<u>Total lost: 758</u>

ARMY PERSONNEL BURIED IN FRANCE

Codes used, when space is not available, for war cemeteries in (brackets) after regiment details, are as follows:

(Ang) = Angoulins. (Bern) = La Bernerie-en-Retz. (Brest) = Brest, Kerfautras Cemetery, Lambézellec. (C) = Le Clion-sur-Mer. (C d'O) = Château d'Olonne.
(C'P) = Chatelaillon Plage. (L-d'Y) = l'Ile-d' Yeu. (L) = La Plaine-sur-Mer.
(L'A) = L'Aiguillon-sur-Mer. (La Bar) = La Barre-de-Monts. (L'H) = L'Herbaudiere.
(M) = Les Moutiers-en-Retz. (N) = Nantes [Pons du Cens].
(N D) = Notre Dame-de-Monts. (N-e-L) = Noirmoutier-en-l'Ile (L'Herbaudiere).

APPENDIX 1: ROLL OF HONOUR

(Pf) = Prefailles. (P s M) = Piriac-sur-Mer. (Sables) = Les Sables-d'Olonne.
(St C) = St Charles de Percy. (St Denis) = St Denis-d'Oleron.
(St Georges) = St Georges d'Oleron. (St M) = St Marie. (Soulac) = Soulac-sur-Mer.
(St P) = St Palais-sur-Mer. (St Trojan) = St Trojan-les-Bains.

Please Note: In many of these cemeteries there are a number of service personnel buried with no known identity. However, these names should appear on the Dunkirk or Runnymede Memorials, and probably appear in the respective list of names researched by the author from the relevant registers.

Abbott Arthur William	(24)	Pte	RASC (Les Moutiers-en-Retz)	S/106859*
Adams Alexander Gray	(20)	Pte	1 Base Ord Depot RAOC (Dolus)	7594089*
Adams William George	(23)	Pte	663 Artisan Works Coy RE (M)	1902499*
Alderson Sydney Flowett	(43)	L/Cpl	116 Road Constr Coy RE (Bern)	2189400*
Aldred Arthur Vernon	(?)	Spr	663 Artisan Works Coy RE (N-e-L)	1910525*
Andrewartha Douglas John	(21)	L/Cpl	RASC (La Bernerie-en-Retz)	T/104001*
Anthony Patrick	(34)	Sgt	AMPC (St Marie)	7606674*
Anthony Robert Cummings	(21)	Pte	RASC (Noirmoutier-en-l'Ile)	S/98410*
Armstrong Walter Herbert	(39)	Pte	AMPC (La Bernerie-en-Retz)	13003423*
Ashworth James	(33)	L/Cpl	AMPC (St Georges d'Oleron)	3381296*
Attwood Albert	(38)	Pte	AMPC (Prefailles)	13005631*
Aynsley George William	(41)	Pte	AMPC (Prefailles)	13005211*
Ayre Robert	(30)	Pte	AMPC (La Bernerie-en-Retz)	13007283*
Baker Albert Sydney	(24)	Spr	663 Artisan Works Coy RE (L-d'Y)	5495828*
Baker Joseph	(34)	Pte	AMPC (Prefailles)	1446738*
Baldwin Thomas	(42)	Sgt	AMPC (La Couarde-sur-Mer)	754746*
Banks Alfred Edward	(36)	Dvr	RASC (Prefailles)	T/107695*
Barclay Stanley Joseph	(23)	L/Cpl	1 Armd Div Provost Coy MP (C)	7686963*
Barrett Herbert	(21)	Gnr	5 Bty 2 AA Regt RA (Bern)	1519234*
Barrick Norman Alfred	(21)	Dvr	Royal Engineers (Prefailles)	1884183*
Barritt William Ernest	(27)	Pte	RASC (La Bernerie-en-Retz)	148581*
Barry Rex Edmund	(35)	Pte	RASC (Les Moutiers-en-Retz)	94912*
Barton Frederick William G.	(29)	Spr	663 Artisan Works Coy RE (Bern)	1903465*
Barty Lewis Stevenson	(25)	Spr	159 Rly Operating Coy RE (Bern)	1887433*
Baum Alfred Isaac	(21)	Pte	2 Bn Buffs (Prefailles)	6288801*
Bean John Hardy	(24)	Spr	663 Artisan Works Coy RE (C)	1903410*
Beaver Frank	(42)	Pte	73 Coy AMPC (La Barre-de-Monts)	13001392*
Beeson Dennis George	(22)	Gnr	158 Bty 53 HAA Regt RA (St Georges)	1490629*
Bell John	(22)	Dvr	116 Road Constr Coy RE (La Plaine)	1882312*
Bennett Frederick John	(39)	WO II (CSM)	159 Rly Constr Coy RE (Yves)	1863807*
Birch Francis James	(33)	Cpl	SWB attd AMPC (La Plaine)	4073087*
Bird Charles Edward	(40)	Spr	663 Artisan Works Coy RE (St M)	1912389*
Bird Lawrence William	(31)	Spr	663 Artisan Works Coy RE (Sables)	1913351*
Blain John	(?)	Pte	6 Bn A&S Highlanders (Ste Marie-de-Re)	2976833*
Blakely Albert	(?)	Spr	663 Artisan Works Coy RE (L)	1904631*
Boardman John Charles	(30)	Sgt	2 Bn N&D Regt (N-e-L)	4971155*
Bolton Frederick Cecil	(20)	L/Cpl	1 HRS RASC (La Bernerie-en-Retz)	T/64906*
Bowen John William	(28)	Spr	675 Artisan Works Coy RE (Dolus)	1911508*
Brain Frederick Henry John	(36)	Cpl	AMPC (La Bernerie-en-Retz)	13000857*
Braisby Reuben	(21)	Pte	1/5 Bn N&D Regt (Les Moutiers)	4975922*

Brampton Victor Sidney	(37)	Pte	AMPC (Les Moutiers-en-Retz)	13005244*
Brand Harry	(38)	WO	II (SQMS) RASC (Dolus d'Oleron)	S/94144*
Breeze John	(36)	Spr	190 Rly Operating Coy RE (M)	1927307*
Broomhead Robert	(36)	Pte	AMPC (Prefailles)	13001398*
Brotherton James	(20)	Spr	1 Movement Control Coy RE (Bern)	1985633*
Brown Douglas Arthur	(21)	Pte	1 Base Sply Depot RASC (L'Epine)	S/115317*
Brown Francis Ernest Raynor	(21)	Pte	N&D Regt (La Bernerie-en-Retz)	4978391*
Bryan James Paton	(?)	Spr	159 Rly Constr Coy RE (Bern)	1899084*
Bryson Stanley George	(22)	Pte	1 Base Supply Depot RASC (N-e-L)	S/137037*
Bullock Harry	(22)	Dvr	RASC (Piriac-sur-Mer)	T/136129*
Burke Daniel Augustus	(32)	Cpl	RASC (Aytré)	52872*
Burrows John	(21)	Gnr	158 Bty 53 AA Regt RA (Bern)	1490673*
Burton Leonard	(39)	Pte	AMPC (Dolus d'Oleron)	13005334*
Calvert Edwin Owran	(33)	Spr	159 Rly Constr Coy RE (Bern)	1899148*
Calvert Ernest	(42)	Cpl	116 Road Constr Coy RE (Bern)	2189402*
Cameron Peter Paterson	(22)	L/Cpl	159 Rly Constr Coy RE (L'Epine)	1899093*
Carchrie Archibald	(36)	Pte	AMPC (La Barre-de-Monts)	13001818*
Carr Robert Ravera	(27)	Pte	RASC dra 23.6.40 (Bretignolles-sur-Mer)	
				S/147487
Carr William	(27)	Pte	AMPC (La Plaine-sur-Mer)	7606923*
Catlin Herbert Edward	(34)	Pte	AMPC (Prefailles)	13006840*
Cavanagh James	(48)	Cpl	AMPC (La Bernerie-en-Retz)	6972252*
Chalmers Charles	(32)	Spr	663 Artisan Works Coy RE (Pf)	1913126*
Chapman Ernest Arthur	(20)	Gnr	158 Bty 53 AA Regt RA (Bern)	879727*
Chapman Gordon Henry L.	(26)	Gnr	158 Bty 53 HAA Regt RA (St Trojan)	2566837*
Chapman William John	(33)	Pte	1 Bn KOSB (Noirmoutier-en-l'Ile)	3183606*
Cheetham Wilfred	(23)	Spr	116 Road Constr Coy RE (L'H)	2189387*
Chipchase John	(33)	Sgt	1 Base Sply Depot RASC (St Trojan)	S/74207*
Clark Herbert	(40)	Pte	AMPC (La Turballe)	13005747*
Clarke Eric William Herbert	(21)	Dvr	12 Armd Persnl Bde RASC (St Sever)	T/77052
Clarke George	(52)	Pte	AMPC (L'Epine)	13002051*
Clarke Harold Edwin	(24)	Pte	1 Base Ord Depot RAOC (Prefailles)	7624737*
Clarke Herbert Henry	(39)	Pte	1 Bn East Surrey Regt (Prefailles)	6448515*
Coats William John	(31)	Spr	116 Road Constr Coy RE (St Denis)	1882256*
Cogger Louis	(37)	Pte	AMPC (Prefailles)	13001140*
Conn-Hall William	(30)	Pte	AMPC (L'Epine)	102591*
Corbett Francis	(21)	Pte	1 Base Ordnance Depot RAOC (M)	7616539*
Crawford William	(36)	Pte	AMPC (Les Moutiers-en-Retz)	13003568*
Cunningham James Dennis	(41)	Pte	AMPC (La Bernerie-en-Retz)	13006008*
Cyples Lawrence	(37)	Sgt	RASC (St Georges d'Oleron)	S/5041642*
Davies Leslie	(21)	Pte	3 Div Supply Col RASC (L'Epine)	S/97270*
Davison John William	(47)	Pte	AMPC (La Bernerie-en-Retz)	1043424*
Denison Frederick Charles	(29)	Dvr	RASC (Prefailles)	T/158277*
Derbyshire Joe	(36)	Cpl	AMPC (Ars-en-Ré)	2188599*
Derham Leslie Gordon	(20)	Pte	1 Base Sply Depot RASC (Prefailles)	S/165631*
Derrick Alfred	(39)	L/Cpl	Royal Engineers (Bern)	3949440*
Dick Duncan	(?)	Spr	159 Rly Constr Coy RE (N-e-L)	1899133*
Dixon George Iley	(38)	Gnr	RA attd HQ 12 AA Bgd (Les Portes)	3703664*
Douglas William James	(23)	L/Cpl	RAOC attd RE (Ars-en-Ré)	7611733*
Dowse Albert James	(40)	Spr	159 Rly Constr Coy RE (Bern)	1854359*

Doyle Martin	(37)	Cpl	AMPC (La Couarde-sur-Mer)	102338*
Doyle William Austin	(34)	Cpl	3 L of C Postal Sec RE (L'Epine)	3522745*
Duck Leslie George	(25)	L/Cpl	1 Base Supply Depot RASC (M)	S/54234*
Dudman Eric Arthur Clifford	(27)	Tpr	12 Royal Lancers RAC (M)	318806*
Duffy Joseph	(28)	Spr	663 Arts'n Works Coy RE (St Denis)	1918081*
Dunning Thomas Nesbet	(25)	L/Cpl	4 Heavy Repair Shop RASC (N)	T/71154*
Dunnington Albert	(39)	Pte	AMPC (Le Clion-sur-Mer)	13005355*
Duquemin Cyril	(23)	Spr	663 Artisan Works Coy RE (Bern)	1903478*
Dyas Leonard William	(33)	Sgt	RASC (Ste Marie-de-Re)	T/33717*
Easom James	(?)	Cpl	AMPC (L'Epine)	5042446*
Eddy Harold Weir	(23)	Pte	1 Base Ord Depot RAOC (N-e-L)	7607390*
Edgeworth Thomas William	(44)	Tpr	12 Royal Lancers RAC (La Plaine)	310772*
Edmondson Thomas Henry	(43)	Pte	AMPC (St Georges d'Oleron)	13005275*
Edwards Albert Henry	(29)	Dvr	RASC (Ars-en-Ré)	T/45585*
Edwards Sidney George	(25)	Pte	RASC (Prefailles)	147447*
Elsdon John James	(37)	Pte	AMPC (La Bernerie-en-Retz)	4337743*
Evans William Henry	(33)	Spr	663 Artisan Works Coy RE (Pf)	1903432
Everett Sidney Herbert	(26)	Pte	QORWK Regt attd AMPC (Bern)	6200532*
Farrar George	(37)	Pte	AMPC (La Bernerie-en-Retz)	13006680*
Fenwick Arthur	(35)	Cpl	116 Road Constr Coy RE (L'H)	2187338*
Fichou Albert Alfred	(30)	Pte	AMPC (L'Epine)	2185530*
Filmer Albert William	(20)	Spr	663 Artisan Works Coy RE (La Bar)	1903520*
Findlay Richard Frederick H.	(22)	Pte	2 Res MT Coy RASC (N-e-L)	63904*
Fleming George	(23)	Spr	663 Artisan Works Coy RE (Pf)	1918047*
Fletcher Frederick Edward	(20)	L/Cpl	159 Rly Constr Coy RE (La Plaine)	1892938*
Foulds Goerge Henry	(40)	Pte	AMPC (Le Clion-sur-Mer)	13005214*
Fowler George	(39)	Pte	AMPC (Olonne-sur-Mer)	13005091*
Frudd Gilbert	(45)	Pte	AMPC (Le Clion-sur-Mer)	13005898*
Gannon Thomas	(34)	Pte	AMPC (Olonne-sur-Mer)	102376*
Garrett Albert Henry	(25)	Sgt	RASC (Prefailles)	94087*
Gibbs Leonard	(24)	Spr	663 Artisan Works Coy RE (Pf)	1904515*
Gibson Robert Henry	(44)	Pte	AMPC (La Bernerie-en-Retz)	13004998*
Gill James	(41)	Pte	AMPC (La Bernerie-en-Retz)	13006666*
Godfrey James Frank	(45)	Pte	AMPC (La Bernerie-en-Retz)	13004210*
Goldie Peter	(42)	Pte	AMPC (La Bernerie-en-Retz)	3123462*
Gompertz Arthur George	(37)	Pte	RASC (Dolus d'Oleron)	T/63358*
Goodwin Thomas	(33)	Cpl	1/5 Bn N&D Regt (Bern)	4968706*
Graham Alexander Thomas	(25)	Pte	RASC (La Bernerie-en-Retz)	S/109062*
Graham William	(41)	Pte	RASC (St Marie)	T/58085*
Graves Harold Ernest	(27)	Pte	2 Field Bakery RASC (Le Clion)	S/158018*
Green William	(41)	Pte	AMPC (La Couarde-sur-Mer)	13001829*
Greenfield Phillip William	(22)	Pte	2 Bn Buffs (Prefailles)	6289187*
Greenfield Silas Anthony	(20)	Pte	1 Base Supply Depot RASC (M)	S/128803*
Gregory Geoffrey Frank	(22)	Pte	2 Bn Buffs (Le Clion-sur-Mer)	6466573*
Grice James	(21)	Pte	2 Field Bakery RASC (Le Clion)	S/97531*
Griffiths Harold Edward	(23)	Spr	RE (St Hilaire-de-Riez)	1898735*
Griggs Roy	(23)	Pte	RAPC (Prefailles)	7667695*
Grimmett Alfred Arthur	(?)	Cpl	AMPC (Les Moutiers-en-Retz)	2306160*
Hadley George	(38)	Pte	AMPC (Barbâtre)	2188513*
Haigh William Alfred	(24)	Spr	663 Artisan Works Coy RE (L)	1910375*

Haines Walter Frederick	(37)	L/Cpl	RASC (Prefailles)	T/60452*
Hall Edwin	(34)	Pte	AMPC (La Bernerie-en-Retz)	2188407*
Hall Kenneth Victor	(22)	Gnr	158 Bty 53 HAA Regt RA (M)	1490818*
Hamper Thomas George	(35)	Spr	663 Artisan Works Coy RE (Bern)	1914224*
Hanson Cuthbert Dennis	(23)	Pte	1 Base Ord Dep RAOC (Prefailles)	7623949*
Harker Henry Austin	(27)	Sgt	Army Educational Corps (M)	7720882*
Harris Gerald Egerton	(23)	Pte	RASC (La Bernerie-en-Retz)	S/158344
Harris John Thomas	(54)	Pte	AMPC (La Bernerie-en-Retz)	13005503*
Harrison Sidney	(41)	Pte	RASC (Prefailles)	147815*
Harrop William	(42)	Pte	AMPC (La Bernerie-en-Retz)	13005648*
Hart Silvester Benjamin	(34)	L/Cpl	663 Artisan Works Coy RE (Bern)	1911276*
Hathway Ronald	(?)	Spr	159 Rly Constr Coy RE (N-e-L)	1892998*
Hayes William	(38)	Pte	AMPC (La Bernerie-en-Retz)	13002457*
Headland Frank	(26)	Pte	RASC (L'Herbaudiere)	S/147864*
Hemingway Robert	(21)	Pte	RAPC (La Bernerie-en-Retz)	7662918*
Hennah John Charles	(41)	Spr	663 Artisan Works Coy RE (Pf)	1904268*
Herman Frederick Jeffrey J.	(21)	Dvr	Royal Engineers (St Trojan)	1884175*
Heron Charles	(25)	Spr	663 Artisan Works Coy RE (P-s-M)	1913129*
Hewitt William	(48)	Pte	AMPC (La Turballe)	13005340*
Hickman Ronald Edward	(21)	Gnr	157 Bty 53 HAA Regt RA (La Bar)	1490842*
Hill Cecil William Joseph	(33)	Tpr	Royal Armoured Corps (St Trojan)	7897002*
Hissey William George R.	(34)	Pte	AMPC (St Georges d'Oleron)	13006799*
Holland Clifford	(27)	Sigmn	2 Air Formation SigsR Sigs (Dolus)	2587556*
Holmes Edward James	(43)	Pte	RASC (Prefailles)	S/94990*
Holroyd Gordon	(?)	Pte	9 Bn N&D Regt (St Marie) 4977771*	
Holt Edward Henry	(22)	Pte	1 Bn N&D Regt (La Plaine)	4977724*
Hopewell Harold	(19)	L/Cpl	N&D Regt (Le Clion-sur-Mer)	4976196*
Hopkins George William	(40)	Cpl	2 Field Bakery RASC (Bern)	S/5876*
Howard Eric	(35)	Pte	AMPC (St Gilles-sur-Vie)	13004957*
Howard Thomas	(29)	Spr	663 Artisan Works Coy RE (C)	1902521*
Hudson George	(38)	Spr	116 Road Constr Coy RE (L'H)	2189411*
Hughes Thomas Henry	(32)	Gnr	204 Bty 51 Anti-Tank Regt RA (Bern)	786739*
Hunt Henry	(36)	Spr	663 Artisan Works Coy RE (M)	1917049*
Hunt Lewis Vincent	(21)	Pte	17 Field Bakery RASC (Pf)	S/114695*
Hunter George	(21)	Gnr	158 Bty 53 AA Regt RA (Bern)	1490859*
Hurley Reginald	(31)	Pte	1 Base Supply Depot RASC (C)	S/830657*
Hurst Edward Charles	(35)	Tpr	Royal Armoured Corps (Le Clion)	7903384*
Ingham Harold	(31)	Pte	AMPC (L'Epine)	2188321*
Ingram Alfred Frederick J.	(23)	Pte	2 Field Bakery RASC (Dolus)	S/161335*
Ings Kenneth Sydney	(23)	Pte	AMPC (La Bernerie-en-Retz)	13002886*
Ireton Henry Arthur	(34)	Spr	663 Artisan Works Coy RE (Pf)	1902675*
Isger Reginald Frederick	(21)	Pte	RASC (Beauvoir-sur-Mer)	T/98927*
Jackson Albert Edward	(49)	Cpl	AMPC (St Marie)	13005617*
Jackson Stanley	(36)	Pte	AMPC (Le Clion-sur-Mer)	13005372*
James Horace	(34)	Pte	C Regt attd AMPC (Bern)	4189138*
Johnson Thomas Taylor	(25)	Sgt	N&D Regt (Bern)	4970786*
Johnson Wilfred Edmund	(21)	Pte	1 Base Supply Depot RASC (L)	S/98267*
Johnston Walter	(24)	Pte	1 Base Ord Dep RAOC (St Trojan)	7603652*
Johnstone George Frank	(35)	Pte	1 Base Sply Depot RASC (Prefailles)	T/58405*
Jones David Meirion	(34)	Sgt	RAOC (Le-Bois-Plage-en-Re)	T/4186951*

Jones John	(26)	Sigmn	2 Air Form Sigs R Sigs (St Trojan)	2587568*
Jones James Henry	(29)	Spr	159 Rly Constr Coy RE (St C)	5333719*
Jones James Lloyd	(57)	Pte	AMPC (St Gilles-sur-Vie)	7605729*
Jones Lewis Ernest Hugh	(21)	Pte	RASC (Le Clion-sur-Mer)	98945*
Jump Joseph	(21)	Sgt	1 Base Ord Dep RAOC (Le-Bois-Plage)	
				7613310*
Kelly James	(47)	Pte	AMPC (La Bernerie-en-Retz)	13001552*
Kennard Francis Leslie	(27)	Dvr	12 AA Bde RASC (N-e-L)	T/72226*
Kennedy Harry	(24)	Pte	AMPC (L'Herbaudiere)	2184605*
Kennedy Robert Brown	(41)	Pte	AMPC (Prefailles)	13005264*
Kent Edgar William	(24)	Pte	1 Base Ord Dep RAOC (Aytré)	7624270*
Kerry John Clifford	(27)	Cpl	RASC (Bouin)	S/54127*
Kershaw Harold	(36)	Pte	AMPC (Noirmoutier-en-L'ile)	13005102*
Kesson Edward	(41)	L/Cpl	AMPC (L'Herbaudiere)	3237769*
Kinch Sidney Joseph	(35)	Gnr	158 Bty 53 HAA Regt RA (N-e-L)	1451993*
King John Frederick	(23)	Pte	1 Base Ord Dep RAOC (L'H)	7623981*
Kingsman George Richard	(20)	Spr	663 Artisan Works Coy RE (St M)	1914308*
Kirkham Walter Morris	(41)	Lt	RASC dra 6.7.40 (Le Bernerie-en-Retz)	113813
Lansley Cyril	(22)	Cpl	RASC (Les Moutiers-en-Retz)	94240*
Lardant John William	(35)	Pte	AMPC (Le Clion-sur-Mer)	13002251*
Lazenby Alfred	(34)	Spr	116 Road Constr Coy RE (M)	4530328*
Lea Sydney	(28)	Spr	663 Artisan Works Coy RE (St M)	1912429*
Leckenby Charles	(37)	Pte	AMPC (Prefailles)	13005233*
Leslie Leonard George	(39)	Pte	AMPC (St Marie)	6195176*
Lewis Horace	(23)	Spr	663 Artisan Works Coy RE (Bern)	1913204*
Lillico William	(27)	Pte	1 Base Ord Depot RAOC (Soulac)	7594242
Lloyd Alfred Douglas	(44)	Lt (QM)	RASC (Ars-en-Ré)	118257*
Lowther Charles	(42)	L/Cpl	AMPC (La Bernerie-en-Retz)	13005051*
MacDonald–Malekin Robert	(24)	Pte	2 Bn Buffs (L'Herbaudiere)	6289068*
Manley Patrick	(45)	CQMS	2 Bn B & H Regt (Brest)	7143482
Manning Ernest George	(31)	Cpr	1 Base Sply Depot RASC (Prefailles)	S/54140*
Marl William Roberts	(38)	Pte	AMPC (Le Clion-sur-Mer)	13002341*
Martin Clarence Eric	(21)	Pte	1/5 Bn N&D Regt (Les Moutiers)	4978633*
McArdle Patrick	(21)	Spr	159 Rly Constr Coy RE (M)	1901802*
McDougall Harry	(42)	Pte	AMPC (St Hilaire-de-Riez)	2744825*
McFeggan William James	(49)	Pte	AMPC (Barbâtre)	13005420*
McGuire Henry James S.	(38)	Pte	AMPC (St Hilaire-de-Riez)	2188489*
McIntyre Archibald Burgess	(23)	Spr	663 Artisan Works Coy RE (M)	1913130*
McMahon Patrick	(37)	Cpl	AMPC (St Gilles-sur-Vie)	13000284*
McMurray Thomas Alexander	(25)	Pte	RASC (La Bernerie-en-Retz)	105151*
McVie George	(27)	Pte	RASC (Les Moutiers-en-Retz)	T/70305*
Meddle John Thomas	(21)	Pte	2 Field Bakery RASC (La Plaine)	S/98256*
Mendham John Graham	(36)	Pte	AMPC (Les Moutiers-en-Retz)	13005734*
Metcalfe Ninion	(40)	Pte	AMPC (Le Clion-sur-Mer)	13003767*
Moore Sydney Ernest	(20)	Pte	1 Base Supply Depot RASC (L)	S/57306*
Morgan David John	(25)	Pte	RASC (L'Epine)	S/147721*
Morgan George James	(20)	Pte	RAPC (La Bernerie-en-Retz)	7663824*
Morgan Thomas	(47)	Pte	AMPC (St Clément-les-Baleines)	13003454*
Morris Arthur Leonard	(25)	Pte	RASC (Prefailles)	147519*
Morris William	(25)	Sgt	EY Regt attd AMPC (Bern)	4342155*

Munnerley Charles	(26)	Pte	1 Base Supply Depot RASC (Pf)	T/127367*
Naylor Donald Ernest	(30)	Dvr	RASC (Les Moutiers-en-Retz)	T/67674*
Neil Robert Henry	(38)	Pte	AMPC (La Bernerie-en-Retz)	2188754*
Newby George	(38)	Sgt	1/6 Bn Lancashire Fusiliers (Pf)	3440142*
Newman Kenneth Arthur	(21)	Gnr	158 Bty 53 HAA Regt RA (Pf)	1490973*
Novis Joseph	(32)	Cpl	RASC (Prefailles)	S/148584*
Nutton Allan Edward	(26)	Dvr	2 Res MT Coy RASC (St Marie)	71268*
Oare Alfred	(26)	Pte	AMPC (St Georges d'Oleron)	2188517*
O'Dowd Michael	(37)	Pte	AMPC (La Bernerie-en-Retz)	13001505*
O'Neil John	(25)	Spr	159 Rly Constr Coy RE (Bern)	1899072*
Oram Thomas Henry	(45)	Pte	AMPC (Les Moutiers-en-Retz)	4848875*
Orme Thomas	(26)	Spr	663 Artisan Works Coy RE (St M)	1913322*
Palmer Sidney Eric	(33)	Pte	AMPC (St Georges d'Oleron)	13000992*
Parker Harold Vincent	(26)	Pte	RAOC (Le Clion-sur-Mer)	7586402*
Parry Noel	(23)	Pte	1 Base Sply Depot RASC (Soulac)	T/109755
Parry Samuel Henry	(25)	Pte	1/5 Bn N&D Regt (Prefailles)	4975823*
Parsons Victor Roye	(20)	Pte	2 Field Bakery RASC (Olonne)	S/934505*
Pates Ronald Charles	(25)	Pte	RASC (Les Moutiers-en-Retz)	T/153057*
Payne Ernest Edwin	(20)	Pte	4 Bn Buffs (L'Herbaudiere)	6286788*
Pennington Arnold	(21)	Dvr	RASC (La Bernerie-en-Retz)	T/114027*
Phillips Reginald John	(25)	Pte	1 Base Ord Depot RAOC (N-e-L)	7594090*
Pickstock George	(26)	Pte	1 Gen Base Depot RAOC (N-e-L)	7620739*
Pilgrim Ernest Edward	(28)	Sgt	RASC (Noirmoutier-en-L'ile)	S/147854*
Pinchon Edward Victor (*served* as Young George) (39)			RASC (St Marie)	S/147042*
Pope Francis	(38)	Pte	AMPC (Noirmoutier-en-L'ile)	13001749*
Porter Joseph Henry	(37)	Pte	AMPC (St Marie)	13005198*
Powell Robert William	(?)	Sgt	AMPC (La Bernerie-en-Retz)	13002346*
Price Trevor Glyn	(21)	Pte	RASC (L'Herbaudiere)	S/97605*
Priddey Peter Basil	(21)	Sgt	1 Base Ord Dep RAOC (St Marie)	7591313*
Prosser Norman James	(21)	Pte	2 Bn Buffs (Prefailles)	6289212*
Quarmby Harry	(32)	Pte	1/5 Bn N&D Regt (Angoulins)	4743839*
Randall Cyril William	(23)	Tpr	44 Royal Tank Regt RAC (Bern)	5184487*
Raper George C. (C de G)	(48)	Sgt	RAPC (Pf) (MID in 1914–18 War)	386297*
Ratcliffe Ernest	(28)	Tpr	(Oldham) Royal Tank Regt RAC (N-e-L) 3525216*
Read Harry William	(39)	Dvr	2 Res MT Coy RASC (Les Moutiers)	T/63985*
Reader Christopher	(21)	Spr	190 Rly Op Coy RE (Bretignolles)	1898252*
Reed Arthur James	(38)	Pte	RASC (Bouin)	105370*
Reese George Edward	(21)	Tpr	Royal Armoured Corps (M)	7905391*
Renner William Maxwell	(23)	Pte	RASC (Le Clion-sur-Mer)	94242*
Reynolds Ernest	(37)	Pte	AMPC (La Bernerie-en-Retz)	13004976*
Richardson Andrew T.	(27)	Pte	RASC (Beauvoir-sur-Mer)	S/90419*
Roberts Charles Henry	(40)	Cpl	AMPC (Prefailles)	13001510*
Robinson Charles William	(43)	Pte	AMPC (Les Moutiers-en-Retz)	13005235*
Rodger William John	(21)	Dvr	6 Res MT RASC (Bern)	121658*
Rudd Bernard George	(?)	Gnr	158 Bty 53 HAA Regt RA (Le Clion)	1491042*
Rushton Thomas	(32)	Pte	AMPC (La Bernerie-en-Retz)	101436*
Sales Joseph William	(22)	Gnr	158 Bty 53 HAA Regt RA (L'H)	1491047*
Savin Ernest James	(45)	WO	II (SSM) 4/7 Ryl Drgn Gds RAC (Bern) 389781*

Sawyer Henry John	(30)	Pte	2 Base Ordnance Depot RAOC (C)	7586299*
Scott Charles Herbert	(28)	Cpl	RASC (Prefailles)	S/94027*
Scougall Joseph	(39)	Pte	AMPC (St Marie)	13009067*
Shannon William John	(36)	Spr	663 Artisan Works Coy RE (Bern)	2207307*
Shepherd William Charles	(22)	Spr	116 Road Constr Coy RE (Le Clion)	1882257*
Shuker Stan Francis	(20)	Fus	RWF attd AMPC (Bern)	4195662*
Siberry Thomas Henry	(34)	Dvr	116 Rly Constr Coy RE (Bern)	2183819*
Silver Ronald Arthur	(24)	Spr	663 Artisan Works Coy RE (Pf)	1911263*
Silvey George Albert	(?)	Spr	663 Artisan Works Coy RE (C)	1917064*
Smedley Ernest	(21)	Pte	N&D Regt (Noirmoutier-en-L'ile)	4978595*
Smith Arthur	(32)	Pte	2 Field Bakery RASC (La Plaine)	S/93011*
Smith Charles Kenneth	(21)	Pte	2 Bn Buffs (Les Moutiers-en-Retz)	6289225*
Smith Douglas	(23)	Pte	159 Rly Constr Coy RE (La Plaine)	1907459*
Smith Duglass Frank	(21)	Dvr	RE (Château-d'Olonne)	1884207*
Smith George Henry	(44)	Cpl	AMPC (La Barre-de-Monts)	7813684*
Smith George Joseph	(36)	Pte	AMPC (St Marie)	13002752*
Smith James	(38)	Pte	AMPC (Le Clion-sur-Mer)	13005236*
Smith John	(48)	Pte	AMPC (La Bernerie-en-Retz)	13001774*
Smith Joshua	(28)	Pte	AMPC (St Hilaire-de-Riez)	2196053*
Smith Walter James	(21)	Dvr	1 Heavy Repair Shop RASC (Triaize)	T/104370*
Spooner John Frederick	(22)	Gnr	157 Bty 53 HAA Regt RA (Pf)	1491085*
Stafford John Henry	(42)	Pte	1 Base Ord Depot RAOC (St Marie)	50441*
Stead Arthur	(45)	Pte	AMPC (L'Epine)	13001992*
Stewart William	(20)	Pte	RASC (La Bernerie-en-Retz)	T/136019*
Street Robert Henry	(20)	Dvr	RASC (Beauvoir-sur-Mer)	T/161023*
Sturgess Thomas Ralph	(31)	Cpl	12 Royal Lancers RAC (Prefailles)	310811*
Sullivan William	(36)	Pte	AMPC (St Marie-de-Re)	101732*
Sutton Cyril Thomas	(30)	Pte	RASC (Prefailles)	S/10516*
Swinn George Henry	(35)	L/Sgt	1 Armd Div Workshops RAOC (Brest)	4968434
Tate Joseph Herbert	(20)	L/Cpl	RASC (L'Aiguillon-sur-Mer)	T/3770619*
Tate Thomas Thompson A.	(?)	Pte	AMPC (Prefailles)	13002832*
Taylor Geoffrey Bavin	(29)	Pte	1 Base Ord Dep RAOC (Ars-en-Ré)	7593554*
Taylor Harold	(?)	Spr	159 Rly Constr Coy RE (Bern)	1899147*
Taylor Thomas	(27)	Pte	AMPC (Le-Bois-Plage-en-Re)	2188408*
Thomas Brinley Clifford	(42)	Spr	154 Rly Operating Coy RE (Pf)	1927008*
Thomas Percy Reginald	(20)	Pte	1 Base Ordnance Depot RAOC (Pf)	7593462*
Thomason Peter	(44)	Sgt	AMPC (Château-d'Olonne)	13002487*
Thompson James	(40)	Pte	RASC (L'Herbaudiere)	17027*
Thompson Joseph	(47)	Pte	AMPC (St Denis-d'Oleron)	13004983*
Thornton James	(25)	Spr	159 Rly Constr Coy RE (Bern)	1899075*
Tonkin Richard George	(24)	Spr	116 Road Constr Coy RE (L'H)	1882243*
Towell Harold	(43)	Spr	663 Artisan Works Coy RE (C)	1007874*
Traviss George	(45)	Pte	AMPC (Prefailles)	13002817*
Tunstall Thomas	(29)	Pte	AMPC (Prefailles)	7605537*
Turner Frank Eardley	(40)	2/Lt	663 Artisan Works Coy RE (M)	115439*
Unsworth Walter (MID)	(45)	Sgt	663 Artisan Works Coy RE (Bern)	1902520*
Viall John Arthur	(46)	Cpl	AMPC (La Plaine)	13000932*
Walker George T.	(48)	Pte	AMPC (Les Moutiers-en-Retz)	13001523*
Wallace John Harry	(20)	Spr	159 Rly Operating Coy RE (M)	1906567*
Walsh Leonard	(40)	Pte	AMPC (La Barre-de-Monts)	13005519*

Warboys Horace	(28)	Spr	156 Transportation Coy RE (Bern)	1987197*
Wardle Philip Sidney	(21)	Pte	2 Bn Buffs (La Bernerie-en-Retz)	6289230
Watson George	(47)	Pte	AMPC (Les Moutiers-en-Retz)	13000409*
Watts Jack	(21)	Pte	Buffs (Le-Bois-Plage-en-Re)	6289267*
Whailing John	(47)	Sgt	AMPC (Château-d'Olonne)	13005166*
White Harold Mathew	(43)	Pte	RASC (Dolus d'Oleron)	S/5721218*
White Thomas Edward	(36)	Pte	AMPC (St Nazaire-sur-Charente)	13005164*
Whitehouse Claude	(40)	Cpl	AMPC (Châtelaillon-Plage)	13002422*
Wickert Christian Ronald	(20)	Spr	159 Rly Constr Coy RE (L'H)	1901792*
Wilkin Eric Cecil	(28)	Spr	663 Artisan Works Coy RE (St M)	1912465*
Wilkins William George	(24)	Cpl	RASC (L'Herbaudiere)	S/94105*
Williams Harold	(22)	Pte	5 Base Supply Depot RASC (Bern)	S/135979*
Williams Harold	(26)	Sgt	1 Base Ord Depot RAOC (Bern)	7594416*
Williams William Edward	(38)	Pte	AMPC (Les Moutiers-en-Retz)	2188686*
Williams William George	(21)	Pte	2 Bn Buffs (La Barre-de-Monts)	6289193*
Wilson Henry	(47)	Pte	AMPC (Le Clion-sur-Mer)	2188847*
Wilson James	(45)	Pte	AMPC (Les Moutiers-en-Retz)	13002815*
Winstanley William V.	(35)	Pte	AMPC (Le Clion-sur-Mer)	2188605*
Wood Arthur Reginald	(40)	Cpl	AMPC (Les Moutiers-en-Retz)	13003439*
Wood Frederick	(21)	Tpr	Royal Armoured Corps (Bern)	7902156*
Woods Charles Albert	(39)	Pte	RASC (St Marie)	S/147603*
Worrall John Hewitt	(39)	Pte	RASC (Yves)	S/105368*
Wright Douglas	(24)	Spr	116 Road Constr Coy RE (Le Clion)	2189406*
Wright George Herbert	(30)	Dvr	116 Road Constr Coy RE (N-e-L)	2189389*
Yates Albert Henry	(25)	Spr	1 Artisan Works Coy RE (M)	1903296*
Young Arthur	(29)	Pte	1 Base Supply Depot RASC (Bern)	S/6344381*

Young George (for details *see* Pinchon E.V. Re. S 147603)

Total lost: 362

ARMY PERSONNEL BURIED IN FRANCE, HAVING BEEN WASHED ASHORE. THOSE LISTED BELOW ARE NOT RECORDED AS BEING ON BOARD HMT *LANCASTRIA* BUT THE DATE, 17 JUNE 1940, IS RECORDED

Applicable codes used for War Cemeteries, after Regiment details, are as follows:
(E) = Escoublac–La–Baule. (P) = Pornic.

Adams Henry John	(31)	Spr	663 Artisan Works Coy RE (Pornic)	1913367
Apetu-Larty Augustus	(43)	Pte	73 Coy AMPC (Escoublac-La-Baule)	13005225
Ashworth Royal	(39)	Pte	73 Coy AMPC (Pornic)	13007657
Auty Lawrence	(21)	Pte	1 Base Supply Depot RASC (P)	S/112888
Axcell Benjamin	(35)	Pte	AMPC (Escoublac-La-Baule)	2188527
Barnaby Arthur Edward	(51)	Pte	50 Coy AMPC (Pornic)	3701642
Barron William Frederick	(23)	Spr	663 Artisan Works Coy RE (Pornic)	1903464
Beever Percy	(39)	Pte	73 Coy AMPC (Pornic)	13005168
Bell Sidney	(29)	Pte	1 Base Ord Depot RAOC (Pornic)	7610715
Beney William George	(28)	Spr	1 Docks Group RE (Pornic)	1984548
Bidgood Thomas	(49)	Pte	AMPC (Pornic)	13003785

Bingham Ronald	(30)	Pte	73 Coy AMPC (Escoublac-La-Baule)	101269
Bishop William Robert	(48)	Pte	53 Coy AMPC (Pornic)	13000444
Bourn George Thomas	(23)	Pte	73 Coy AMPC (Pornic)	13005833
Bowles William (MC)	(51)	Capt	Royal Engineers (Pornic)	120002
Bradford Albert John	(44)	Pte	50 Coy AMPC (Pornic)	13001137
Bray Leslie Percy	(39)	Dvr	RASC (Pornic)	T/16921
Brewis Forster Anderson	(25)	Cpl	RASC (Pornic)	S/147960
Briggs Joseph	(27)	Pte	73 Coy AMPC (Pornic)	1452391
Brook Stanley	(32)	Pte	73 Coy AMPC (Escoublac-La-Baule)	13004948
Butcher Charles Henry	(41)	Cpl	67 Coy AMPC (Escoublac-La-Baule)	13003637
Button George Thomas	(20)	Pte	4 Bn Buffs (Escoublac-La-Baule)	6288041
Cameron-Waller Arthur E.	(31)	L/Cpl	1 Base Supply Depot RASC (Pornic)	S/52890
Cannell Horace Frederick H.	(40)	Spr	663 Artisan Works Coy RE (Pornic)	1914062
Cannon Frederick Thomas C.	(37)	L/Sgt	RAPC (Pornic)	5172653
Carr Thomas	(36)	L/Cpl	73 Coy AMPC (Pornic)	13005181
Carver Charles F.K.	(28)	Tpr	2 General Base Depot RAC (E)	4268313*
Chambers John Alfred	(22)	Spr	159 Rly Constr Coy RE (E)	1891908
Chapman Henry John	(36)	Pte	73 Coy AMPC (Escoublac-La-Baule)	13005966
Clark John	(39)	Pte	53 Coy AMPC (Pornic)	13001820
Colquitt James Richard	(?)	Cpl	663 Artisan Works Coy RE (Pornic)	1918148
Cooke Robert Charles	(32)	Pte	RASC (Escoublac-la-baule)	S/94318
Cooper Richard	(19)	Pte	7 Bn A&S Highlanders (E)	2984114
Cope Arthur	(40)	Cpl	73 Coy AMPC (Escoublac-La-Baule)	1001001
Copsey Frederick	(28)	Spr	663 Artisan Works Coy RE (Pornic)	1918032
Cowin Percy	(38)	Spr	663 Artisan Works Coy RE (Pornic)	1904286
Danks Edward John	(24)	Cpl	RASC (Pornic)	105081
Davis Goodwin Julian (MID)	(52)	Capt	RAOC (Pornic)	120327
Dawson Norman	(23)	Pte	2 Field Bakery RASC (Pornic)	S/162752
Deacon Arthur	(23)	Spr	159 Rly Constr Coy RE (E)	1899035
Delaney Robert	(37)	Pte	39 Coy AMPC (Pornic)	13000110
Diamond Thomas George	(44)	Sgt	10 Royal Hussars RAC (Pornic)	6600
Doherty William Jackson	(19)	Spr	116 Road Constr Coy RE (E)	1917143
Doughty Jack	(21)	Pte	N&D Regt (Escoublac-La-Baule)	497894
Downes Claude Cyril M.	(20)	Pte	RASC (Escoublac-La-Baule)	S/133108
Doyle Frederick	(30)	Cpl	RASC (Escoublac-La-Baule)	T/94304
Draper Frederick	(24)	Spr	116 Rly Constr Coy RE (Pornic)	1882316
Duncan David Alexander	(29)	Pte	75 Coy AMPC (Pornic)	2191368
Dunn John	(36)	Pte	53 Coy AMPC (Pornic)	13002830
Dunstall Cyril George	(35)	Cpl	RAPC (Pornic)	7258100
Dyer Eric	(22)	Sigmn	2 Air Form Sigs R Sigs (Pornic)	2587086
Easterbrook Walter H.	(42)	Pte	AMPC (Escoublac-La-Baule)	1023063
Edwards Douglas Malcolm	(26)	Pte	RASC (Escoublac-La-Baule)	147926
Escreet William	(46)	Pte	75 Coy AMPC (Pornic)	1012280
Essen Charles Arthur	(20)	Spr	159 Rly Constr Coy RE (Pornic)	5382598
Etheridge James	(21)	Spr	159 Rly Constr Coy RE (E)	3132238
Evans David Emelyn	(21)	Pte	2 Field Bakery RASC (Pornic)	S/98705
Evans John	(37)	Pte	50 Coy AMPC (Pornic)	13002056
Farrall Arthur	(23)	Spr	Royal Engineers (Pornic)	1898823
Farrar Edward	(37)	Pte	115 Coy AMPC (Pornic)	2182004
Farrell Donald	(?)	Pte	RASC (Pornic)	147431

Fielding Walter	(20) Spr	159 Rly Constr Coy RE (Pornic)	1891796
Firkins Harry	(48) Pte	50 Coy AMPC (Pornic)	13004019
Forde Robert	(20) Pte	AMPC (Pornic)	7606888
Gaskell George	(60) Cpl	AMPC (Pornic)	13002431
Gellatly Samuel	(32) Pte	46 Coy AMPC (Pornic)	2188300
Gigg Arthur George	(34) Pte	QORWK attd AMPC (E)	6196256
Gillies Walter	(40) Pte	AMPC (Pornic)	13005262
Ginns Joseph Edwin	(22) Spr	159 Rly Constr Coy RE (Pornic)	1889874
Golby Gerald Herbert	(22) Pte	RAPC (Pornic)	7663694
Gorman Michael	(35) Pte	73 Coy AMPC (Pornic)	4529713
Gorman Trevor	(23) Cpl	1 Base Supply Depot RASC (Pornic)	S/7604551
Goudy Francis Gerard	(28) L/Cpl	663 Artisan Works Coy RE (E)	1881687
Gowers Maurice	(28) Pte	Essex Regt attd AMPC (E)	6009238
Griffiths Charles	(21) Pte	N&D Regt (Pornic)	4978379
Hailstone Joseph George	(38) Spr	29 Rly Survey Coy RE (Pornic)	1848828
Hanley Martin	(43) Pte	73 Coy AMPC (Pornic)	13005215
Hare Ernest Victor	(37) Pte	AMPC (Pornic)	13004621
Harrison Frederick Georges	(42) L/Cpl	73 Coy AMPC (Escoublac-La-Baule)	13005010
Hickling Joseph Walter	(35) Pte	RASC (Pornic)	S/49460
Highley Arthur Thomas	(41) Pte	75 Coy AMPC (Pornic)	3123314
Hill Thomas William	(22) Spr	159 Rly Constr Coy RE (Pornic)	1909657
Hingle Oliver	(37) WO	II (SSM) 15/19 KRH RAC (Pornic)	529839
Hireson Kenneth Ernest	(21) Gnr	158 HAA Regt RA (E)	1490846
Holland Arthur	(21) Pte	2 Field Bakery RASC (E)	S/4803846
Holliday Albert	(?) Spr	663 Artisan Works Coy RE (Pornic)	1903357
Hood John	(35) Spr	663 Artisan Works Coy RE (Pornic)	1902517
Hopper John	(36) Gnr	5 Bty 2 AA Regt RA (E)	777446
Houghton Thomas Edward	(24) Pte	AMPC (Pornic)	13001247
Howcroft Tom	(24) Spr	176 Rly Constr Coy RE (Pornic)	2189413
Humphreys George Dory	(22) Pte	5 Base Supply Depot RASC (Pornic)	136004
Hunter William	(24) Pte	RASC (Pornic)	S/54649
Hurley Cecil Edward	(43) Lt	RAMC (E) dra 16.6.40	104538
Hutchinson Philip Douglas C.	(27) Sgt	158 Bty 53 HAA Regt RA (E)	804709
Inkpen Frederick Ernest	(36) Spr	663 Artisan Works Coy RE (Pornic)	1911260
Jackson Frederick	(45) Pte	73 Coy AMPC (Escoublac-La-Baule)	13005099
Jamison Thomas Joseph	(43) Pte	RASC (Pornic)	S/147734
Jinks Robert Leslie	(21) Tpr	Royal Armoured Corps (Pornic)	7902192
Johnson Ernest Victor	(22) Dvr	Royal Engineers (Pornic)	1884182
Johnson John William	(38) Pte	N&D Regt (Escoublac-La-Baule)	4975967
Jones David Leslie	(23) L/Bdr	158 Bty 53 HAA RA (E)	1447752
Jones Ernest	(40) Cpl	1 Base Supply Depot RASC (E)	S/9333
Jones James	(50) Pte	50 Coy AMPC (Pornic)	13001000
Jones Tom W.	(21) Pte	2 Field Bakery RASC (Pornic)	S/114677
Kearney Hugh	(24) Pte	RASC (Pornic)	S/153717
Kelgy Francis	(30) Pte	RASC (Pornic)	S/105471
Kelly Daniel	(22) Pte	AMPC (Pornic)	2188572
Kenton John William C.	(43) Cpl	RASC (Pornic)	94049
Khan Peter	(35) Cpl	53 Coy AMPC (Escoublac-La-Baule)	13000584
Knowles George Frederick	(38) Pte	53 Coy AMPC (Pornic)	4380742
Langford Peter	(41) Pte	AMPC (Escoublac-La-Baule)	3233186

Laing William Robert	(41)	Cpl	AMPC (Pornic)	2867468
Ledger William	(35)	Spr	159 Rly Constr Coy RE (Pornic)	5490408
Lewis Albert	(38)	Pte	Cheshire Regt (Pornic)	4188602
Lewis David Thomas	(40)	Pte	50 Coy AMPC (Pornic)	13002060
Lewis William Trevor	(32)	Pte	1 Base Suppy Depot RASC (Pornic)	S/7604555
Liversidge Edgar	(43)	Pte	73 Coy AMPC (Pornic)	13005217
Lowe Charles Bowyer	(46)	S/Sgt	RAPC (Pornic)	7658213
McColl James Porter	(37)	Pte	73 Coy AMPC (Pornic)	13005252
McDonald John	(34)	Cpl	82 Coy AMPC (Pornic)	13006692
McIntyre Thomas	(22)	Spr	159 Rly Constr Coy RE (Pornic)	2079112
McKee James	(33)	Pte	1 Base Ord Depot RAOC (Pornic)	7593725
McKinnon Angus	(?)	Sgt	159 Rly Constr Coy RE (E)	2923178
McPhee William	(31)	Pte	12 Salvage Unit AMPC (Pornic)	13011021
McPhun Walter Samuel	(33)	WO	III (PSM) N&D Regt (Pornic)	4967178
McQuade Joseph	(40)	Pte	AMPC (Pornic)	13005220
Maloney James	(33)	Pte	2 Bn Buffs (Escoublac-La-Baule)	6285455
Maguire Thomas	(20)	Spr	663 Artisan Works Coy RE (Pornic)	1903526
Marchant Charles Frederick	(48)	Cpl	AMPC (Pornic)	13000265
Marson Luke	(?)	L/Cpl	116 Road Constr Coy RE (Pornic)	2189416
Melvin George Alfred	(41)	Pte	AMPC (Escoublac-La-Baule)	3179660
Miller Terence George	(22)	Pte	46 Coy AMPC (Pornic)	2188361
Mills George	(42)	Pte	50 Coy AMPC (Escoublac-La-Baule)	13003869
Morris Alfred David	(35)	Pte	1 Base Supply Depot RASC (E)	T/50522
Morris Hartley Kirby	(?)	Cpl	RASC (Pornic)	148152
Mouat Andrew Walker	(28)	Pte	RAOC (Pornic)	7603207
Murray James Kerr	(25)	Spr	159 Rly Constr Coy RE (E)	1899076
Newbon Charles	(25)	Pte	RASC (Escoublac-La-Baule)	S/147653
Newsham James	(24)	Spr	159 Rly Constr Coy RE (E)	1899067
Nicholls Cyril	(?)	L/Cpl	Royal Engineers (Pornic)	1894080
Nixon William	(47)	Pte	AMPC (Pornic)	13005508
Nock Roland	(36)	Pte	A&S Highlanders (Pornic)	2974230
Olley John Frederick	(38)	Bdr	159 Bty 53 AA Regt RA (Pornic)	834885
O'Loughlin John	(21)	Pte	N&D Regt (Pornic)	4978347
O'Neill William	(28)	Pte	108 Coy AMPC (E)	13004153
Orgee Percy Samuel	(40)	Sgt	Royal Armoured Corps (E)	398311
Paltridge Ambrose Maurice	(39)	Spr	156 Transportation Coy RE (P)	3514516
Parks Dennis Frederick	(26)	Dvr	RASC (Escoublac-La-Baule)	T/133468
Parry Osborne Charles	(22)	Spr	159 Rly Constr Coy RE (E)	1901404
Parsons Edward Charles Owen	(39)	Dvr	RASC (Pornic)	T/74659
Paterson Eric Roy	(21)	Pte	RAPC (Pornic)	7662453
Pattison Herbert (MM)	(51)	Cpl	AMPC (Escoublac-La-Baule)	4381206
Paton Gavin Browning	(39)	Pte	RASC (Pornic)	147707
Phillips Gervase Robert	(21)	Spr	159 Rly Constr Coy RE (E)	1891958
Pitcher Joseph	(?)	L/Cpl	Royal Engineers (Pornic)	1894169
Pond Ralph Frederick	(41)	Spr	663 Artisan Works Coy RE (Pornic)	1041271
Potton Herbert Victor	(43)	Pte	53 Coy AMPC (Escoublac-La-Baule)	13001316
Pringle John	(29)	Gnr	51 Lt AA Anti-Tank Regt RA (P)	1464847
Pugh Charles Stanley	(21)	Gnr	158 Bty 53 HAA RA (E)	1491012
Queen Andrew Sutherland	(24)	Pte	RAOC (Pornic)	2978605
Ralley James Frederick	(46)	Pte	50 Coy AMPC (Pornic)	3301428

Rawle Clifford	(22)	Spr	159 Rly Constr Coy RE (Pornic)	1892992
Reeve Charles	(33)	Cpl	663 Artisan Works Coy RE (Pornic)	1904428
Renton Edgar Joseph	(32)	Pte	46 Coy AMPC (Pornic)	2188356
Renwick David Leslie	(39)	L/Cpl	AMPC (Pornic)	13004944
Richards Edward	(26)	Fus	Royal Welch Fusiliers (Pornic)	4032408
Richardson Geoffrey	(24)	Spr	663 Artisan Works Coy RE (Pornic)	1914381
Ridley John	(25)	Pte	53 Coy AMPC (Escoublac-La-Baule)	64682
Robinson Thomas Henry	(41)	Pte	AMPC (Pornic)	13004832
Rowe Herbert Edward	(30)	Sgt	1 Base Supply Depot RASC (Pornic)	S/37833
Rowe Reginald Clifford	(26)	L/Cpl	663 Artisan Works Coy RE (E)	1902498
Rowe William	(25)	Dvr	Royal Engineers (Pornic)	1878857
Shaw Victor	(21)	Spr	663 Artisan Works Coy RE (Pornic)	3599756
Skaife Edwin	(37)	Spr	116 Road Constr Coy RE (Pornic)	2186742
Skilton Reginald Walter	(33)	Pte	AMPC (Pornic)	6138778
Slade Roland Edmund	(21)	Dvr	RASC (Pornic)	T/71115
Smith Ernest Frederick C.	(23)	Spr	Royal Engineers dra 18.6.40 (Pornic)	2199870
Smith Hector Thomas	(23)	Spr	663 Artisan Works Coy RE (Pornic)	1911362
Smith Thomas Edward	(33)	Pte	46 Coy AMPC (Escoublac-La-Baule)	2188416
Spriddle David William	(22)	Pte	RAPC (Escoublac-La-Baule)	7663512
Staniland Albert Henry C.	(24)	Spr	663 Artisan Works Coy RE (Pornic)	1918055
Stocks John	(28)	Pte	46 Coy AMPC (Pornic)	2188566
Swan William Charles	(37)	Pte	AMPC (Pornic)	2188964
Taylor John Samuel	(27)	L/Cpl	2 Field Bakery RASC (Pornic)	S/73997
Temple Thomas Turnbull	(24)	Pte	RASC (Pornic)	S/159121
Thompson Albert W.	(28)	Cpl	RASC (Pornic)	S/4912570
Thorpe Harold D.	(27)	Spr	663 Artisan Works Coy RE (E)	1902527
Toon Leon Owen	(26)	Pte	115 Coy AMPC (Pornic)	2182447
Truscott Francis Leonard	(31)	Pte	1 Base Ord Depot RAOC (Pornic)	7589108
Turpin Arthur (MM)	(43)	WO	II (CSM) AMPC (Pornic)	13002079
Tyler James Alfred	(42)	Pte	AMPC (Pornic)	13006068
Wadsworth Fred	(21)	Pte	1 Base Ord Depot RAOC (Pornic)	7593614
Walker Haydn	(28)	Pte	RAOC (Escoublac-La-Baule)	7609845
Walker Leslie	(26)	Spr	159 Rly Constr Coy RE (E)	1887585
Walters Clifford	(21)	Spr	159 Rly Constr Coy RE (Pornic)	1909662
Walters Thomas Gordon	(34)	Pte	RASC (Escoublac-La-Baule)	T/53610
Watkins Albert Thomas	(35)	Dvr	RASC (Pornic)	T/7875947
Watson Cecil Edward	(42)	Sgt	349 Bty 37 Searchlight Regt RA (E)	766990
Webb Alfred Charles	(27)	Pte	RASC (Pornic)	S/147410
Whitehead Philip	(33)	WO	II (SQMS) 1 Base Ord Depot RAOC (P)	7593922
Wilkins John	(40)	Pte	50 Coy AMPC (Pornic)	13001447
Williams Ernest George	(35)	Sgt	Royal Engineers (Pornic)	1853873
Williamson Frederick John	(25)	Pte	50 Coy AMPC (Pornic)	2190162
Wilson Francis Herbert	(34)	Pte	RAPC (Pornic)	74731
Wright John	(21)	Pte	2 Bn N&D Regt dra 6.7.40 (E)	4978392
Wyber Frederick Leonard	(44)	L/Cpl	159 Rly Constr Coy RE (Pornic)	6077834
Yielder John Railton	(22)	Sgt	11 Ord Ammn Coy RAOC (Pornic)	7612206
Zapp Victor Irving	(?)	Sgt	RASC (Pornic)	147889

<u>Total lost: 208</u>

83. One of the many graves at the Pornic Cemetery.

84. General view of the Pornic Cemetery.

MERCHANT NAVY PERSONNEL COMMEMORATED AT TOWER HILL MEMORIAL

Adams Thomas A.	(36)	Steward*
Amos Thomas	(56)	Steward*
Austin James	(48)	Steward*
Boyle Michael	(19)	Sailor*
Bradley Herbert	(43)	Sectionman*
Briscoe Norman Lord	(49)	Chief Steward*
Clarke Thomas Lonsdale	(44)	Barkeeper*
Coffey Joseph	(57)	Sectionman*
Coman William J.	(40)	Assistant Steward*
Connor Albert Michael	(23)	Sailor*
Croft Ernest James	(35)	Trimmer*
Cunningham Albert	(23)	Assistant Steward*
Darley John Frederick	(17)	Deck Boy*
Devlin Thomas	(55)	Greaser*
Dingle Robert	(30)	Porter*
Duck Edward Douglas	(25)	Steward*
Duncan James	(51)	Snr 2nd Eng Offr (King's Commendation for Bravery)*
Dunmore Herbert Richard	(53)	Waiter*
Eades John	(39)	Steward*
Fraser Alexander Irvine	(34)	Chief Master at Arms*
Frodsham Thomas Henry	(46)	Steward*
Gilbert Henry	(54)	Steward*
Green Joseph	(20)	Asst Cook*
Hawes Arthur Lawson	(63)	Able Seaman*
Hayden William	(51)	Boatswain*
Haynes James	(23)	Assistant Steward*
Hill John	(44)	Surgeon*
Hughes James	(44)	Waiter*

Illidge Harry A.	(57)	Waiter*
Imlach Jacob Cowie	(30)	Seaman*
Jackson Harry	(55)	Steward*
Kelly James Ernest	(49)	Steward*
Key Stanley Louis Frederic	(34)	Captain's Steward*
Major Robert George	(38)	Greaser*
Marshallsay Joseph	(62)	Barkeeper*
Mason John	(50)	Trimmer*
McCaw Samuel Alexander	(30)	Storekeeper*
McGorrin Owen	(55)	Cook*
Mottershead Walter	(31)	Assistant Cook*
Oliver Thomas John	(57)	Steward*
Owen Frederick	(52)	Assistant Baker*
Pearse Joseph	(51)	Chef*
Porter Cuthbert Edgar	(31)	Junior Assistant Purser*
Read Thomas Douglas	(53)	Chief Butcher*
Roberts Richard Goronwy	(54)	1st Officer*
Rogerson Arthur	(60)	Steward*
Rowe Thomas	(58)	Porter*
Ryan Edward John	(23)	Waiter*
Shepherd Fred	(36)	Dispenser*
Slater William H.	(48)	Steward*
Smith Joseph Edwin	(47)	Steward*
Snowdon John Herbert	(61)	Steward*
Stanton Patrick	(61)	Assistant Steward*
Surtees Robert	(18)	Ordinary Seaman*
Taylor Thomas	(26)	Steward*
Temby Edgar	(60)	Porter*
Tilston George Henry	(30)	Able Seaman*
Walsh Patrick J.	(33)	Fireman*
Walton Joseph	(27)	Trimmer*

<u>Total lost: 59</u>

MERCHANT NAVY PERSONNEL BURIED IN FRANCE

McDonald John	(60)	Steward (P)*
Rogers Herbert	(48)	Steward(L'A)*
Rumney Reginald Gordon	(45)	3rd Officer (P)*
Smith Wilfred George	(29)	Steward (E)*

<u>Total lost: 4</u>

PERSONNEL BURIED IN UNITED KINGDOM

Richardson William, MN (39)   Assistant Butcher   dra 23.1.47 (Liverpool – West Derby)*
(William Richardson died at Broadgreen Emergency Hospital, Liverpool. His cause of death is given as: (a) Congestive cardiac failure (b) Mitral valvular disease. Whether this is

linked with the *Lancastria* sinking is unknown. However, he is listed by the CWGC as a casualty of the ship–therefore his inclusion).
Campbell Gordon Grant (21)   Cpl RAMC   dra 11.1.41   7517192 (St Pancras)*

Total lost: 2

ROYAL AIR FORCE PERSONNEL BURIED IN FRANCE

Alston Hugh Durbin   (?)   Flt Sgt   RAF 98 Squadron (Pornic)   370706
Ashley Alfred   (38)   Cpl   RAF 73 Squadron (Pornic)   350089
Baker Leslie George   (19)   Sgt   RAF 98 Squadron (Bern)   581492*
Boniface Ronald John   (?)   Sgt (W Op/Air Gnr) 98 Sqdn RAF (VR)(St M) 751838*
Clifford Norman John   (27)   Cpl   RAF (Noirmoutier-en-L'ile)   753581*
Childs Thomas Harry   (20)   AC 2   RAF (VR) 98 Squadron (Pf)   906929*
Crane Lionel James   (43)   LAC   RAF 73 Squadron (La Plaine)   408226*
Cranston James   (19)   AC 1   RAF BAFF (Château-d'Olonne)   618536*
Griffiths Daniel Myrddin (24)   AC 2 (W Op/Air Gnr) RAF 98 Sqdn (L'A)   627989*
Guymer Hugh Percy F.   (33)   LAC   RAF 98 Squadron (St Trojan)   624110*
Handley Colin Wright   (20)   Pilot Offr (Pilot) RAF dra 18.6.40 (Charroux) 42343
Hatherly Frank Henry   (?)   AC 2   RAF HQ BAFF(La Bernerie-en-Retz)
                                                                                904276*
Higgins John   (?)   AC 1   RAF (Le Clion-sur-Mer)   638025*
Hoskins Ernest Daniel C. (19)   Sgt   RAF (VR) 98 Squadron (C)   759330*
Kent James Edwin   (34)   AC 1   RAF 73 Squadron (Pornic)   624350
Kevan Robert   (26)   Cpl   RAF 98 Squadron (Pornic)   545496
Lusty Wilfred   (20)   AC 1   RAF HQ BAFF (Prefailles)   631821*
McKelvie John   (27)   Sgt   RAF (VR) 98 Squadron (Pf)   761198*
Moore Ralph   (30)   Cpl   RAF 73 Squadron (Pornic)   508119
Parton Frederick   (43)   AC 1   RAF (VR) HQ BAFF (St Palais-sur-Mer)
                                                                                743143*
Price Thomas   (20)   AC 2   RAF HQ BAFF (Pornic)   643721
Reeves Eric Charles   (23)   AC 2   RAF 98 Squadron (L'ile-d' Yeu)   642662*
Rushton William Charles   (25)   Cpl   RAF (St Nazaire sur Charente)   523638*
Stokes Lawrence Jesse   (27)   Sgt   RAF (VR) 98 Squadron (Pornic)   740503
Thomas James Gilbert B.   (26)   LAC   RAF (VR) dra 18.6.40 (Charroux)   936495
Trahearn Henry Cornelius (40)   LAC   RAF (Aux VR) 73 Squadron (E)   805215
Tredgett Edward   (21)   AC 1   RAF 73 Squadron (Pornic)   614428
Watkin Francis William   (19)   LAC   RAF 98 Squadron (Prefailles)   625205*
Watts Alfred John   (22)   Cpl   RAF HQ BAFF (L'Epine)   525119*
Whitehead Eric Charles   (35)   Fly Off (Air Gnr) RAF (VR) 217 Sqdn (E)   79200
Wilson Walter   (20)   Cpl   RAF (L'Herbaudiere)   591172*
Windle Alec   (23)   Sgt (Air Gnr) RAF (VR) 217 Squadron (E)   942630

Total lost: 32

ROYAL AIR FORCE PERSONNEL COMMEMORATED AT
RUNNYMEDE MEMORIAL

Adams Alfred Alexander   (27)   AC 1   RAF (VR)   747551*

Alston William	(?)	AC 1	RAF dra 25.6.40	637973
Anderson Frederick Lawrence	(?)	Sgt	RAF (VR) dra 20.6.40	743074
Appleby William	(26)	LAC	RAF HQ BAFF	630625
Applin Edward Charles S.	(20)	AC 2	RAF (VR) 98 Squadron	906916
Ardern Walter	(?)	Sgt	RAF 98 Squadron	581488
Arnott Eustace Thomas	(?)	AC 1	RAF dra 25.6.40	532387
Ashard Ernest Francis	(19)	AC 2	RAF (VR) 98 Squadron	907022
Ashby Kenneth William	(23)	AC 2	RAF HQ BAFF	940345
Bardgett Joseph Edward C.	(20)	AC 1	RAF 73 Squadron	542802
Barrie George Wellesley	(22)	LAC	RAF 98 Squadron	547360*
Bassam George William	(30)	LAC	RAF 73 Squadron	510961
Bateman George	(?)	LAC	RAF 98 Squadron	535546
Baxter John Robert	(32)	Cpl	RAF 73 Squadron	505311*
Beckington Bernard Oliver	(34)	AC 1	RAF (VR) dra 25.6.40	901322
Bell Edmund	(39)	LAC	RAF	641894
Bell Joseph Dixon	(23)	Sgt	RAF	522900
Bellamy Charles Victor	(20)	AC 2	RAF (VR) 98 Squadron	947377
Best John Robert	(?)	AC 2	RAF (VR) dra 25.6.40	749226
Biddle Ernest Reginald	(26)	AC 1	RAF (VR) dra 25.6.40	942880
Bird Sidney Alfred	(23)	AC 2	RAF (VR) HQ BAFF dra 25.6.40	922154
Blackett George	(24)	AC 1	RAF (VR) 98 Squadron	954766*
Blackwell Frank James	(34)	LAC	RAF (VR) 98 Squadron	935698*
Bodden Richard Raymond (MID)	(32)	Cpl	RAF HQ BAFF	525364*
Booth Thomas Gervais	(20)	AC 1	RAF 73 Squadron	624402*
Bott Kenneth Victor	(25)	AC 2	RAF (VR) 98 Squadron	913271
Boumphrey Arnold	(22)	AC 1	RAF 73 Squadron	624815
Broadbent Raymond	(?)	LAC	RAF HQ BAFF	614898*
Brown Douglas	(?)	AC 2	RAF 98 Squadron	627081*
Brown George Oswald	(?)	AC 2	RAF (VR) 98 Squadron	943513
Brunton John	(23)	AC 2	RAF (VR) 98 Squadron	946579*
Burdett Geoffrey George	(25)	Cpl	RAF dra 25.6.40	520421
Burrows Harry	(18)	AC 2	RAF (VR) 98 Squadron	973456
Cannar Basil Richard	(?)	AC 1	RAF 73 Squadron	940077
Cartwright James	(32)	Cpl	RAF 98 Squadron	510279*
Chard William Francis	(48)	Flt Sgt	RAF	21476
Chart George Arthur	(?)	AC 2	RAF (VR) HQ BAFF	963218*
Chave Frederick Stanley Hubert	(?)	AC 1	RAF	508618*
Child Arthur George	(?)	LAC	RAF dra 25.6.40	616033
Christie James Balfour	(19)	AC 1	RAF	625723*
Clarke Donald Basil	(?)	AC 1	RAF 98 Squadron	640028
Clarke Horace	(26)	Cpl	RAF HQ BAFF	652931*
Clarke Sydney	(25)	LAC	RAF 98 Squadron	518910
Cleary Richard	(19)	AC 1	RAF dra 25.6.40	631845
Cocking Norman	(21)	Cpl	RAF HQ BAFF	542816*
Cook Albert Charles	(24)	Cpl	RAF 98 Squadron	532979
Cooper James William	(?)	AC 1	RAF 98 Squadron	633627
Cormack-Beatson Charles Edward	(?)	LAC	RAF	534033
Cross Reginald Alfred Richard	(39)	LAC	RAF (VR) 98 Squadron	900352
Currie Joseph	(?)	AC 1	RAF dra 25.6.40	34350
Daniel Henry	(21)	Cpl	RAF 98 Squadron	568835

Dean Henry William	(19)	AC 2	RAF (VR)	975058
Denton Thomas Frederick	(34)	Sgt	RAF 98 Squadron	509566
Derwin Harry Duhamel	(33)	LAC	RAF 73 Squadron	509271
Diamond George MacDonald	(23)	LAC	RAF HQ BAFF	535631
Dignan George Alfred	(19)	AC 2	RAF 98 Squadron	619976
Donaghy Alexander James	(26)	LAC	RAF dra 25.6.40	544946
Dowding John Henry	(?)	LAC	RAF (VR) 98 Squadron	751081
Edwards Herbert George	(?)	LAC	RAF	551107*
Eldred William George	(?)	Cpl	RAF HQ BAFF	354733*
Fisher Harry	(27)	AC 1	RAF	639435
Fisher Harry	(20)	LAC	RAF 98 Squadron	551310
Fitzpatrick Thomas	(20)	AC 1	RAF 98 Squadron	629004
Fleming Alexander Crabbe	(?)	AC 1	RAF (VR) dra 25.6.40	743827
Fothergill James Ernest	(46)	AC 1	RAF 73 Squadron	212009
Frost John	(34)	Cpl	RAF 73 Squadron	505130
Garside Cyril	(23)	AC 2	RAF 98 Squadron	978500
Gavin Patrick	(19)	AC 1	RAF 98 Squadron	637128*
Gavis James Percy	(30)	Cpl	RAF dra 25.6.40	512854
Gleave Walter	(?)	LAC	RAF	623072*
Glover Dennis William	(20)	LAC	RAF HQ BAFF	544145*
Golding Charles Alfred	(31)	Cpl	RAF 73 Squadron	509633
Gordon Francis Lowson	(31)	Cpl	RAF 98 Squadron	511338
Greenman Wilfred James	(20)	AC 2	RAF (VR) 98 Squadron	977406
Griffin Kenneth Willoughby	(19)	AC 2	RAF 98 Squadron	636117
Grove Reginald George Bishop	(31)	Cpl	RAF 73 Squadron	505901
Groves George Edward	(20)	AC 1	RAF 98 Squadron	569713
Gunn Henry Charles	(33)	AC 1	RAF HQ BAFF	617121
Hall George Thomas	(?)	Cpl	RAF	529271
Hamilton Andrew George	(29)	Cpl	RAF 73 Squadron	561175
Hardisty William	(23)	LAC	RAF 73 Squadron	544667
Harpham Wilfred	(?)	AC 1	RAF 98 Squadron	623494
Harris Stanley Louis	(20)	Sgt	RAF (VR) 98 Squadron	751759
Hayes Thomas Alfred	(34)	AC 1	RAF 73 Squadron	624731
Hedger Harold James	(?)	AC 2	RAF (VR)	908440
Hepplewhite James Isaac	(21)	LAC	RAF HQ BAFF	549266
Hill Albert Dennis	(20)	AC 2	RAF (VR) 98 Squadron	908668
Hills George Gresham Stanley	(24)	Sgt	RAF 98 Squadron	631209
Hodgetts Albert Henry James	(23)	AC 2	RAF (VR) 98 Squadron	908944
Hoe Alfred Frederick Gordon	(25)	Cpl	RAF HQ BAFF	612270*
Holland Reginald Alfred	(40)	LAC	RAF 73 Squadron	253638
Honderwood William Stewart	(20)	LAC	RAF 73 Squadron	569469*
Hopkinson John Frederick	(20)	AC 2	RAF	617338
How Victor Hugh	(19)	AC 1	RAF 98 Squadron	653766*
Howell Robert	(20)	AC 1	RAF	630740
Humphreys Owen	(21)	AC 1	RAF 73 Squadron	639529
Hunter Ronald Wallace	(21)	LAC	RAF (VR)	760014
Hutchinson James	(34)	LAC	RAF 73 Squadron	357304
I'anson Leonard Addy	(23)	Cpl	RAF HQ BAFF	618392
Ingraham Ian	(?)	LAC	RAF 98 Squadron	521686
Jamieson Robert Watson	(24)	AC 2	RAF (VR) HQ BAFF	967699

Jarvis Patrick Joseph (served as Kirk W.H.) (20) AC 2 RAF (VR) 98 Sqdn 974666
Jary Robert Samuel (21) LAC RAF 524483*
Jones Charles Phillips (?) Sgt RAF 98 Squadron 536553
Jones Douglas Walter (?) LAC RAF 98 Squadron 533484
Jones Richard Thompson (22) LAC RAF 544901*
Jones Tegwyn Davies (?) Cpl RAF 98 Squadron 528052
Joy Fred (38) Cpl RAF 73 Squadron 347116*
Kelly Robert Miller (24) LAC RAF 542978*
Kemp Dudley George (22) LAC RAF dra 25.6.40 535214
Kerr John (22) AC 1 RAF 639579
King George Roland (26) Cpl RAF 98 Squadron 564874*
Kirk William Henry (*see* Jarvis P.J.)
Lansdowne Marcus Miller (40) AC 1 RAF 73 Squadron 278360*
Latter Gordon Albert (20) LAC RAF 98 Squadron 571314
Lawson Thomas Edward (27) AC 2 RAF (VR) 908388
Lloyd Trevor David Samuel (19) AC 1 RAF 73 Squadron 613179*
Lunnun William Edwin (24) AC 2 RAF (VR) HQ BAFF 977727*
Lunt Harold (?) AC 2 RAF (VR) 98 Squadron 909562*
Macauley Alexander (?) AC 1 RAF HQ BAFF 629386*
Macpherson William (19) LAC RAF 98 Squadron 642192*
Marron Stephen Joseph (25) LAC RAF 73 Squadron 536654*
Martin Edgar (20) LAC RAF HQ BAFF dra 25.6.40 633385
Martin William Walter (38) AC 2 RAF (VR) 98 Squadron 913127*
Mason Thomas (?) AC 2 RAF HQ BAFF dra 25.6.40 549132
Mawson John Henry (38) AC 2 RAF 73 Squadron 334379*
McCall Robert (48) LAC RAF dra 25.6.40 286815
McFarlane James (23) AC 2 RAF (VR) 98 Squadron 975628*
McLeod Henry George (21) AC 1 RAF 98 Squadron 613055*
McMahon Roy Patrick Walter (19) Cpl RAF 591398*
McNaughton Norman (?) LAC RAF (VR) 98 Squadron 749340
Mitchell William Reekie (?) AC 2 RAF (VR) HQ BAFF 968374*
Moore Alfred William (26) Cpl RAF HQ BAFF 653337*
Munn Cunningham (23) AC 1 RAF dra 25.6.40 627591
Musgrave Arthur (20) AC 1 RAF dra 25.6.40 653443
Niall James Dominic (19) AC 1 RAF 619958*
Norris John Harry (21) AC 1 RAF 616532*
Odgers John Arthur (24) LAC RAF (VR) HQ BAFF 799580*
Olsen Nelson William (?) AC 2 RAF (VR) HQ BAFF 940188*
Park Albert (?) Cpl RAF 98 Squadron 526717
Pearson Harry Vincent (27) AC 2 RAF (VR) 98 Squadron 947539*
Peters John Edward (20) AC 2 RAF (VR) 98 Squadron 900985*
Petrie Edward (36) Cpl RAF 73 Squadron 358147*
Plumb Eric George (?) AC 1 RAF 98 Squadron 615972*
Pugh William (20) AC 1 RAF 98 Squadron 542863*
Radford William Edward (?) AC 1 RAF 98 Squadron 618627*
Ramsey Dennis Joseph (?) AC 1 RAF 73 Squadron 551305*
Ranson Morrison Wilfred Joseph (?) AC 2 RAF 98 Squadron 621890*
Rayner Ernest Edward (?) AC 2 RAF 73 Squadron 354527*
Reading George (23) AC 2 RAF (VR) 98 Squadron 908528
Reading Redvers George (36) LAC RAF (VR) HQ BAFF 770880

Record George Arthur Thomas	(?)	LAC	RAF HQ BAFF	122726*
Redfern Leslie	(21)	AC 2	RAF 98 Squadron	644120*
Richardson Douglas Henry	(20)	AC 1	RAF 98 Sqdn dra 25.6.40	550743
Richardson William	(38)	LAC	RAF	357083*
Riddell Robert	(19)	LAC	RAF 98 Squadron	615860*
Ridley George Thomas	(?)	AC 1	RAF dra 25.6.40	629767
Rigby Geoffrey Arthur	(23)	Cpl	RAF 98 Squadron	532880*
Rigby George Henry	(?)	Cpl	RAF 73 Squadron	354586*
Roberts John Malcolm	(18)	AC 1	RAF dra 25.6.40	634663
Robinson Herbert	(?)	AC 1	RAF 98 Squadron	625691*
Rodgers John Burton	(41)	Cpl	RAF 73 Squadron	347547*
Roe Andrew Garbutt	(43)	LAC	RAF 73 Squadron	348238*
Rogers John	(18)	AC 1	RAF 98 Squadron	591650*
Roxborough James Henry	(?)	Cpl	RAF (VR) 98 Squadron	937857
Ruck Gordon	(22)	AC 2	RAF (VR) 98 Squadron	907056
Sargent Harry Victor	(20)	LAC	RAF	629753*
Saunders Peter Wardlaw	(?)	AC 1	RAF	547248*
Scoins Douglas Jack	(21)	AC 1	RAF	624090
Scott-Kiddie Andrew John	(24)	AC 2	RAF 98 Squadron	628742*
Sellick Harold William Bertie	(22)	AC 1	RAF (VR) 73 Squadron	701311
Sibborn Joseph Alan	(21)	AC 2	RAF (VR) 98 Squadron	702682*
Slater Clarence Frederick	(19)	AC 1	RAF 98 Squadron	631548*
Small Walter Lochrie	(22)	AC 1	RAF 98 Squadron	612896*
Smith Frederick Horatio	(19)	AC 2	RAF 98 Squadron	626102*
Smith Harold Vincent	(26)	AC 1	RAF	654382*
Smith Sydney	(22)	AC 2	RAF	623477*
Smyth Nicholas	(20)	AC 1	RAF HQ BAFF	628225*
Stocker Frank	(20)	LAC	RAF (VR) 98 Squadron	935588*
Stones Dennis	(?)	AC 1	RAF 98 Squadron	628640*
Storrar John Reid	(?)	LAC	RAF HQ BAFF	619703*
Swift George	(?)	LAC	RAF dra 25.6.40	551391
Symmonds Albert Leslie	(21)	AC 1	RAF 98 Squadron	628702*
Taws Stanley	(?)	LAC	RAF 98 Squadron	614845*
Taylor Albert John	(36)	LAC	RAF HQ BAFF	356773*
Taylor George Henry	(?)	LAC	RAF dra 25.6.40	352704
Telford Charles George	(20)	AC 1	RAF dra 25.6.40	627498
Thomas James Victor Lewis	(28)	LAC	RAF	516061*
Thorp Leslie Charles	(24)	AC 1	RAF dra 25.6.40	633277
Thorpe Albert Edward	(37)	Cpl	RAF dra 25.6.40	326629
Tidy Gordon Keable	(28)	Flt Sgt	RAF HQ BAFF	590139*
Timms Cyril	(19)	AC 2	RAF 98 Squadron	573560*
Troth George	(41)	LAC	RAF dra 25.6.40	62712
Waite James Albert	(?)	LAC	RAF 98 Squadron	524140*
Walker Keith Mensforth	(18)	AC 1	RAF 73 Squadron	570036*
Ward Wilfred Arnold	(22)	AC 1	RAF (VR) HQ BAFF	905570*
Watson Albert	(23)	AC 1	RAF 98 Squadron	620691*
Wayman Alfred William	(20)	LAC	RAF HQ BAFF	632799*
Webb Douglas Cyril	(19)	AC 1	RAF (VR) dra 25.6.40	966677
White Victor John	(35)	LAC	RAF dra 25.6.40	352129
Whitmarsh Kenneth Ronald	(32)	LAC	RAF (VR) 98 Squadron	742095*

Whittet James	(20)	Cpl	RAF	591163*
Williamson John Arkell	(22)	LAC	RAF	530579
Williamson William John	(23)	LAC	RAF 98 Squadron	532511*
Willmington Sydney Victor	(20)	LAC	RAF dra 25.6.40	610598
Wilson Frederick James	(19)	AC 1	RAF 98 Squadron	636044*
Wright John Noble	(?)	AC 2	RAF (VR) 98 Squadron	908737*
Wyatt Kenneth Leslie	(?)	AC 2	RAF 98 Squadron	640245*

Total lost: 207

AVIONS FAIREY PERSONNEL

Arnold Mr	(?)	
Beufays Mr	(35–45)	
Legroux Marcel	(36)	Foreman Tinsmith
Thiry Mr	(35–45)	
Thiry Mrs	(35–45)	

Total lost: 5

Overall total of **known** personnel lost: 1637

Below is listed possible names whose death is recorded between two dates that embrace 17 June 1940; there is no certain way of knowing if they were on board the *Lancastria*, but regimental details suggest that most of them were.

ARMY PERSONNEL BURIED IN FRANCE (SAME CODES APPLY)

Alliston Edward George	(26)	Pte	B&H Regt (Le Clion)	5948188
Barnard Victor Wilfred	(22)	Pte	2 Field Bakery RASC (E)	S/6402133
Barnhouse Frederick George	(34)	Pte	Cheshire Regt attd AMPC (Bern)	4188009
Bell William Shaw	(30)	L/Cpl	QORWK Regt (St Hilaire-de-Riez)	6198302
Bellenger William Hunt	(27)	Cpl	RASC (Le Clion)	148582
Bishop Frederick William	(20)	Pte	RASC (L'ile-d' Yeu)	T/146503
Borrowdale James	(20)	Pte	1 Bn Tyneside & Scottish BW (E)	4454676
Bourne Wilfred E.	(22)	Spr	159 Rly Constr Coy RE (Le Clion)	1889970
Brady Patrick Anthony	(22)	Pte	2 Bn Buffs (Sables)	6466503
Bray George	(28)	Cpl	RASC (Escoublac-La-Baule)	S/105931
Brooks Joseph	(27)	Pte	N&D Regt (St Marie)	4971989
Brown Albert Edward	(50)	Pte	50 Coy AMPC (Escoublac-La-Baule)	13002413
Brown Herbert Frank	(24)	Dvr	2 Works Coy RASC (Pornic) dra 7.6.40	
				T/158266
Buchan John Strachan Russell	(37)	Pte	AMPC (La Plaine)	7606917
Burnip Harold	(24)	Pte	RASC (Pornic)	T/153235
Cain John Andrew C.	(41)	Pte	46 Coy AMPC (Pornic)	4441270
Campbell George William	(22)	Spr	Royal Engineers (E)	1891755
Campbell James	(24)	L/Cpl	159 Rly Constr Coy RE (Pornic)	1899086
Cheeseman Ronald Edgar	(21)	Pte	2 Bn Buffs (La Bernerie-en-Retz)	6288856
Collett Walter James	(36)	L/Cpl	MP (Olonne)	6619226

Cocks Edgar	(49)	Sgt	RASC dra 16.7.40 (Bern)	S/94309
Cook Robert Watson	(21)	Pte	1 Bn Black Watch (C d'O)	2755899
Coulston Henry Charles	(49)	Capt	1 Bn KORR dra 14.6.40 (E)	42161
Coward Thomas Luke	(?)	Pte	RASC (L'Epine)	S/147495
Cross Aloysuis	(22)	Dvr	RASC (Le Clion)	T/99449
Cunnah Gwynfryn	(29)	Pte	Cheshire Regt attd AMPC (L)	4190085
Davidson James	(24)	Pte	RAOC (La Bernerie-en-Retz)	7622849
Done Bernard	(22)	Pte	AMPC (L'ile-d' Yeu)	7606948
Drake Edward William	(35)	Pte	10 General Hospital RAMC (N)	5564503
Ecott John Bertram	(25)	Pte	RASC (Pornic)	147974
Everett Francis Dennis	(21)	Pte	2 Bn Buffs (L'ile-d' Yeu)	6288674
Felton-Brant Cyril William	(20)	Pte	RASC (St Trojan-les-Bains)	T/152193
Ffoulkes Reginald	(30)	Pte	South Wales Borderers (L'H)	3907327
Garner John Clifford	(33)	Pte	South Staffordshire Regt (Olonne)	4798983
Gillard Samuel	(39)	Pte	50 Coy AMPC (Pornic)	13001626
Gilleece Norman	(?)	Pte	2 Bn Buffs (St Hilaire-de-Talmont)	6466569
Grassby George Harold	(38)	Cpl	AMPC (La Bernerie-en-Retz)	4380370
Griffiths George	(41)	Pte	AMPC (Les Moutiers)	13011221
Griffiths Harry	(26)	Pte	RASC (Pornic)	/147483
Grocock Arthur W.	(23)	Spr	159 Rly Constr Coy RE dra 19.7.40 (P)	869109
Groombridge George Jack	(33)	Cpl	4 Bn Buffs (Escoublac-La-Baule)	6396019
Hawley Enoch Edward	(26)	Gnr	1 General Base Depot RAC (E)	821660
Hayward William Charles	(34)	L/Cpl	MP (La Couarde)	310766
Hickling Joseph Walter	(35)	Pte	RASC (Pornic)	S/49460
Hinks Horace	(41)	Pte	AMPC (La Bernerie-en-Retz)	13002606
Holmes Robert William	(26)	Pte	RASC (Pornic)	147108
Hopkins George Edward	(30)	Tpr	Royal ArmouredCorps dra 28.5.40 (La T)	
				7886476
Hudson Harry William George	(25)	Spr	663 Artisan Works Coy RE (E)	1904265
Hudson John George	(22)	Pte	10 Bn Durham Light Infantry (P)	4455391
Ingham Albert	(23)	Pte	AMPC (St Trojan les Bains)	2188401
Ingham Arthur	(24)	Spr	663 Artisan Works Coy RE (E)	1912431
Jordan Joseph Raymond	(20)	Tpr	Royal Armoured Corps (Pornic)	557509
Keefe George	(25)	Cpl	RASC (St Gilles-sur-Vie)	105815
Lapworth Leonard Henry	(21)	Spr	Royal Engineers (E)	2194204
Lewis Cecil Sheridan	(27)	Cpl	RASC (Les Moutiers)	148780
Lomax Alexander	(21)	Pte	2 Bn Buffs (Le Clion)	837812
Long Walter	(39)	Pte	46 Coy AMPC (Pornic)	3435841
McConnell Robert (*served* as Sinclair Robert) (25) Pte RASC (Bern)				/105947
McLean William	(32)	Pte	A&S Highlanders (Le Clion)	2976528
McLeod James	(22)	Bdr	75 Field Regt RA (Pornic)	864995
Matthews David Charles James (19) Sgt			RASC (Les Moutiers)	S/94330
May Arthur Henry	(40)	Pte	RASC (L'ile-d' Yeu)	94748
Mills James Kenneth Cyril	(24)	Pte	RASC (Le Clion)	/152598
Minchin George Job	(29)	Tpr	Royal Armoured Corps (Châteillon)	7896085
Morgan William Stanley C.	(24)	Pte	RASC (L'Herbaudiere)	105547
Newbitt Walter	(21)	Pte	N&D Regt (Les Moutiers)	4978228
Newman Douglas	(21)	Pte	2 Bn Buffs (Escoublac-La-Baule)	6288729
Organ Francis Charles	(34)	Pte	4 Coy AMPC (Pornic) dra 13.5.40	7606845
Paterson Angus Murdoch	(22)	Cpl	4 Bn QOCH (La Bernerie-en-Retz)	2929190

Phillips David	(29)	Pte	1 Bn Black Watch (Bern)	4447299
Porter William Samuel	(33)	Pte	RASC (L'ile-d' Yeu)	T/58418
Powell James Wilson	(20)	Spr	159 Rly Constr Coy RE (Ste Marie)	1892994
Ramsay William Armstrong	(21)	Pte	RASC (Escoublac-La-Baule)	S/120300
Rickerby James	(38)	WO II	(SQMS) RASC (Le Clion)	S/94387
Ridley Harrison Richard	(35)	Cpl	AMPC (L'ile-d' Yeu)	4338778
Robertson George Stoddart	(21)	Pte	RASC dra 6/8.7.40 (Pornic)	120303
Rogers Ernest Albert	(21)	Pte	Buffs (St Hilaire-de-Riez)	6289036
Rolfe Philip Eric Penfold	(26)	Pte	RASC (Le Clion)	147101
Rowlands Joseph Idris	(20)	Fus	Royal Welch Fusiliers attd AMPC (M)	4195636
Sands Albert Edward	(38)	Pte	AMPC (La Bernerie-en-Retz)	13006381
Scott Charles	(?)	Pte	2 Bn Buffs (Ste Marie)	6288709
Scott Walter Edward	(21)	Pte	2/5 Bn N&D Regt (Le Clion)	4978244
Sellen James Alec	(24)	Pte	4 Bn Buffs (Pornic)	6285362
Shaw Frank	(?)	L/Cpl	RASC attd 40 Field Regt RA (Bern)	S/100772
Sheppard William Alfred	(21)	Cpl	2 Field Bakery RASC (E)	S/99290
Sinclair Robert (*see* McConnell Robert)				
Smith Ernest William	(25)	Pte	RASC (Le Clion)	S/94010
Smith Sydney Lewis	(21)	Pte	N&D Regt (La Plaine)	4978954
Taylor Walter H.E.	(28)	Cpl	RASC (La Plaine)	S/94115
Taylor William John Norton	(30)	Sgt	RASC (Le Bois Plage)	148062
Tebble Frank Stephen	(26)	Pte	4 Bn Buffs (La Plaine)	6284494
Thomas Julian	(29)	Spr	663 Artisan Works Coy RE (Pornic)	1914198
Thorley James William	(32)	Pte	2 Field Bakery RASC (Bern)	S/52590
Thorpe Howard John	(24)	Cpl	RASC (La Bernerie-en-Retz)	S/147765
Timms Frederick Albert	(20)	Sgt	RASC (Pornic)	S/880834
Tipper Wilfred Frank	(29)	Sgt	RASC (Pornic)	147477
Tooke William Charles	(39)	L/Cpl	2 Res MT Coy RASC (E)	/5766793
Vidler Charles Edward	(37)	Sgt	RASC (Les Moutiers)	S/94220
Walk Frederick Celestine	(38)	Pte	RASC (La Bernerie-en-Retz)	S/105064
Watson Thomas	(20)	Pte	N&D Regt (Ste Marie)	4978878
Wheeler Christopher Ernest	(25)	Pte	RASC (Ars-en-Ré)	S/147099
Wood Joseph Richard	(25)	Spr	663 Artisan Works Coy RE (Pornic)	1912468
Woodland Isaac Frederick	(32)	Pte	Cheshire Regt attd AMPC (M)	4186887
Worrall Cyril George	(23)	Pte	2 Ord Workshop Coy RAOC (Ste Marie)	
				7624405
Worsfold James William	(38)	Pte	RASC (Pornic)	S/94064
Wright Alexander	(33)	Rfn	2 Bn Royal Ulster Rifles (Le Clion)	7009511
Wright Robert	(20)	Pte	4 Bn Buffs (Les Moutiers)	6287876

Total lost: 106

The following list of names are recorded on the Dunkirk Memorial. No body, or recognisable body, was found; therefore, the date of death is, as the above list, recorded between two dates that embrace 17 June 1940. It must be pointed out that this list is much more unreliable than the former. This is because of the vastness of the area of combat. There is no certain way of knowing if any of the names recorded below were on board the *Lancastria* but, again, some regiment details suggest that some of these personnel were.

DUNKIRK MEMORIAL

Bacon Percy	(21)	Pte	5 Bn QORWK Regt	5727190
Baker Graham Edward	(21)	Pte	Royal Sussex Regt	6401844
Barnes Ronald Jack	(22)	Pte	7 Bn Royal Sussex Regt	6403295
Beer Harry	(22)	Pte	2 Bn Buffs	6466496
Bennett Harry	(26)	Pte	1 Bn Royal Scots (Royal Regt)	3058102
Blake Alfred Victor	(20)	Pte	Royal Norfolk Regt	5773023
Buck Reginald Robert	(26)	Pte	Royal Norfolk Regt	5771188
Carter Frank Thomas	(21)	Pte	2 Bn Gloucester Regt	5185799
Chandler Arthur Roy	(22)	Pte	2 Bn Royal Norfolk Regt	5772972
Cooper John W.	(25)	Pte	2 Bn Royal Norfolk Regt	5770783
Cuthbert James Gordon	(20)	Pte	2 Bn Seaforth Highlanders	2821052
Daniel Francis Kenneth	(22)	Dvr	RASC	T/124231
Davies Leslie	(26)	L/Cpl	2 Bn Royal Norfolk Regt	5770937
Davison Walter James	(26)	Pte	6 Bn Durham Light Infantry	4456767
Day Reginald	(26)	Pte	2 Bn Royal Norfolk Regt	5770934
Dick William	(27)	Pte	2 Bn Seaforth Highlanders	2818491
Forbes Daniel	(21)	Pte	5 Bn QORWK Regt	6346408
Ford Roy Robert	(20)	Pte	2 Bn Royal Norfolk Regt	5772007
Gardiner Robert	(28)	Pte	2 Bn Durham Light Infantry	4448398
Gibson William	(39)	Pte	13 Salvage Unit AMPC	13011144
Gotobed Leonard Gilbert	(24)	Spr	678 General Construction Coy RE	1917076
Griffin James Edmund	(27)	L/Cpl	2 Bn Royal Norfolk Regt	5770633
Hadler Norman Stanley	(21)	Pte	Royal Sussex Regt	5622191
Harrison Cyril H.	(31)	Pte	2 Bn Middlesex Regt	6198391
Heley Alfred Francis	(35)	Pte	5 Bn QORWK Regt	3906591
Hill George Douglas	(?)	Major	7 Queen's Own Hussars RAC	18403
Howlett Walter George	(27)	Pte	2 Bn Royal Norfolk Regt dra 18.6.40	5770475
Huddleton James Leo	(36)	Pte	29 Coy AMPC dra 16.6.40	2191601
Hughes Edward William	(20)	Pte	2 Bn Dorsetshire Regt	5726236
Humphreys John Morley	(26)	L/Cpl	Royal Engineers	1910177
Jackson Harold Ernest	(28)	Pte	2 Bn Royal Norfolk Regt	5770065
Jarvis William Albert	(21)	Pte	Royal Warwickshire Regt	5112894
Jeoffroy Alfred William	(31)	Pte	2 Bn Royal Norfolk Regt	5771258
Jones Daniel Brynmor	(32)	Pte	5 Bn QORWK Regt	3955492
Keely Leslie Herman	(21)	Gnr	17 Field Regt RA	935401
Knight Joseph William (MM)	(26)	L/Bdr	151 Bty 51 Lt AA Regt RA	823640
Lake Edward James	(34)	Pte	2 Bn Royal Norfolk Regt	5769417
Lashmar Frederick Charles	(20)	L/Cpl	5 Bn QORWK Regt	6344285
Lawler Duncan Campbel	(21)	Pte	2 Bn Seaforth Highlanders	2981590
Mace James Arthur	(20)	Pte	5 Bn QORWK Regt	6345873
McInnes William Austin	(23)	L/Cpl	6 Bn Black Watch	2757852
McNally Anthony	(40)	Pte	347 Coy AMPC	13009618
Martin Thomas George	(20)	Pte	5 Bn QORWK Regt	6344491
Mercer George Lawrence R.	(21)	Pte	2 Bn Royal Norfolk Regt	5776506
Mills Alfred James	(21)	L/Cpl	2 Bn Gloucester Regt	5186324
Monaghan Charles Joseph	(31)	Cpl	5 Bn QORWK Regt	5726221
Moulden Allan Bert	(28)	Pte	2 Bn Gloucester Regt	5181793

Pierce Eric William	(25)	L/Sgt	239 Bty 101 Lt AA/Anti-Tank Regt RA	
				1454607
Piggott Albert William James	(23)	Pte	1 Bn Princess Louise's Kens'tn Regt	2032237
Pratt Alfred Francis	(32)	L/Cpl	2 Bn Royal Norfolk Regt	5769229
Price William Henry	(21)	Pte	1 Bn Gloucester Regt 5	186243
Pursey Charles Henry	(?)	Cpl	RASC	148596
Reeve Arthur Harold	(27)	Pte	2 Bn Royal Norfolk Regt	5770587
Roberts Albert	(30)	Pte	2 Bn Royal Norfolk Regt	5768951
Salmon Gordon Noel	(21)	Pte	2 Bn Royal Norfolk Regt	5772735
Sear Charles Albert	(20)	Gnr	1 Bty 4 AA Regt RA	1439199
Sheppard Kenneth Arthur	(21)	Pte	5 Bn QORWK Regt	5727404
Sissons Thomas Allwyn	(34)	Pte	5 Bn KOSB	4263794
Smalls Frederick Cyril	(36)	WO II (PSM)	2 Bn Royal Norfolk Regt	5766889
Stagg Norman Llewellyn	(32)	L/Cpl	7 Royal Tank Regt RAC	7882223
Storey John Ernest	(20)	Fus	1/8 Bn Lancashire Fusiliers	3449561
Sturgeon Herbert Michael	(20)	Pte	2 Bn Royal Norfolk Regt	5773340
Thompson Joseph	(36)	Pte	6 Bn King's Own Royal Regt (Lancs)	2055258
Tilley George Henry	(20)	Pte	2 Bn Royal Norfolk Regt	5772296
Tilney Hector Stanley	(29)	WO III (PSM)	2 Bn Royal Norfolk Regt	5773699
Twynham Oliver George	(21)	Pte	4 Bn Oxford and Bucks LI	5387141
Wallbridge Charles William	(21)	Pte	2 Bn Buffs	6288686
Watson Frederick	(19)	Tpr	13/18 Royal Hussars RAC	558479
Webb Alan Conningsby	(37)	Gnr	43 Bty 101 Lt AA/Anti-Tank Regt RA	1432709
Williams Richard	(21)	Gnr	140 Field Regt RA	947066
Wise Francis Herbert	(32)	Cpl	4 Bn East Yorkshire Regt	4340688

<u>Total lost: 71</u>

<u>Total of possible additional names: 177</u>

<u>Total gained from Commonwealth War Graves Commission's Registers = 1816</u>

**'In Proud Memory of those who died with the troopship *Lancastria*
on 17 June 1940. At the going down of the sun, and in the morning.
We will remember them.'**

(Above is the inscription written on The *Lancastria* Association's wreath placed
at the Cenotaph, on Remembrance Day, every year).

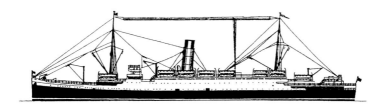

APPENDIX 2

HONOURS AND AWARDS GIVEN TO CREW MEMBERS OF SS *LANCASTRIA*, WHEN THE TROOPSHIP WAS BOMBED AND SUNK ON 17 JUNE 1940

(Published in the *London Gazette*, 8 October 1940)

Dunbar, James	Chief Engineer	OBE (Civil)
Grattidge, Harry	Chief Officer	OBE (Civil)
Sharp, Rudolf	Captain	OBE (Civil)
Beattie, Frederick Entwistle	Chief Steward	BEM (Civil)
Stone, William Herbert	Gunner	BEM (Civil)
Thomson, David Irvine Jardine	Boatswain's Mate	BEM (Civil)
Dover, Arthur	Extra 2nd Steward	Commendation
Hyde, Wilfred John	Senior Assistant Purser	Commendation
Murphy, Michael	Quartermaster	Commendation
Duncan, James	Snr 2nd Engineer	Posthumous Commendation
Hill, John	Surgeon	Posthumous Commendation
Roberts, Richard Goronwy	Senior 1st Officer	Posthumous Commendation

SS *Lancastria* had embarked a large number of troops and some refugees at Saint-Nazaire, and was waiting for her escort when attacked. She was struck by a salvo of four high-explosive bombs, which hit her simultaneously in the most vital parts, and she sank in ten minutes (*sic*). Some 2,000 were saved by lifebelts and 500 by boats and rafts.

* * *

HONOURS AND AWARDS GIVEN TO CREW MEMBERS OF SS *DUNDRUM CASTLE* FOR THE RESCUE OF SURVIVORS OF SS *LANCASTRIA* ON 17 JUNE 1940

(Published in the *London Gazette*, 23 August 1940).

Klasen, David Patrick Horndon	Chief Officer	OBE (Civil)
Shannon, William Gardiner	2nd Officer	MBE (Civil)

223

THE FORGOTTEN TRAGEDY

When HM Troopship *Lancastria* was sunk by enemy aircraft off Saint-Nazaire, fine work was done by *Dundrum Castle*'s two lifeboats, under Chief Officer D.P. Klasen and Second Officer W.G. Shannon. They rescued over 120 men. Oil on the surface of the water made rescue work very dangerous, but these two Officers made repeated trips with survivors of *Lancastria* to ferry boats which were standing by. After these gallant and successful efforts, *Dundrum Castle*'s boats were the last to leave the scene.

* * *

HONOURS AND AWARDS GIVEN TO CREW MEMBERS
OF SS *ORONSAY*

(Published in the *London Gazette*, 8 October 1940).

Nicholls, Arthur Edward	Captain	OBE (Civil)
Goldsworth, Ivan Ernest Goodman, RD.	Staff Commander	Commendation

The transport *Oronsay* was engaged in withdrawing troops from France and rescued a large number of military officers and other ranks, many of whom proved to be survivors of HMT *Lancastria*. *Oronsay* was heavily attacked from the air and hit at the moment of her arrival at Saint-Nazaire. The embarkation took some four or five hours during which five bombing attacks were made on this vessel. Captain Nicholls was ably assisted by Staff Commander Goldsworthy who had been injured. The Master's resource and coolness were outstanding and he brought his ship home without any bridge instruments or charts.

* * *

AWARD GIVEN TO CREW MEMBER OF HMS *PUNJABI*

(Published in the *London Gazette*, 1 January 1941)

Thomas, John,	Surgeon Lieutenant	DSC

* * *

There was a list of names sent in by Captain W. G. Easton, the Commanding Officer of HM Trawler *Cambridgeshire*. The crew of *Cambridgeshire* played an important part in the rescue of *Lancastria* survivors. Unfortunately, Captain Easton thought that the recommendations would be forwarded by either the NOIC or the Group Commander. When he eventually discovered that the responsibility was his own, he tried to redress the situation, writing a letter to the Flag Officer in Charge at Cardiff on 21 April 1942. The men listed below never did receive their awards; awards that they undoubtedly should have received, hence their inclusion here.

Note: they are only recommendations, but had been authorised on 1st July 1942 by Rear Admiral Rudolf Burmester, Flag Officer in Charge, Cardiff. The recommendations were received by Admiral Sir Percy Noble, Commander in Chief, Western Approaches, on 4 July 1942. On 14 July 1942 Admiral Noble sent the following letter to the Admiralty:

Forwarded for Their Lordships' consideration.

2. It is not known whether HMT *Cambridgeshire* was included in the report of the Senior Officer at the time but if not I consider that these men and their Commanding Officer are worthy of recognition.

APPENDICES

Admiral Noble had even included Captain W.G. Easton in his letter of recommendation. Below are the crews recommendations:

HM Trawler *Cambridgeshire*

Drage, Arthur (new recruit)****	OS Patrol Service	Operational Decoration
Kingett, Stanley (X/20095A) ***	Cox'n, RNR	Operational Decoration
Baxter, John (No. X/9483B)*	LS, RNR	Mention in Despatches
Elliot, William Henry (X/19916A)*	AB, RNR	Mention in Despatches
Morrison, Malcolm (K/17560A)*	AB, RNR	Mention in Despatches
Perrin, William Reeves (D/164)**	AB, RFR	Mention in Despatches

Citations made by Captain Easton were as follows:

*   For courage and devotion to duty while under enemy fire, as crew of ship's boat while engaged in rescue work.

**   For courage and devotion to duty, keeping up continuous machine-gun fire, in an attempt to prevent enemy planes machine-gunning men in water. Probably brought down one plane, but this cannot be confirmed.

***   For courage and devotion, making repeated journeys in ship's boat to rescue exhausted men from water while under machine-gun fire from enemy planes.

****   For courage and initiative, in taking charge of lifeboat from *Lancastria*, and persuading some of the survivors to act as boat's crew, thereby being directly responsible for saving some 50 men from drowning. (This boat was unavoidably left when I withdrew, the occupants being picked up by a destroyer and landed at Devonport).

(KNOWN) HONOURS AND AWARDS GIVEN TO ARMY PERSONNEL

(Published in the *London Gazette*, 20 December 1940).

Medlicott–Vereker, John Cayler	Lt	RASC	Military Cross
Durrant Jack	Sgt	RASC	Military Medal
Brooke, Sir Alan F., KCB, DSO	LtGen (actg Gen)		MID
de Coudray Tronson, Norman G.P.	Maj (actg LtCol)	NS Regt	MID
Studdy, E. S., AMIME	LtCol	RASC	MID
Green, T. (No. 1870955)	Dvr	RE	MID

Note: It has only been possible to check the known names of Army recipients of awards given for acts of bravery throughout the sinking of the *Lancastria* on 17 June 1940. To check the individual names of every survivor is an impossible task. This is because most of the Army awards published in the appropriate editions of the *London Gazette* do not give a citation or a reason for the award. Some Members of 1 HRS, RASC, who manned guns aboard the *Lancastria* were recommended for awards, but these were squashed by their commanding officer, Lieutenant Colonel E. S. Studdy, RASC. His argument being, that either they all got awards, or none of them did.

An Interesting Coincidence: Jack Durrant's brother, Sergeant Thomas Frank Durrant, RE/1 Commando, was awarded a posthumous Victoria Cross on 15 June 1945 for his part in the famous raid on Saint-Nazaire during the early hours of 28 March 1942. The *London Gazette* recorded the following citation:

225

On 28 March 1942 HM motor launch *306* was heavily attacked while proceeding up the River Loire in the raid on Saint-Nazaire. Sergeant Durrant, in charge of a Lewis gun in a completely exposed position, engaged enemy guns and searchlights on shore. He was severely wounded in the arm, but refused to leave his gun.

Later, when the launch was attacked at close range by a German destroyer, Sergeant Durrant fired coolly and continuously at the destroyer's bridge, drawing on himself the enemy fire and suffering many further wounds. When so weak that he had to support himself on the gun mounting, he went on firing until his gun was silenced, and the enemy boarded the motor launch and took prisoner those still alive. This very gallant NCO died later of his wounds.

NUMBERS AND AWARDS GIVEN TO ARMY AND ROYAL NAVY PERSONNEL AFTER THE SUCCESSFUL ATTACK ON SAINT-NAZAIRE ON 27/28 MARCH 1942

The following decorations were given to nearly one man in eight who took part in the famous raid on Saint-Nazaire docks on 27/28 March 1942: VCs (5; 2 posthumously); DSOs (4); DSCs (17); MCs (11); CGMs (4); DCMs (5); DSMs (24); and MMs (15). Another 51 men were Mentioned in Despatches (22 posthumously).

STATISTICS OF THE RAID ON SAINT-NAZAIRE ON 27/28 MARCH 1942

From the 611 men who took part in the raid 169 were killed, a proportion of more than one in four. Approximately 200 men were taken prisoner and the remainder (around 240 men) managed to retreat and return to England.

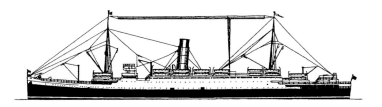

APPENDIX 3

LIST OF HRS (RASC) GUNNERS ON DUTY AT THE TIME OF THE SINKING OF THE *LANCASTRIA*

Private Cockburn
Private Morris Lashbrook
Private McColl
Private Samson
Lance Corporal F.C. Bolton (missing)
Lance Corporal Mayl
Corporal Knight
Corporal G. Touzel

Private Jenkins
Private Mackintosh
Private Alan Moore
Private Stafford
Lance Corporal C.F. Coe
Corporal Hopgood
Corporal Old
Corporal Waterfall

Commanding Officer of 1 Heavy Repair Shop (motor transport) RASC Overseas: Lieutenant Colonel E. Studdy.

Officer in charge of HRS gunners: Captain D.F. Abbott (RASC).

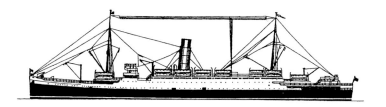

APPENDIX 4

CAREER DETAILS OF EXTRA MASTER RUDOLPH SHARP

Born in Liverpool in 1880. Passed Masters Certificate (No. 039503) in 1908 (Liverpool). Passed Extra Masters Certificate in 1909. Sub Lieutenant RNR on 1 April 1911. Lieutenant RNR on 2 August 1915. Lieutenant Commander RNR 27 October 1923. Commander RNR (Retired) on 27 October 1930. Served in HMS *Havelock* from September 1915 to January 1919. Awarded Reserve Decoration. Apart from First World War service with the Royal Navy, Captain Sharp served explicitly with the Cunard company.

Abbreviations used below (for destinations):
US = United States (East coast and Gulf ports).
For = Foreign (not further identified).
M = Mediterranean, Black Sea, Sea of Azoff, Adriatic.
NA = British North America, Greenland, Iceland.
FPS = France (south of Brest), Portugal, Spain (outside the Strait of Gibraltar), Azores.

CAPTAIN RUDOLPH SHARP'S CAREER DETAILS:

Vessel/Number	Dates of Appointment/Re-appointment (Class of Voyage)
Campania (102086) (2nd or 3rd Mate)	17. 12. 1913 (US), 6. 2. 1914.
Mauretania (124093) (2nd or 3rd Mate)	4. 3. 1914 (US), 15. 5. 1914.
Lusitania (124093) (2nd or 3rd Mate)	6. 9. 1914 (US), 16. 12, 1914.
Mauretania (124093) (2nd or 3rd Mate)	19. 5. 1915 (For), 23. 8. 1915.
Saxonia (110648) (2nd or 3rd Mate)	15. 5. 1919 (US), 17. 6. 1919.
Brescia (118021) (1st mate)	25. 7. 1919 (M), 21. 11. 1919, 2. 3. 1920, 16. 6. 1920.
Venusia (142627) (1st mate)	20. 10. 1920 (NA), 9. 12. 1920 (US), 14. 2. 1921, 18. 5. 1921 (NA), 14. 11. 1921 (US), 28. 12. 1921.

Andania (145934)   29. 5. 1922 (NA), 30. 6. 1922, 2. 8. 1922, 17. 11. 1922 (US)
(1st mate)   1. 12. 1922, 23. 1. 1923, 31. 5. 1923 (NA), 20. 11. 1923,
                         21. 1. 1924 (US), 14. 4. 1924, 17. 6. 1924.

Caronia (120826)   20. 8. 1924 (NA), 19. 12. 1924 (US), 28. 1. 1925, 22. 7. 1925.
(1st mate)

Ascania (147307)   25. 8. 1925 (NA), 22. 9. 1925.
(1st mate)

Ausonia (145970)   3. 3. 1926 (US).
(1st mate)

Antonia (145937)   2. 6. 1926 (US), 29. 6. 1926 (NA), 23. 11. 1926 (US),
(1st mate)   9. 2. 1927, 1. 6. 1927 (NA), 15. 12. 1927 (US), 5. 4. 1928 (NA),
                         27. 8. 1928.

Ausonia (145970)   28. 9. 1928 (NA), 19. 11. 1928 (US), 21. 1. 1929,
(1st mate)   1. 5. 1929 (NA), 29. 9. 1929, 25. 11. 1929 (US), 18. 3. 1930.

Lancastria (145943)   16. 6. 1930 (US), 28. 10. 1930, 10. 2. 1931.
(1st mate)

Caronia (120826)   10. 4. 1931 (US), 4. 5. 1931.
(1st mate)

Franconia (147216)   29. 6. 1931 (US).
(1st mate)

Lancastria (145943)   16. 2. 1932 (US), 19. 9. 1932 (M), 21. 12. 1932 (US).
(1st mate)

Lancastria (145943)   10. 4. 1933 (FPS).
(Staff Captain)

Lancastria (145943)   20. 6. 1933 (M).
(1st mate)

Lancastria (145943)   6. 9. 1933 (M).
(Staff Captain)

Franconia (147216)   12. 12. 1933 (US), 10. 7. 1934.
(Staff Captain)

Scythia (143730)   3. 1. 1935 (US), 30. 1. 1935.
(1st mate)

Olympic (131346)   5. 3. 1935 (US).
(1st mate)

Olympic (131346)   2. 3. 1935 (US).
(Staff Captain)

Samaria (145923)   28. 5. 1935.

(1st mate)	
Franconia (147216)	
(Staff Captain)	9. 7. 1935 (US), 24. 9. 1935 (M), 29. 11. 1935 (US).
Franconia (147216)	9. 6. 1936 (US), 6. 7. 1936
(1st mate)	
Carinthia (147318)	5. 1. 1937 (US), 12. 4. 1937, 3. 6. 1937, 6. 7. 1937.
(1st mate)	
Queen Mary (164282)	2. 2. 1938 (US), 12. 4. 1938, 23. 7. 1938, 31. 8. 1938
(Staff Captain)	25. 10. 1938.
Antonia (145937)	7. 2. 1939 (US), 7. 3. 1939, 19. 4. 1939 (NA), 30. 5. 1939,
(Captain)	26. 6. 1939.
Samaria (145923)	27. 6. 1939 (US), 24. 7. 1939, 21. 9. 1939, 3. 10. 1939,
(Captain)	3. 11. 1939. Last appointment not taken up.
Antonia (145937)	23. 11. 1939 (NA), 23. 12. 1939, 31. 1. 1940 (US). Last
(Captain)	appointment not taken up.
Lancastria (145943)	5. 3. 1940 (US), 14. 4. 1940.
(Captain)	Bombed and sunk at Saint-Nazaire on 17 June 1940 (survived sinking).
Antonia (145937)	6. 8. 1940 (For), 16. 9. 1940, 29. 9. 1940.
(Captain)	Awarded the OBE for War services (Lloyd's List, 10. 10. 1940, page 5, column 1).
Laconia (145925)	31. 12. 1941 (For).
(Captain)	Torpedoed and sunk by *U–156* (Lieutenant Commander Werner Hartenstein) on 12 September 1942. (Captain Rudolph Sharp and his First Officer, George Steel, chose to stay with the doomed liner and went down with the ship).

Captain Rudolf Sharp, OBE, RD, RNVR, was five feet eleven inches tall, stout in build and looked older than his age. He was rich in seafaring experience and tradition, coming from a seagoing family. His grandfather and uncle had both served with Cunard Line. First impressions, apparently, revealed a serious nature to his personality and when faced with unexpected aggravation his expression took on a certain weariness. He was married (wife's name was Florence) with two sons, the eldest serving in the Royal Navy in the cruiser HMS *Cape Town*.

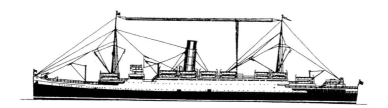

APPENDIX 5

DATES RECORDED ON LLOYD'S VOYAGE RECORD CARDS AND AGREEMENTS AND CREW LISTS WHEN MASTERS JOINED THE SS *TYRRHENIA / LANCASTRIA* 9 JUNE 1922 – 17 JUNE 1940

CAPTAIN'S NAME	DATE HE JOINED SHIP
F. G. Brown	9 June 1922
W. H. Hossack	13 November 1922
F. G. Brown	7 March 1925
R. G. Malin	12 April 1926
B. B. Oram	17 June 1927
R. G. Malin	13 December 1927
B. B. Oram	17 January 1928
J. C. Townley	6 September 1928
H. A. L. Bond	3 October 1929
J. C. Townley	5 February 1930
B. B. Oram	17 June 1930
P. A. Murchie	17 April 1931
H. A. L. Bond	13 June 1931
G. R. Dolphin	18 February 1932
E. Edkin	5 March 1935
J. G. P. Bisset	21 January 1937
C. G. Illingworth	1 February 1938
W. C. Battle	29 March 1938
C. G. Illingworth	2 May 1938
E. M. Fall	7 June 1939
H. R. Oulsnam	23 January 1940
R. Sharp	5 March 1940

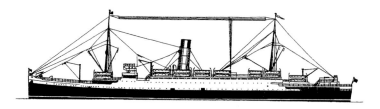

APPENDIX 6

SHIPS INVOLVED IN THE EVACUATION OF HARSTAD JUNE 1940

(The numbers in brackets denote the personnel capacity of each ship as recommended by the Ministry of Shipping)

GROUP 1
Troopships:
Batory [Polish] (2,420)
Franconia (2,880)
Georgic (2,600)
Lancastria (2,600)
Monarch of Bermuda (2,460)
Sobieski [Polish] (1,700)
Royal Scotsman (900)

GROUP 2
Troopships:
Arandora Star (2,000)
Duchess of York (?)
Ormonde (2,600)
Oronsay (2,600)
Irish Channel packet-boats:
Royal Ulsterman (900)
Ulster Monarch (900)
Ulster Prince (900)
Armed merchant cruiser (on stand-by):
Vandyck (1,500)
Troopship (surplus to requirement and ordered to return home empty by Admiral Vivian):
Orama (2,600) [19,840 tons, she was short of 500 tons of fuel oil and 300 tons of water]. She was sunk by a German fleet, under the command of Admiral Marschall, on 8 June 1940.

NAVAL ESCORT

GROUP 1
Cadet training ship:
Vindictive

GROUP 2
Cruisers:
Coventry
Southampton (Lord Cork and Vice Admiral Layton)
Destroyers:
Beagle
Delight
Fame
Firedrake
Havelock

APPENDIX 7

COPY OF MENU FOR THE INTENDED LUNCH ON BOARD SS *LANCASTRIA* ON THE DAY OF SINKING

Please note that although the menu was actually printed for that day, it is highly improbable that it was fully implemented, due to the amount of preparation required by most crew members during the massive embarkation. In wartime circumstances, this menu would only apply to the ship's officers and possibly some high ranking passengers. However, it does make interesting reading.

HMT Lancastria   *Monday June 17 1940*

LUNCHEON

Hors d'Oeuvre Varie
Consomme Massena   Thick Oxtail Soup
Fried Fillet of Cod Colbert
(cold) Crab Salad, Mayonnaise
Macaroni au Gratin
Saute of Oxtail, Nohant
To order from the Grill:
Minute Steak, Maitre d'Hotel
Boiled Knuckle of Veal and Bacon, Parsley Sauce
Green Lima Beans
Baked Jacket and Mashed Potatoes
Cold Buffet:
Braun Luncheon Sausage, Ox Tongue
Riat Beef   Roast Lamb
Lettuce, Tomatoes, Beetroot
Rusk Pudding   Apricot Flan
Ice Cream and Wafers
Cheese, Biscuits, Coffee

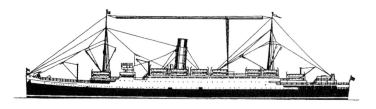

APPENDIX 8

NUMBERS OF MILITARY SURVIVORS KNOWN TO HAVE BEEN LANDED IN ENGLAND

HMS *Havelock*:	460	Plymouth
HMT *Oronsay* and trawlers (unnamed)	1,566	Plymouth
HM Destroyer *Beagle*	600	Plymouth
SS *John Holt*	820	Plymouth
MV *Cymbula*	243	Plymouth
HM Yacht *Oracle*	44	Plymouth
SS *Fabian*	Numbers unknown	Plymouth
SS *City of Mobile*	20	Plymouth
MV *Royal Ulsterman*	150	Falmouth
MV *Ulster Prince*	Numbers unknown	Falmouth
Queen Emma	4	The survivors were transferred to another ship near England and landed in Weymouth
HMS *Punjabi*	9 (including 6, who were badly burnt)	Plymouth

Total: 3,916

Note: a small number of men, additional to these, were taken prisoners of war; because they were hospitalised and unfit to travel before the German occupation, i.e., at least the two referred to on page 155.

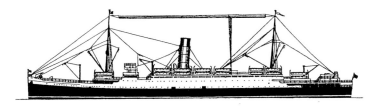

APPENDIX 9

THE MOST NOTABLE MERCHANT SHIPPING
DISASTERS OF THE SECOND WORLD WAR

	Name of Ship	Nationality	Date of Loss	Casualties
1.	*Goya*	German	16 April 1945	*c.* 6,800
2.	*Cap Arcona*	German	3 May 1945	5,594
3.	*Wilhelm Gustloff*	German	30 January 1945	*c.* 5,400
4.	*Steuben*	German	10 February 1945	3,608
5.	*Petrella*	German	8 February 1944	2,647
6.	*Lancastria*	MoWT–British	17 June 1940	*c.* 2,000
7.	*Awa Maru*	Japanese	1 April 1945	*c.* 2,000
8.	*Salzburg*	German	1 October 1942	*c.* 2,000
9.	*Sinfra*	German	19 October 1943	1,998
10.	*Lisbon Maru*	Japanese	1 October 1942	*c.* 1,800
11.	*Laconia*	British	12 September 1942	1,614
12.	*Slamat*	Dutch	27 April 1941	1,384
13.	*Rakuyo Maru*	Japanese	12 September 1944	*c.* 1,350
14.	*Khedive Ismail*	MoWT–Egyptian	12 February 1944	1,297
15.	*Conte Rosso*	Italian	24 May 1941	1,212
16.	*Rohna*	British	26 November 1943	1,149
17.	*Arandora Star*	British	2 July 1940	847
18.	*Leopoldville*	MoWT–Belgian	24 December 1944	819
19.	*Francesco Crispi*	Italian	19 April 1943	*c.* 800
20.	*Taiyo Maru*	Japanese	8 May 1942	780
21.	*Nova Scotia*	British	28 November 1942	762
22.	*Cap Guir*	German	16 April 1945	756
23.	*Ceramic*	British	6 December 1942	655
24.	*Moero*	German	22 September 1944	582
25.	*Inster*	German	3 May 1945	560
26.	*Antares*	German	10 April 1940	*c.* 500
27.	*Yoma*	British	17 June 1943	484
28.	*Calabria*	MoWT–British	8 December 1940	472
29.	*Bremerhaven*	German	31 October 1944	410
30.	*Benalbanach*	British	7 January 1943	410

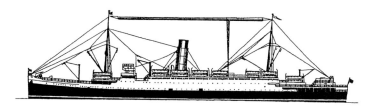

APPENDIX 10

DETAILS OF SHIPS INVOLVED IN 'OPERATION AERIAL'

SS *Oronsay*
Built in 1925, gross weight: 20,043 tons and owned by Ocean Steam Navigation Co. Ltd. Registered in Glasgow and built by John Brown & Co. Ltd., Glasgow. Dimensions: 633.6 ft long × 75.2 ft wide × 33.0 ft deep. Call sign: GJRZ. Six steam turbines, twin screw.

MV *Ulster Prince*
Built in 1930, gross weight: 3791 tons and owned by Belfast Steamship Co. Ltd. Registered and built in Belfast by Harland & Wolff. Dimensions: 346.0 × 46.2 × 15.2. Call sign: GLFM. Oil engines, twin screw.
Grounded off Návplion on 25 April 1941 and attacked by aircraft during evacuation from Greece.

MV *Ulster Monarch*
Built in 1929. Details identical to the *Ulster Prince*, except call sign: GBXS.

MV *Royal Scotsman*
Built in 1936, gross weight: 3,244 tons and owned by Burns & Laird Lines Ltd. Registered in Glasgow and built by Harland & Wolff, Belfast for Channel service. Dimensions: 327.9 × 47.7 × 13.6. Call sign: GYTM. Oil engines, twin screw.

MV *Royal Ulsterman*
Details identical to the *Royal Scotsman*, except: Call sign: GYWW and registered in Belfast.

SS *Dundrum Castle*
Built in 1919, gross weight: 5,259 tons and owned by Union-Castle Mail Steamship Co. Ltd. Built by Harland & Wolff Ltd., Greenock. Dimensions: 400.3 × 52.3 × 28.5. Call sign: GNWT. Triple expansion steam engine, single screw.

SS *Baharistan*
Built in 1928, gross weight: 5,479 tons and owned by Strick Line (1923) Ltd. Registered in London and built by Readhead & Sons Ltd., South Shields. Dimensions: 415.0 × 54.2 × 27.6. Call sign: GSLF. Triple expansion steam engine, single screw.

SS *Marslew*
Built in 1926, gross weight: 4,542 tons and owned by Walmar Steam Ship Co. Ltd. Registered in London and built by Lithgow's Ltd, Port Glasgow. Dimensions: 385.0 × 52.0 × 26.6. Call sign: GMPZ. Triple expansion steam engine, single screw.
Sunk by Commander Gerd Schreiber in *U-95* at 00.27 GMT on 24 February 1941. Position: 59° 18´N 21° 30´W.

SS *Teiresias*
Built in 1914, gross weight: 7,405 tons and owned by Ocean Steam Ship Co. Ltd. Registered in Liverpool and built by Hawthorn Leslie & Co. Ltd., Newcastle. Dimensions: 455.3 × 56.3 × 32.5. Call sign: GQBC. Triple expansion steam engine, single screw.
Sunk by aircraft near Saint-Nazaire on 17 June 1940. Position: 47° 07´N 02° 23´W.

SS *Clan Ferguson*
Built in 1938, gross weight: 7,347 tons and owned by The Clan Line Steamers Ltd. Registered in Glasgow and built by Greenock Dockyard Co. Ltd. Greenock. Dimensions: 463.3 × 63.0 × 29.5. Call sign: GLLJ. Two triple expansion steam engines plus two LP turbines, twin screw.
Sunk by Commander Puccini in Italian U-boat *Alagi* at 21.05 GMT on 12 August 1942, 'Operation Pedestal', 20 miles north of Zembra Island, 37° 28´N 10° 38´E.

SS *Fabian*
Built in 1919, gross weight: 3,059 tons and owned by Ellerman Lines Ltd. Registered in Liverpool and built by W. Gray & Co. (1918) Ltd., West Hartlepool. Dimensions: 331.2 × 46.8 × 23.2. Call sign: GBWS. Triple expansion steam engine, single screw.
Sunk by Commander Herbert Wohlfarth in *U-137* at 14.29 GMT on 16 November 1940. Position: 02° 49´N 15° 29´W.

SS *Floristan*
Built in 1928, gross weight: 5,478 tons and owned by Strick Line (1923) Ltd. Registered in London and built by J. Readhead & Sons Ltd., South Shields. Dimensions: 415.3 × 54.2 × 27.6. Call sign: GSPW. Triple expansion steam engine, single screw.

SS *City of Lancaster*
Built in 1924, gross weight: 3,041 tons and owned by Ellerman Lines Ltd. Registered in Liverpool and built by Palmers' Co. Ltd., Newcastle. Dimensions: 335.2 × 45.0 × 22.6. Call sign: GJZV. Triple expansion steam engine, single screw.

MV *David Livingstone*
Built in 1930, gross weight: 5,013 tons and owned by Elder Demster Lines Ltd. Registered in Liverpool and built by A. McMillan & Sons Ltd., Dumbarton. Dimensions: 370.6 × 51.6 × 20.1. Call sign: GSJT. Oil engine, single screw.

SS *Glenlea*

Built in 1930, gross weight: 4,252 tons and owned by Cliffside Shipping Co. Ltd. Registered in Newcastle and built by Sir J. Priestman & Co., Sunderland. Dimensions: 367.5 × 51.5 × 25.1. Call sign: GSML. Triple expansion steam engine, single screw.

Sunk by Commander Gerhard Remus in *U-566* at 14.36 GMT on 7 November 1942. Position: 50°N 30°W.

SS *Glenaffric*

Built in 1920, gross weight: 7,782 tons and owned by Glen Line Ltd. Registered in Liverpool and built by Caledon S.B. & E. Co. Ltd., Dundee. Dimensions: 459.2 × 56.3 × 32.5. Call sign: GDPS. Triple expansion steam engines, single screw.

MV *Cymbula*

Built in 1938, gross weight: 8,082 tons and owned by Anglo-Saxon Petroleum Co. Ltd. Registered in London and built by N.V. Nederland Schps. Maats., Amsterdam. Dimension: 465.3 × 59.3 × 33.8. Call sign: GTGV. Oil engine, single screw.

SS *John Holt*

Built in 1938, gross weight: 5,007 tons and owned by J. Holt & Co. (Liverpool) Ltd. Registered in Liverpool and built by Cammell Laird & Co. Ltd., Birkenhead. Dimensions: 370.4 × 52.8 × 20.6. Call sign: GMGY. Triple expansion steam engine plus LP turbine, single screw.

Sunk by Commander Günther Hessler in *U-107* at 06.31 GMT on 24 September 1941. Position: 31° 12′N 23° 32′W.

SS *Robert L. Holt*

Built in 1926, gross weight: 2,918 tons and owned by J. Holt & Co. (Liverpool) Ltd. Registered in Liverpool and built by Smith's Dock Co. Ltd., Middlesborough. Dimensions: 310.0 × 44.6 × 24.3. Call sign: GMDS. Triple expansion steam engine, single screw.

Sunk by Commander Jost Metzler in *U-69* on 4 July 1941. Position: 24° 15′N 20° 00′W.

SS *City of Mobile* (ex-*Kentucky*)

Built in 1912, gross weight: 6,614 tons and owned by Ellerman & Bucknall Steam Ship Co. Ltd. Registered in North Shields and built by Workman Clark & Co. Ltd. Dimension: 447.3 × 56.4 × 31.4. Call sign: GMWC. Quadruple cylinder steam engine, single screw.

HMS *Cambridgeshire*

Trawler, built in 1935, gross weight: 443 tons and originally owned by Cambridgeshire Steam Fishing Co. (Shire Trawlers) Grimsby. Built by Smith's Dock Co. Ltd., Middlesborough. Dimensions: 162.3 × 26.7 × 14.4. Purchased by the Admiralty in August 1939. Pennant No. FY 142. Complement: 16. Sold in 1945 to Kingston S.F. Co., Hull and renamed *Kingston Sapphire* (H 206). Scrapped in 1954.

HMS *Highlander* (ex-*Jaguaribe*)

Destroyer, launched on 17 October 1939 and built by Thornycroft. Displacement: 1,340 tons. Dimensions: 312 (pp) 323 (oa) × 33 × 8.5. Armament: 4 – 4.7 in. (4 × 1), 8 – 0.5 in. AA (2 × 4) guns; 8 – 21 in. torpedo tubes (2 × 4). Pennant No. H 44. Complement: 145. Steam turbines, twin screw. Speed: 35½ knots. SHP: 34,000. Scrapped at Rosyth on 27 May 1946.

HMS *Havelock* (ex-*Jutahy*)

Destroyer, launched on 16 October 1939 and built by White. Pennant No. H 88. All other details are the same as HMS *Highlander*. Scrapped at Inverkeithing on 31 October 1946.

HMS *Punjabi*

Destroyer, launched on 18 December 1937 and built by Scott Shipbuilding & Engineering Co. Ltd., Greenock. Completed on 29 March 1939. Displacement: 1,870 tons. Dimensions: 355.5 (pp) 377.5 (oa) × 36.5 × 9. Armament: 8 – 4.7 in. (4 × 2), 4 – 2 pdr. AA (1 × 4), 8 – 0.5 in. AA (2 × 4) guns; 4 – 21 in. torpedo tubes (1 × 4). Pennant No. F 21. Complement: 190. Rammed and sunk after collision, in fog, with battleship HMS *King George V* in Russian convoy PQ 15 on 1 May 1942.

HMS *Beagle*

Destroyer, launched on 26 September 1930 and built by Clydebank. Displacement: 1,360 tons. Dimensions: 312 (pp) 323 (oa) × 32.25 × 8.5. Armament: 4 – 4.7 in. (4 × 1), 2 – 2 pdr. AA (2 × 1) guns; 8 – 21 in. torpedo tubes (2 × 4). Pennant No. H 30. Complement: 138. Scrapped at Rosyth in June 1946.

HMS *Vanoc*

Old destroyer, launched on 14th June 1917 and built by Clydebank. Displacement: 1,090 tons. Dimensions: 300 (pp) 312 (oa) × 29.5 × 10.75. Armament: 2 – 4 in. 2 – 20 mm. AA guns; 3 – 21 in. torpedo tubes and 1 ATW (Hedgehog). Pennant No. H 33. Lost near Penryn en-route to shipbreakers in June 1946.

Queen Emma

Not listed in Lloyd's Register of Shipping. No details known.

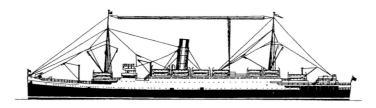

APPENDIX 11

OTHER NEWSPAPER REPORTS OF THE DISASTER PUBLISHED ON 26 JULY 1940, LETTERS CONCERNING THE RAF AND A REPORT BY A NAVAL OFFICER

Daily Telegraph:

LANCASTRIA SANK WITH 5,300 ABOARD

2,477 SAVED: SURVIVORS TELL OF NAZI MACHINE-GUNNING

Details were released last night of the sinking by enemy action on June 17 of the 16,243-ton Cunard-White Star liner *Lancastria* off Saint-Nazaire.

The *Lancastria* was being used as a transport in the evacuation of British troops and civilian refugees from France. Nearly 2,500 are known to have been saved from a total of about 5,350 on board. It is thought, however, that others may have made their way ashore and fallen into enemy hands.

The first news of the loss of the *Lancastria*, given in the later editions of *The Daily Telegraph* yesterday, was cabled from New York, where a report had appeared in the *New York Sun*. The undisclosed facts had been in the possession of British newspaper offices for some weeks.

French tenders were returning empty to the port when a number of enemy 'planes flew over, one of them dropping a salvo of bombs or aerial torpedoes across the harbour, where the *Lancastria* was about to weigh anchor.

SANK IN 30 MINUTES

There are conflicting statements as to whether the line received two or three direct hits, but so badly stricken was she that she sank within 30 minutes.

One woman, Mrs Tips, wife of the Belgian branch of the Fairey Aviation Company, floated about for three hours before she reached the safety of a warship. She, her daughter Fernande, and her two boys Martin and Maurice, had been thrown into the water from one of the lifeboats which capsized while being lowered. All survived, and, by coincidence, were picked up by the same ship.

Mr and Mrs Clifford Tillyer, also refugees from Belgium, were hurled into the water with their two and a half year old daughter Jacqueline. Both parents had lifebelts, and swam for a mile and a half holding the little girl up between them.

TROOPS JUMP OVERBOARD

Many of the soldiers lost their lives by striking wreckage as they jumped headlong from the decks of the sinking ship. There were about 100 unable to swim who clung to the ship to the last, and as the battered remains of the liner plunged under the waters roared out "Roll out the barrel."

One survivor said that Bren gunners stayed on the sinking ship firing at enemy 'planes overhead till the very last. The majority of those rescued were transferred to another troopship which, just before the attack on the *Lancastria*, had been hit by a bomb launched by a low-flying Dornier. She crossed the Channel without further incident.

Survivors' stories tell of heroism and coolness in the face of disaster.

Two Church Army workers, Sisters Trott and Chamley, told how they were taken aboard the *Lancastria* after a dash for the coast in a military convoy which was attacked five times by German 'planes.

"Through an open porthole," the said, "we saw a black cloud in the sky moving very fast. It turned out to be five or six aeroplanes which, as soon as they were over the ship, released bombs. We rushed on deck and, hearing the order 'Women and children first,' got into a lifeboat while men were sliding into the sea by ropes and others leapt overboard."

"The German 'planes swept down and we saw the spurts as their bullets struck the water where men were swimming for their lives. Twenty-five men were hanging like grim death to a piece of wood which was too small to float, but none of them would let go."

"As our boat moved away from the side of the ship, soldiers watching through a porthole saw that we were wearing lifebelts. They shouted, 'Give us a chance,' and we took off the belts and flung them into the sea. The soldiers jumped in after them."

A cook told how he saw one soldier grab a young girl, both of whose legs had been broken. He swam with her and both were picked up, but she died later on the rescuing ship and was buried on the voyage over.

COVERED WITH OIL

Most of the men who survived were swimming in the oily water for an hour or more before they were picked up and when they were landed in England they were in a pitiable condition.

Scores of badly injured men were brought ashore on stretchers and for two or three hours every available ambulance in the port was pressed into service to take the wounded to hospital.

One member of the crew said: "I was reading a book and had got too tired of the continuous alarms to get up on deck so I stayed where I was. Then suddenly there came a terrific explosion as the first bomb fell not far from where I was sitting. In complete darkness I groped my way to a companionway, my only means of escape.

We scrambled up on deck eventually, stripped, and jumped overboard into the sea. Beneath where I had been sitting I know there were at least 200 RAF men and they must have been lost.

They just hadn't a chance. Their means of escape was cut off and I heard the terrible sound of their cries as I scrambled away to safety."

GRIM SCENES IN WATER

Another member of the crew who tried to get one of the lifeboats over the side, described the scenes on deck:

"As soon as we were struck," he said, "I pushed my way through the mass of soldiers towards one of the lifeboats. Already it was full right up with men and when I eventually moved them, the others all surged towards the boat hoping they would get a place aboard.

Just then the *Lancastria* gave a terrific lurch to port and all the men were thrown from one side of her to the other. I slid on my back down the deck which was at an enormous slant. I was flung into the sea, which can only be described as being one almost solid mass of men clinging together like flies and covered with thick black oil.

Men clung to others in the hope of survival. Some of them were horribly burnt by the explosion, others were hanging on to debris, others were swimming until they finally sank, it was every man for himself."

MEN IN WATER FIRED AT

"All this time the three aeroplanes were still above us and they continually swooped and bombed the oily waters and their machine-gunners fired on the men struggling for their lives in the water."

The bearing of the troops was described as "simply magnificent."

"We were so tightly packed on board," said one officer, "that we could not move when the 'plane came over, so the men just jeered. When the bomb struck us some were killed by the force of the explosion, but there was not the least sign of panic, and as the ship heeled over those who were not thrown into the sea clambered on to her side and actually began to sing. But when they heard the cries from the men in the water the singing suddenly stopped. When the ship suddenly went down it was a dreadful sight to see all those heads bobbing about in the water."

Some of the survivors spent five hours in the water, clinging to upturned boats and any piece of wreckage they could find. They were covered in thick oil when they were brought ashore at a west country port.

————

Addendum to *The Times:*

STORY OF THE DISASTER

MISHAPS WITH LIFEBOATS
FROM OUR CORRESPONDENT
A SOUTH-WEST PORT, JUNE 19
[DELAYED BY CENSOR]

The *Lancastria*, which was bombed and sunk off Saint-Nazaire on the afternoon of Monday, June 17, was carrying about 5,000 troops and between 40 and 50 civilians. An early estimate here was that probably about half of them were saved, but since survivors reached port in a variety of vessels, anything like an exact total of casualties proved impossible.

The *Lancastria* had been lying about five miles off shore filling with troops, which came out from early morning in tugs and tenders. Not far off lay another liner turned troopship. Just before the attack occurred the *Lancastria* had reached her full complement, and a small boat containing a dozen men made instead for the other ship. Just previously this transport had been hit by incendiary bombs, dropped by a low-flying Dornier.

CIVILIAN REFUGEES FIRST

Three aeroplanes were seen swooping over the *Lancastria*, and one dropped a bomb which struck the ship. Another, following quickly, also struck the ship. In a few minutes she began to take on a list, and showed signs of sinking quickly.

Many people, including a number of officers, were in the dining room eating a late lunch. Some of them escaped to the upper deck, where preparations were being made to lower the boats. One major had a miraculous escape. A bomb dropped right through his cabin. He was thrown against the ceiling by the force of the explosion, but escaped injury. A lieutenant who was on deck, standing within a few feet of where the first bomb fell, also came off without a scratch. A number of men below decks were killed. Hundreds were crushed by falling metal and debris or trapped by the swift inflow of water.

Of those on deck or who reached the deck from below only a few managed to get away safely in lifeboats. Boats on one side of the ship could not be lowered at all. On the other only two or three appear to have been lowered without mishap. Civilian refugees were given the first chance in the boats. One of the fortunate families were Mr and Mrs Goodwin and their daughter, aged 10, who got into a boat and reached a rescue craft soon after the ship foundered.

Other families were separated when lifeboats tipped up before reaching the water, and they were flung into the sea. Mr and Mrs Clifford Tillyer, who were among a party of refugees from Belgium, were thrown out of their boat and swam for over a mile holding up their daughter, Jacqueline, aged 2½. Mrs Tips, whose husband, Mr Ernest Tips, is manager of the Belgian branch of the Fairey Aircraft Company, was separated from her daughter and two young sons, and floated in the water, sustained by her lifebelt, for three hours before being picked up. She was reunited with her children on reaching a British warship. Mr Tips, who had flown to London to arrange for their evacuation, met them in the port where they landed today.

Hundreds of troops lost their lives because they were unable to swim. About 100 of them clung to the ship until the last, and went down singing at the top of their voices.

————

It is believed that one of the aeroplanes whose bombs made direct hits on the *Lancastria* was shot down later by another British vessel, and that the pilot, who was uninjured, was taken prisoner.

————

SINKING OF SS *LANCASTRIA* ON 17 JUNE 1940, INVOLVING THE LOSS OF THIRTY-SEVEN PERSONNEL OF NO. 73 SQUADRON

The following account has been prepared solely for the benefit of the next of kin of the missing personnel of No. 73 Squadron, and must not be communicated to the Press.

————

On the evening of 16 June, the ground personnel of No. 73 Squadron arrived at Nantes from Saumur. A thunderstorm was in progress at the time of arrival but everybody set-to with a will on the job of unloading the transport when they were informed that many of them would be leaving for England that night.

Transport by road was provided to the port of departure, and about 200 men left for the ports of Brest and Saint-Nazaire ahead of the others. Sixty of these embarked at 6 o'clock on the morning of the 17th on board the SS *Lancastria*, at port Saint-Nazaire. The process of embarking approximately 5,000 took until about midday, and many of the men, wearied by their overnight journey, proceeded to their bunks or bed-spaces for a rest.

At approximately 3.45 p.m., the ship was attacked by enemy aircraft, two bombs falling quite close to the ship and giving it a list to port. On a second attack, a bomb hit amidships, and the ship sank about an hour afterwards. Many escaped by swimming, but a number of men remained on board until the ship sank and must have drowned.

A destroyer and other ships were quickly on the scene, and rescue work was promptly undertaken, but it was impossible to save all those who survived the actual bombing.

Whilst the SS *Lancastria* was still afloat, men were heard singing 'Roll out the Barrel' and many individual cases of gallantry have been reported.

Signed by J. C. More
Squadron Leader, Commanding, No. 73 Squadron, RAF.

————

EVACUATION OF NO. 98 SQUADRON FROM CHATEAU BOUGON ON 16 JUNE 1940
REPORT BY PILOT OFFICER J. F. CASTLE

On 16 June 1940, at approximately 02.03, No. 98 Squadron moved off in convoy from Chateau Bougon. The party consisted of 14 officers and 240 airmen (approx.) and arrived at Saint-Nazaire at approx. 05.03. They returned to an uncompleted airport and passed the day waiting for a troopship.

It was learned from the Movement Control Officer that a troopship would be off Saint-Nazaire early on Monday morning.

Marching off according to timetable at 02.25 on Monday, 17/6/40, we arrived at the docks at 04.30, with about 63 personnel from No. 67 wing attached to our party. We embarked on a tender at 06.03, arriving on board the SS *Lancastria* at about 08.00. All troops were aboard by 12.00, including units of BAFF Headquarters and 73 Squadron.

Just after 13.30, the first air raid alarm was sounded in which enemy aircraft bombed the SS [*Oronsay*] hitting the bridge. The 'all clear' was given at about 15.00. At 15.45 another alarm was sounded. Two bombs were dropped apparently not hitting the ship. Later other bombs were dropped, one hitting the bridge and another dropping through the ship, which sank the ship. I was in the dining room at the time and it seemed only a few feet away. Plaster work on the [deckhead] fell down and officers in the room immediately hurried the women and children and a few wounded people up the main [companionway], at the same time trying to stem the rush from the decks below. Fumes from the bomb filled the dining room almost immediately.

The ship took a list to port and on reaching the boat deck, great confusion existed as to the lowering of the boats, due to the fact that all control seemed to have been wiped out by the bomb, hitting the bridge, although all boat crews were at their stations no orders were given. The list made it impossible to lower more than six boats, one of which was later overturned. The bows by then under water, and it was then I left the ship. By the time I was 100 yards away, the ship was lying on its side, men standing on it. Steam then began to blow out of the side plates in the centre, many men being badly burned. The ship finally settled down until only a few feet were above the water line. The scene then was very reminiscent of the pictures of the *Blücher* in the last war, with men standing in a long line on what was left of the [ship]. The spirit of the men was wonderful, those left on the [ship] were singing lustily 'Roll out the Barrel'.

Survivors made for various ships around. Several of us reaching the minesweeper *Cambridgeshire* which cruised around for an hour or more and eventually picked up 819 survivors. Bombs were still being dropped by Junkers 88 and Heinkel 111K machines, which appeared to be aimed very badly again at the [*Oronsay*] owing to the fighters patrolling. These seemed to find it impossible to engage the bombers closely because of the clouds between 4 and 5,000 feet. Anti-Aircraft fire also seemed inaccurate because of the short time the enemy were visible.

The men of our Squadron were mostly in the lower hold. One bomb dropped straight down a hatch bursting though the [deck] of this [lower] hold, probably killing a large number of them by the explosion. The hold was filled immediately by flames and fumes. A few managed to get out and it would seem that those that did get clear in the first few minutes were trapped under the water.

From a Sergeant Observer who was on the upper deck, it seems that the bombers adopted a shallow dive attack from the cloud to about 2,000 feet.

I have heard several reports of men who last saw Flight Lieutenant A. Martin, who was OC [of] our party, helping men over the side of the ship.

One Hurricane pilot flew low over the men swimming in the water and threw out his life jacket.

The 819 survivors from the *Cambridgeshire* were put on board the *John Holt* and left for England about 20.00. The officers and men of this [ship] did everything in their power to help us with kit and food. We arrived in England at about 21.00 on 19/6/40.

Signed John I. Castle.
Pilot Officer.

REPORT OF THE DISASTER BY LIEUTENANT MOSSE, WHO WAS ON BOARD THE DESTROYER *HIGHLANDER*, ALONG WITH THE NAVAL OFFICER IN CHARGE OF THE EVACUATION

The air raid was still in progress, and we made our way to the bridge just in time to see (the liner) *Lancastria* hit by two bombs. She had embarked five thousand troops. We watched her roll over and sink. For a while, the side of her hull remained above water with hundreds of men sitting on it, singing lustily before they floated off. Soon there were thousands to be rescued. Yet two thousand in *Lancastria* perished. Some undoubtedly were bomb casualties, but many more must have been trapped below in a strange ship, unable to find their way out in the darkness. It was the worst individual sea disaster of the War, and, not surprisingly, the least publicised

Lieutenant Mosse

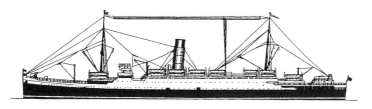

APPENDIX 12

REPORT OF AN INTERVIEW WITH CAPTAIN SHARP
BY THE SHIPPING CASUALTIES SECTION,
TRADE DIVISION, 26 JUNE 1940:
(ADM 199/2133)

We left Liverpool on the 14 June at 17.00, arriving at Plymouth on the 15 June. We left Plymouth at midnight on the 15th for Quiberon Bay where we arrived at 18.00 on the 16th. We left Quiberon Bay that night at midnight and anchored in the Charpentier Roads, Saint-Nazaire at 04.00 on the 17 June.

We lay at anchor in 12 fathoms of water and from 08.00 on the 17th until noon we embarked 5200 troops and a number of refugees including women and children. After 12.00 we had to wait for completion of our embarkation and for the other ships and the destroyers which were to escort us to our destination.

The *Oronsay* was lying 4 cables from us at anchor. At 13.48 the enemy flew over and dropped bombs which hit the *Oronsay*. After that, we expected an air attack at any time. The boats were turned out ready for lowering, and the crew divided into two watches with instructions to do nothing else but stand by the boats, except when the ARP signal was sounded, when they were to go down to their fire stations, clearing everyone off the upper deck.

Our own planes were flying over all the time. The crew had been going to and from their ARP stations at intervals from 14.00. At about 15.45 the ship's ARP alarm was blown on mouth whistles and the electricity operated gongs were rung below. At this signal everyone was to take cover but we had so many on board that actually it was impossible for everyone to get under cover.

I was in my cabin when the officer on watch gave the alarm. I immediately went on to the bridge and had just reached the wheelhouse when the ship was struck by a salvo of four bombs which cut off all communication and started fires fore and aft. I did not even see the aeroplane. The four bombs, which were all high explosive, struck the ship simultaneously in the most vital parts, one went down the funnel, the other three striking No. 2, No. 3 and No. 4 hatches, shattering the hatch boards, which were covered with steel plates, timbers and ladders.

We had a number of 3-inch high-angle guns on board and at least a dozen machine guns. The two officers on watch, one on the bridge and another on the after bridge, let go all their ammunition, and the rest of the guns were all blazing away.

From that time until the ship sank the scene was one of confusion and disorder, as I could make no communication with any part of the ship. Some of the soldiers who were unable to swim became somewhat panicky and came to the bridge for lifebelts. I did my best to reassure them, although I knew we only had 2,000 lifebelts on board.

The ship began to sink rapidly by the head, listing from side to side, probably caused by the passengers rushing from port to starboard as the ship rolled. About ten minutes after we had been hit, at about 16.00, the ship heeled over on to her port side and sank.

I had on my kapok lifejacket and for the next 3 or 4 hours I was in the water, surrounded by those who had managed to escape with lifebelts, or by hanging on to rafts and floating debris. The loss of life amongst the troops must have been high, I should think between 3,000 or 4,000, principally due to shortage of lifebelts, and also to the 1,407 tons of oil fuel from the deep tank which rose to the surface and was the cause of many casualties, adding greatly to the difficulties of the rescue workers.

There were numbers of ships and several destroyers all round us, but the air attack was still going on, so they were unable to help while this lasted. I could hear all the surrounding ships firing at the enemy; the attack lasted for 2 hours after we were in the water. Several calcium flares which had become detached from lifeboats and rafts were drifting on the sea of oil, and I was afraid they would set it on fire. I had asked, when at Glasgow, to be relieved of this surplus oil, but there had never been time to discharge it. This oil proved to be fatal in the end.

A number of small boats, operating from the beach, were carrying out rescue work, but their work was greatly impeded as the rescuers could not get a grip on the men owing to the greasy oil. I saw many men in the water with me who had slipped through their lifebelts, probably through not having time to tie them on properly. The troops had been on the ship so short a time that we had no time to give them instructions. The first thing they had needed was food and they were at their fourth sitting when the ship was attacked.

Whilst I was in the water, boats would come within 20 feet of me and then go away, they were picking up everyone they could find. The spirit of the men in the water was wonderful, they even managed to sing and make jokes whilst waiting to be picked up.

After about 3 or 4 hours, I suddenly recognised my quartermaster, Murphy, in one of our boats, No. 10a. I hailed him and he immediately came along and picked me up. Apparently ten of our boats had got away from the ship. He himself had been picked up out of the water soon after the ship sank, he had somehow managed to get hold of a boat and was assisting in the rescue work. There were a number of naked soldiers in the boat who were covered with oil. We went over to a French Trawler and they sent us to the destroyer *Havelock*. I could not help myself at all for a time, but soon recovered after getting on board. A number of women and children were already there. I was waiting my turn for the bathroom when the order was given that the crew of the *Lancastria* were to go on board the *Oronsay*, which had not been sunk, although hit. Her bridge was wrecked by the bomb which struck her, eventually exploding in the officers' quarters. No one on board had been hurt. She brought us safely back to England, by means of a boat's compass on the bridge.

I spoke to many of the engine-room ratings of the *Lancastria* to enable me to form some opinion as to why a 17,000 ton vessel with her bulkhead door closed should sink in so short time. My conclusion is that each of the bombs which struck the ship passed through the upper deck and hatches, bursting inside the ship and blowing holes in her sides. Then, apparently, a further bomb exploded in the water close to her side, just after abaft the bridge, which probably added to the damage.

The weather at the time was light north-westerly wind, slight sea and swell, cloudy with bright periods. We were heading west-north-west with the sun in that quarter.

Not everyone who had a lifebelt was saved. A lot of men were hurt. I should estimate that 2,000 were saved by lifebelts and another 500 in boats and rafts, so that 2,500 people were saved out of a total of about 5,500. I lost 70 of my crew of 330.

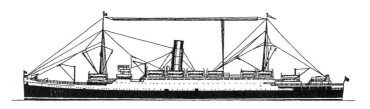

PICTURE CREDITS

1. Harry Grattidge, photographed whilst Commodore aboard the *Queen Mary*, 29 November 1952, *courtesy of University of Liverpool* (frontispiece).

1(b) Anchor Line's new 'T'-class liner, the *Tuscania*, sister to the *Tyrrhenia*, from an old postcard, *publisher's collection* (p. xii).

1(c) The new Cunard liner, *Ascania*, one of the six 'A'-class ships built to replace Cunard's heavy losses in World War I. All were similiar in design to the *Lancastria*, illustrated in a Cunard postcard, showing he rleaving Liverpool. *Author's collection* (p. xii).

2. Lady Invernairn poses for the official photographer on 18 May 1920, pretending to push the launching button. The launch was delayed, however, because of very high winds. No doubt to save face, she named the ship. Lord Invernairn is looking up at the *Tyrrhenia*'s towering bow while the Marquis of Graham, with the bowler hat and brolly, stands to her left, *source unknown* (p. 6).

3. The *Tyrrhenia, Cameronia* and *Conto Rosso* in the fitting out berth on 7 April 1921, delayed by the joiners strike which lasted nearly nine months, *courtesy of University of Newcastle-upon-Tyne* (p. 7).

4. The *Tyrrhenia* in No. 3 graving dock at Govan in 1922. She is undergoing a hull inspection before receiving a fresh coat of anti-fouling paint prior to delivery. A Glasgow tramcar, which is travelling along Govan Road, illustrates the enormity of the new liner, *source unknown* (p. 8).

5. Plan of SS *Tyrrhenia, by Brian Crabb for Paul Watkins Publishing* (p. 10).

6. Deck plans of SS *Tyrrhenia, by Brian Crabb for Paul Watkins Publishing* (p. 11).

7. Deck plans of SS *Tyrrhenia, by Brian Crabb for Paul Watkins Publishing* (p. 12).

8. *Tyrrhenia*'s sister ship *Cameronia*, in Liverpool, boasting her Admiralty cowled funnel; the easy way of distinguishing either ship, *author's collection* (p. 13).

9. One of Cunard Line's early postcards depicting the *Lancastria* with an 'exaggerated' funnel, *author's collection* (p. 15).

10. An impressive view of the *Lancastria* at top speed in choppy weather off Liverpool, *courtesy of National Museums & Galleries on Merseyside* (p. 16).

11. Stern view of the *Berengaria*; she was involved in a collision with the *Lancastria* in Ocean Dock, Southampton, *courtesy of Jim Crissup* (p. 16).

31. Cunard advertisement depicting the *Lancastria*. It was possibly this poster that some of the survivors saw when they landed back in England in June 1940, *author's collection* (p. 31).

32. Port side view of the *Lancastria* at anchor and bunkering through the gunport doors. She is dressed overall for the Coronation Fleet Review in May 1937, *courtesy of National Museums & Galleries on Merseyside* (p. 31).

33. *Lancastria's* last trip to New York in March 1940 three months before she was sunk. Note her grey hull, blacked out port holes and 4-inch low-angle gun, *courtesy of National Archives of Canada/*Copy negative number: PA 149838 (p. 33).

34. An interesting picture showing the *Lancastria* leaving Glasgow as part of convoy 'Alabaster' on 14 May 1940, while a Scottish band plays them off. Her decks are crammed with troops, a scenario that would be repeated almost three-fold in June the same year, *courtesy of Ian Johnston* (p. 35).

34(b) Rare aerial photograph of the *Lancastria*, in peacetime. From *The War Illustrated*, vol. 3 (August 9, 1940), p. 137, *author's collection* (p. 43).

35. View inside the cockpit of a Ju 88 showing the observer pointing to the map while the pilot checks his position, *courtesy of Ted Hooton* (p. 46).

36. HMS *Ark Royal*, seen here going astern. She was reported by the German Propaganda Ministry as being bombed and sunk by Gefreite Carl Francke – a claim that was to cause him great embarrassment, *courtesy of the late Percival Crabb* (p. 48)

37. Reconnaissance picture taken of the attack on the cruisers *Southampton* and *Edinburgh* on 16 October 1939. The Firth of Forth railway bridge and Inch Garvie Island are on the left, while the accuracy of the bombing is very evident, *courtesy of Aerospace Publishing archive* (p. 51)

38. *Franconia* boasting Cunard's white cruising livery, anchored at Liverpool, *courtesy of Jim Crissup* (p. 60).

39. Map showing the probable route of the *Lancastria* and *Franconia* from Plymouth to France, *by Brian Crabb for Paul Watkins Publishing* (p. 61).

40. Another view of the *Franconia*; she was near missed by a Ju 88 as she entered the twisting channel leading to Quiberon Bay. She took no further part in the evacuation. This photograph was taken on 1 March 1948, as she enters Valletta harbour carrying a large number of troops, *courtesy of Michael Cassar* (p. 62).

41. Motto and badge of 1 HRS (MT) RASC. It was painted on the sides of their lorries, *courtesy of Stan Flowers* (p. 63).

42. Groups of troops line the quay and the inner (north) caisson of *Normandie* dock at Saint-Nazaire, awaiting embarkation on board the *Highlander*. The ships in the background are inside the port in Penhouet Basin, the larger part of the docks at that time, *attributed to Frank Clements* (p. 73).

43. Troops boarding HMS *Highlander* from the quayside, most of whom are carrying their rifles, *attributed to Frank Clements* (p. 77).

44. HMS *Highlander* fully loaded and on her way out to the *Lancastria*, *attributed to Frank Clements* (p. 78).

45. Scene on the foredeck of the *Highlander* as troops begin to board. A and B turrets and the open bridge are clearly visible in the background, *attributed to Frank Clements* (p. 80).

46. *Highlander* closes the damaged *Oronsay* in readiness to embark the troops she had originally taken to the *Lancastria*, after being refused permission to board. Note the gun mounted on the stern, *attributed to Frank Clements* (p. 86).

47. Captain Rudolf Sharp, OBE, RD, RNVR, who survived the sinking of the *Lancastria* but was lost in the *Laconia* on 12 September 1942, when she was torpedoed by *U-156*, *source unknown* (p. 88).

48. View of the demolished bridge of the *Oronsay* and the port for'd lifeboat, which is hanging precariously from its davits, *attributed to Frank Clements* (p. 90).

49. A dramatic view of a Ju 88 bomber in a steep dive. Its four bombs are ready to drop – a sight that Fred Coe, George Crew and many others who were on deck will probably never forget, *courtesy of Ted Hooton*, (p. 93).

50. *Lancastria* down by the head with her forefoot resting on the sea bed. The *Highlander* has been forced to manoeuvre into the open sea to avoid further bombing. The French lighter from which Edgar Blant had so nearly boarded the *Lancastria* is still alongside the *Oronsay*, which is anchored, *attributed to Frank Clements* (p. 109).

51. Private Sidney Dunmall, No. 7662664 Royal Army Pay Corps, in July 1940, *supplied by himself* (p. 112).

52. Stanley Flowers pictured in 1939 when he was with 1 HRS, RASC, *supplied by himself* (p. 123).

53. Walter 'Wally' Smith stood in the same yard in 1939. He joined 1 HRS, RASC, as a replacement driver the following year, *supplied by Stanley Flowers* (p. 123).

54. Map of the Loire Estuary showing the coastline in relation to where the *Lancastria* sank, *by Brian Crabb for Paul Watkins Publishing* (p. 124).

55. One of the *Highlander*'s lifeboats is being prepared for rescue work, as the *Lancastria* lists over to her port side, *attributed to Frank Clements* (p. 126).

56. Closer view showing hundreds of men clambering down her starboard side, while others huddle on the stern tube. Hundreds more are already in the water. The 'Welin' davits protrude above the ship's side; oil is just visible on the port side of the wreck, *attributed to Frank Clements* (p. 128).

57. Oil painting of the scene, painted from memory, by survivor Corporal Robert W. May, 1 HRS, RASC whilst he was recovering in hospital. Unfortunately, the *Lancastria* is shown here sinking on her starboard side; an easy mistake to make, *attributed to Robert W. May* (p. 129).

58. Some of the survivors picked up by the *Highlander*, *attributed to Frank Clements* (p. 132).

59. Hot tea is poured into Sapper Percy Brown's cup, who is sat beside the *Highlander*'s torpedo tubes, and a naval rating attends others. Most of them are covered in oil, *attributed to Frank Clements* (p. 133).

60. Leading supply rating, Dennis Maloney; without his fortitude many more people would have died, *supplied by himself* (p. 139).

61. HM trawler *Cambridgeshire* comes alongside the Commodore's ship *John Holt* and disembarks her human cargo into her. Her captain and crew had performed a miracle, *attributed to Mr Stannard* (p. 142).

62. Another dramatic view showing the last of the *Lancastria*'s survivors boarding the *John Holt, attributed to Mr Stannard* (p. 143).

63. A couple of survivors pose for a photograph on board the *Cambridgeshire* before joining the *John Holt*. The injured man was taken back to Saint-Nazaire, *attributed to Mr Stannard* (p. 144).

64. The *Cambridgeshire* steams away towards Saint-Nazaire. The French coast is visible in the distance, *attributed to Mr Stannard* (p. 145).

65. Blue Funnel Line's steamship *Teiresias*. She too was sunk off Saint-Nazaire on 17 June 1940, *courtesy of Jim Crissup* (p. 146).

66. Captain A.E. Nicholls, master of the *Oronsay*. This photograph was taken on 5 September 1945, shortly before he retired, *courtesy of Dennis Knights-Branch* (p. 149).

67. General Sir Alan F. Brooke on board the *Cambridgeshire* with other senior officers who were to take passage back to Plymouth, *attributed to Mr Stannard* (p. 154).

68. The beautiful memorial window at St Katharine Cree Church by Mr M. C. Farrar Bell, *courtesy of Brian Reynolds* (p. 158).

69. Major Cyril V. 'Peter' Petit, survivor and founder member of the *Lancastria* Survivors Association, *courtesy of Brian Reynolds* (p. 161).

70. The wooden plaque which commemorates many of the ships involved in the rescue, *author's collection* (p. 163).

71. Stan Flowers lays a wreath on Walter James Smith's grave at Triaize communal cemetery on 12 June 2000, *author's collection* (p. 166).

72. Survivors of 1 HRS (MT) RASC at Triaize. From the left: Fred Coe, Morris Lashbrook, Tom Hutchison and Stan Flowers, *author's collection* (p. 166).

73. Memorial to those lost in the *Lancastria*. It was designed by Brian Reynolds and stands, facing in the direction of the wreck, at Saint-Nazaire, *courtesy of Robert Miller* (p. 167).

74. Survivor Harry Pettit who I met for the first time on the 60th Anniversary of the sinking, *author's collection* (p. 168).

75. The splendid model of the *Lancastria*. Fred Coe (left) and Denis Holland (right) describe their experiences to the author while Henry Harding points to the position where he was stood, when the ship was bombed (he still has his watch – it stopped at 16.05), *courtesy of Dennis Maloney* (p. 169).

76. Gaston Noblanc and his charming wife Jacqueline. Gaston had helped in the rescue when he was 16 years old and went on to join the resistance. His

face still bears the scars, after interrogation by the Gestapo, *author's collection* (p. 168).

77. HMS *Chiddingfold* moves in over the wreck carrying the survivors of the *Lancastria*, who are stood on the starboard side behind the bridge. A French priest, who is stood on the prow of the Pornic lifeboat, blesses the grave at the exact time of the sinking, sixty years before, *author's collection* (p. 170).

78. Dennis Maloney throws a wreath from HMS *Chiddingfold* while the mayor of Saint-Nazaire and survivors, Stan Flowers and Michael Sheehan, look on, *courtesy of Steve Reigate* (p. 171).

79. General sonar image of the *Lancastria* taken by the FS *Verseau*, showing that the ship's hull is still intact, *author's collection* (p. 174).

80. Sonar image, revealed by the FS *Verseau* on 17 June 2000 from the port quarter, showing the bow section of the *Lancastria*. The curvature of the starboard side is clear to see, while the profile of the port side of the ship is not so well defined, because that side of the hull is partially buried in soft undulating mud. This picture verifies that the *Lancastria* is now virtually upright, *author's collection* (p. 174).

81. Jacqueline Tanner (*née* Tillyer) and Arthur Snow at Pornic's vin d'honneur. The youngest and the oldest survivors to attend the ceremonies marking the 60th anniversary of the loss of HMT *Lancastria*, *courtesy of Colin Clarke* (p. 175).

82. The Dunkirk Memorial is situated on the eastern outskirts of the town of Dunkirk (Dunkerque) alongside the canal-verged road to Veurne in Belgium. Here a total of 4,516 soldiers of the British Expeditionary Force are commemorated, who have no known grave and fell in the campaign of 1939–40. Over 800 of *Lancastria*'s Army victims are listed here, *author's collection* (p. 179).

83. A typical Commonwealth War Graves Commission's headstone at Pornic War Cemetery. This one marks the grave of driver William Rowe. The epitaph says everything, *author's collection* (p. 211).

84. Pornic War Cemetery during the evening of 20 June 2001. There are 395 World War II graves here, of which three-quarters are victims of the *Lancastria* disaster (181 identified and 112 unidentified), *author's collection* (p. 211).

85. Michael Stafford lays a wreath on his father's grave at St Marie communal cemetery on 15 June 2000, *author's collection* (p. 261).

86. The French local people meet the members of the 2000 pilgrimage at Triaize prior to going to Walter Smith's grave in the communal cemetery, *author's collection* (p. 262).

87. Survivors of the *Lancastria* at St Katharine Cree Church on Sunday 17 June 2001 – the 61st anniversary of the sinking, *author's collection* (p. 262).

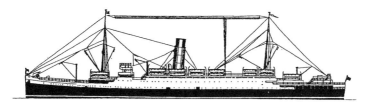

UNPUBLISHED SOURCES AND BIBLIOGRAPHY

PUBLIC RECORD OFFICE

ADM 1/10710: Letters concerning the retention of information about the sinking of the *Lancastria* and HMAS *Hobart*.

ADM 1/12264: Brief report, HMS *Cambridgeshire*, made on 1 July 1940, dealing with the rescue of survivors from the *Lancastria* and awards to personnel (in *Cambridgeshire*).

ADM 12/1742: Admiralty indexes and digests, A – L.

ADM 187/8: Navy List (Pinkies) traces HMS *Highlander*.

ADM 199/76: Particulars of attack by enemy aircraft; re: sinking of the SS *Lancastria*.

ADM 199/371: War Diary. Western Approaches.

ADM 199/486: Evacuation of Norway.

ADM 199/487: Evacuation of Norway.

ADM 199/489: Evacuation of Norway.

ADM 199/672: Occupation of Iceland by British and American forces; including convoy 'Alabaster'.

ADM 199/2133: Report of interviews with Captain Rudolph Sharp (*Lancastria*) and Captain J.R. Davies (*Teiresias*).

ADM 199/2206: War Diary. Home Command.

ADM 199/2207: War Diary. Home Command. 'Operation Aerial'.

ADM 223/127: Naval Intelligence 16–19 June 1940.

AIR 2/4593: Sinking of the *Lancastria* by Wing Cdr D. Macfadyen, RAF.

AIR 35/190: Lists of RAF casualties and survivors with related correspondence; other nominal lists of RAF personnel.

BT 100/579–593: Agreements and Crew Lists for SS *Lancastria* (ex-*Tyrrhenia*) 1922–December 1938.

CAB 65/7: War Cabinet Report.

CAB 65/8: War Cabinet Report.

CAB 100/4: Cabinet Records. War Situation Daily Reports.

Hansard (House of Commons): 31 July 1940, columns 1218–1220.

Hansard (House of Lords): 1 August 1940, column 93.

Letter from Captain Nicholson, in *Oronsay*, to the Superintendent, Mercantile Marine Office, Board of Trade, Liverpool, dated 24 June 1940.

Official Log of the *Oronsay*, 17/18 June 1940.

PREM 3/175: War Cabinet Report 18 June 1940.

PREM 3/188/3: War Cabinet Report 15–18 June 1940 – Allan Brooke.

WO 32/18802: SS *Lancastria*: Army Casualties Resulting from the Sinking of the Troopship After Enemy Bombing Attacks at Saint-Nazaire, 17 June 1940.

WO 106/1615: Instigation of 'Operation Aerial'.

WO 106/1683: Intelligence Report.

WO 167/96: War Diary – RAOC.

WO 167/97: War Diary – HQ, Nantes.

WO 167/117: War Diary – Garrison, Saint-Nazaire.

WO 167/918: War Diary – 29 Railway Survey Company, Royal Engineers.

WO 167/1155: War Diary – No. 1 HRS, RASC.

WO 197/105: Movements, 'Operation Aerial'.

WO 222/483: Medical Reports, casualties etc.

WO 222/1520: Medical Reports, casualties etc.

WO 222/1529: General Instructions.

WO 222/2143: General Instructions.

WO 222/2144: Report on hospital conditions at La Baule.

GUILDHALL LIBRARY

Captain's Certificate: No. 039503.

Confidential Shipping Movements: 1940.

Lloyd's "Captains Registers": (Ms 18569/34).

Lloyd's Voyage Record Cards: *Lancastria* 1927–40.

Lloyd's List: October – December 1929.

Lloyd's List: April – June 1930.

Lloyd's List: April – June 1932.

Lloyd's List: October – December 1932.

Lloyd's List: April – September 1933.

Lloyd's List: March – September 1934.

Lloyd's List: February 1936.

Lloyd's List: October – December 1936.

Lloyd's List: July 1937.

Lloyd's List: September – December 1937.

Lloyd's List: January and June 1940.

Lloyd's List: April – September 1951.

Lloyd's Register: page 86.

Lloyd's Shipping Gazette: June 22 and 24 1940.

Lloyd's Weekly Casualty Reports: June – December 1923.

Lloyd's Weekly Casualty Reports: July – September 1925.

Lloyd's Weekly Casualty Reports: December 1926 – March 1927.

Lloyd's Weekly Casualty Reports: September – December 1927.

BRISTOL CENTRAL LIBRARY

Lloyd's Registers of Shipping: 1922–23, 1923–24, 1939–40 and 1940–41.

London Gazette for period of June 1940 – January 1941.

MINISTRY OF SHIPPING (CARDIFF)

Documents, including Captain's statement, wireless messages from Captain (D9) etc.

REGISTERS ISSUED BY THE COMMONWEALTH
WAR GRAVES COMMISSION

FRANCE 1507–1580, Cemeteries in Finistere, Cotes-du-Nord and Morbihan.

FRANCE 1583–1584, Escoublac-La-Baule and Pornic War Cemeteries.

FRANCE 1585–1598, Cemeteries in Loire-Atlantique.

FRANCE 1601–1699, Cemeteries in Vendee, Maine-et-Loire, Deux-Sevres, Charente, Charente-Maritime, Vienne, Haute-Vienne, Indre-et-Loire, Indre, Loire-et Cher, Cher and Loiret.

FRANCE 1700–1738, Cemeteries in Allier, Ardeche, Aude, Aveyron, Pyrenees Atlantiques, Dordogne, Gironde, Haute-Garonne, Herault, Landes, Lot-et-Garonne, Nievre, Puy-de-Dome and Rhone.

The RUNNYMEDE MEMORIAL, Memorial Register 7, Parts 1 to 15, 1939–1945.

The DUNKIRK MEMORIAL, Memorial Register 11, Parts 1 to 4, 1939–1945.

The TOWER HILL MEMORIAL, Memorial Register 22, Parts 1 to 16, 1939–1945.

COMMONWEALTH WAR GRAVES COMMISSION

Report listing all casualties of the SS *Lancastria*. Please note: according to CWGC records, there were no Royal Navy casualties.

BIBLIOGRAPHY OF PUBLISHED SOURCES

Alanbrooke, Field Marshal, Lord, *War Diaries 1939–45* (London: Weidenfield & Nicolson, 2001).

Atkin, Ronald, *Pillar of Fire, Dunkirk 1940* (London: Sidgwick and Jackson, 1990).

Austen, John with Carter, Nick, *The Man Who Hit the Scharnhorst* (London: Seeley Service & Co. Ltd., 1973).

Bennett, Geoffrey, *The Battle of Jutland* (London: B.T. Batsford Ltd., 1964).

Barnett, Correlli, *Engage the Enemy more Closely, The Royal Navy in the Second World War* (London: Hodder and Stoughton, 1992).

Baumbach, Werner, *Broken Swastika. The Defeat of the Luftwaffe* (London: Robert Hale Ltd., 1960).

Bekker, Cajus, *The Luftwaffe War Diaries* (London: Corgi Books, 1969).

Bond, Geoffrey, *Lancastria* (London: Oldbourne Press, 1959).

Bonsor, N.R.P., *North Atlantic Seaway*, Volume I (London: David & Charles (Holdings) Ltd., 1975).

Boutin, Emile, *Les Grands Naufrages de l'Estuaire* (France: Rives Reines).

British Vessels Lost at Sea 1939–1945 (London: HMSO, 1947).

Buckley, Christopher, *Norway*, part of a short military history series of the Second World War, 1939–45 (London: HMSO, 1977).

Chant, Christopher, *Encyclopedia of Codenames of World War II* (London: Routledge and Kegan Paul, 1986).

Chesterton, Neville, *Crete was my Waterloo* (London: Janus Publishing Company, 1995).

Churchill, Winston, *The Second World War*, Volume III, Chapter IX, The French Agony, page 172 (London: Heron Books, 1950).

Crabb, Brian James, *In Harm's Way, The Story of HMS Kenya, a Second World War Cruiser* (Stamford: Paul Watkins Publishing, 1998).

Crabb, Brian James, *Passage to Destiny, The Sinking of the SS Khedive Ismail* (Stamford: Paul Watkins Publishing, 1997).

de Kerbrech, Richard P. & Williams David L., *Cunard White Star Liners of the 1930s* (London: Conway Maritime Press Ltd., 1988).

Fraser, David, *Alanbrooke* (London: Collins, 1982).

Grattidge, Captain Harry and Collier, Richard, *Captain of the Queens* (London: Oldbourne Press, 1956).

Grossmith, Frederick, *The Sinking of the Laconia* (Stamford: Paul Watkins Publishing, 1994).

Hammerton, Sir John (Editor) *The War Illustrated*, Volume Three (London: The Amalgamated Press Ltd., 1940).

Haws, Duncan, *Merchant Fleets – Anchor Line* (Burwash, East Sussex: Travel Creatours Ltd., 1986).

Haws, Duncan, *Merchant Fleets – Blue Star Line* (Hereford: Travel Creatours Ltd., 1988).

Haws, Duncan, *Merchant Fleets – Cunard Line* (Burwash, East Sussex: Travel Creatours Ltd., 1987).

His Majesty's Regiments of the British Army (London: Metro-Provincial Publications Ltd., 1949).

Hocking, Charles F. L. A., *Dictionary of Disasters at Sea During the Age of Steam. 1824 – 1962*, Volume I, A–L (London: London Stamp Exchange, 1969).

HMT Lancastria – Narratives, compiled by The HMT *Lancastria* Association, containing nearly 60 different eye-witness accounts.

Isherwood, J. H., Steamers of the Past – Cunard Liner *Tyrrhenia/Lancastria* of 1922 (featured in Vol. 45, No. 307 of *Sea Breezes*, pages 495–498, July 1971).

Johnston, Ian, *Beardmore Built. The Rise and Fall of a Clydeside Shipyard* (Clydebank District Libraries & Museums Department, 1993).

Jordan, Roger W., *The World's Merchant Fleets 1939*. The Particulars and Wartime Fates of 6,000 Ships (London: Chatham Publishing, 1999).

Karslake, Basil, *1940 The Last Act. The Story of the British Forces in France After Dunkirk* (London: Leo Cooper Ltd., 1979).

Keegan, John, *Encyclopedia of World War II* (London: Hamlyn, 1977).

Lenton, H.T. and Colledge, J. J., *Warships of World War II* (London: Ian Allan Limited, 1965).

Laffin, John, *British VCs of World War 2; A Study of Heroism* (Sutton Publishing Limited, 1999).

Lucas Phillips, C. E., *The Greatest Raid of All. The Story of the Famous and Very Successful Raid on Saint-Nazaire, 28 March 1942* (Odhams Press, 1958).

Macintyre, Donald, *Narvik* (Evans Brothers, 1959).

McCart, Neil, *Atlantic Liners of the Cunard Line, from 1884 to the Present Day* (Wellingborough: Patrick Stephens Limited, 1990).

McLeod, William A., *The Bosun's Manual* (Glasgow: Brown Son & Ferguson Ltd., 1944).

McMurtrie, AINA (Editor) *Jane's Fighting Ships – 1940* (London: Sampson Low, Marston & Co., Ltd, issued January 1941).

Mitchell, W.H., *The Cunard Line, a Post War History* (Kent: Marinart Ltd., 1975).

Monsarrat, Nicholas, *Monsarrat at Sea* (London: Cassell & Company, 1975).

Niven, David, *Go Slowly Come Back Quickly* (Hamish Hamilton Ltd., 1981).

Roskill, S.W., *The War at Sea*, Volume I, *The Defensive* (London: HMSO, 1954).

Roskill, S.W., *The War at Sea*, Volume II, *The Period of Balance* (London: HMSO, 1954).

Rohwer, Jürgen, *Axis Submarine Successes of World War Two, German, Italian and Japanese Submarine Successes, 1939–1945* (London: Greenhill Books, 1999).

Rohwer, J. and Hummelchen, G., *Chronology of the War at Sea 1939–45*, Volume One *1939–42* (Surrey: Ian Allen Ltd., 1972).

Sharpe, Peter, *U-boat Factfile, 1939–1945* (Leicester: Midland Publishing Limited, 1998).

Stahl, Peter, *The Diving Eagle, a Ju 88 Pilot's Diary* (London: William Kimber 1984).

Talbot-Booth, E. C., *Ships and the Sea* (London: Sampson Low, Marston & Co., Ltd., 1938).

The Medical Directory, 97th Edition (London: J. A. Churchill Ltd., 1941).

Taylor, Eric, *Combat Nurse* (London: Robert Hale, 1999).

Tennent, Alan J., *British and Commonwealth Merchant Ship Losses to Axis Submarines 1939–1945* (Stroud: Sutton Publishing Ltd., 2001).

Thompson, Julian, *The Imperial War Museum Book of the War at Sea* (London: Sidgwick & Jackson, 1996).

Weal, John, *Ju 88 Kampfgeschwader on the Western Front* (Oxford: Osprey Publishing, 2000).

West, John L. (compiler) *The Loss of Lancastria* (Lancashire: Millgate Publishing Ltd., 1988).

Williams, David, *Wartime Disasters at Sea* (Sparkford: Patrick Stephens Limited, 1997).

85. Michael Stafford lays a wreath on his father's grave at St Marie communal cemetery on 15 June 2000 (John Henry Stafford is recorded on p. 205). Sadly, Michael died on 5 March 2001.

86. The French local people meet the members of the 2000 pilgrimage at Triaize
prior to going to Walter Smith's grave in the communal cemetery.

87. Survivors of the *Lancastria* at St Katharine Cree Church on Sunday 17 June
2001 – the 61st anniversary of the sinking.

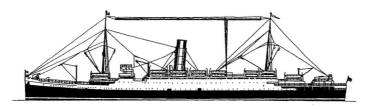

INDEX

Note: the index attempts to cover the main text of the book comprehensively, but it does not cover the alphabetical lists of names in the appendices. The compiler was the author.

GLOSSARY

SHIPPING TERMINOLOGY USED IN THIS BOOK

Alleyway: passageway along the deck of a vessel giving access to different parts of the ship.

Ballast: additional weight carried in a ship, either in solid or liquid form, to give stability.

Bulkhead: an upright partition separating the compartments.

Companionway: staircase to a cabin or another deck.

Cross Alleyway: any corridor which runs athwartships, i.e., port to starboard.

Deck: a platform in a ship covering all or part of the hull area at any level and serving as a floor.

Deckhead: the nautical term for a ceiling.

Fo'c'sle: forecastle, the forward part of a ship where the crew has quarters. Historically, a short raised deck at the bow.

For'd: Forward.

Double Bottom: the space between the outer and inner plating at the bottom of the ship which contain the frames.

Double Bottom Tanks: the area formed by the double bottom which is sub-divided to contain fuel or ballast.

Gunport Door: Side loading door usually leading into a cross alleyway or a hold.

Gunwale: In a wooden vessel, such as a lifeboat, it is the top strake.

Handrail: a rail secured to a bulkhead, companionway or ladder.

Rail: guard rail around the ship's side placed there for the safety of the crew and passengers.

Scuttle: A small housed and elevated entrance on the main deck with doors facing aft, leading to a lower deck, via a companionway.

Settling Tank: Fuel tank used gravitationally to separate oil from water, after being pumped from a double bottom or bunker tank.

281